The Hardcore Diaries

The Hardcore Diaries

MICK FOLEY

POCKET BOOKS

New York   Toronto

Sydney   London

Pocket Books
A Division of Simon & Schuster, Inc.
1230 Avenue of the Americas
New York, NY 10020

First Pocket Books trade paperback edition April 2008

POCKET and colophon are registered trademarks of Simon & Schuster, Inc.

For information about special discounts for bulk purchases, please contact Simon & Schuster Special Sales at 1-800-456-6798 or business@simonandschuster.com.

Designed by Richard Oriolo

Manufactured in the United States of America

10 9 8 7 6 5 4 3 2

ISBN-13: 978-1-4165-3157-9
ISBN-10:   1-4165-3157-2
ISBN-13: 978-1-4165-5678-7 (pbk)
ISBN-10:   1-4165-5678-8 (pbk)

To Vince McMahon.
Thanks for the bumps
in the road.

Introduction

I originally pitched an idea for a new book to Vince McMahon back in June of 2005, after reading Buzz Bissinger's book *Three Nights in August*. I had been captivated by Bissinger's ability to allow the readers unprecedented access into the mind of St. Louis Cardinals manager Tony La Russa, and how much insight was gained from that access—a seemingly irrelevant three-game series against the Chicago Cubs (sure, it wasn't irrelevant at the time, but would be if looked at from a historical perspective) took on such magnitude when seen through the eyes of La Russa.

I wanted to write that same type of book about WWE. I wanted to be like Buzz Bissinger, but I wanted to create a WWE equivalent to *Three Nights in August*—bigger, badder, undoubtedly not as well researched or well written. I wanted to write *Maniac—Inside the Mind of Vince McMahon at WrestleMania*.

Vince seemed to like it, and tentative plans were made to publish the book in the spring of 2007.

Without the snowstorm, it's questionable *The Hardcore Diaries* would even exist. A huge blizzard blanketed much of the Northeast in the second week of February in 2006, grounding thousands of flights and casting a shadow of doubt onto the probability of my appearing as scheduled on the February 13 edition of *Raw*—the designated time for me to kick-start my *WrestleMania* angle (or storyline, in non-wrestling-speak) with Edge. I really needed to make that show. And Vince McMahon made sure I got there—by giving me a seat on the WWE corporate jet.

While en route to *Raw* in Greensboro, North Carolina, Vince asked me about the book idea. I tried to let him down as gently as I could.

"I'm not sure I can really write a book about *WrestleMania* if I'm playing a major role in it."

Vince nodded his head, empathizing with my literary lamentation. "You know, Mick," he said, "why don't you just forget about that idea and write another autobiography."

"That's just what the world needs, Vince," I joked, "a third volume of my memoirs."

But Vince was not to be swayed. With much of the WWE creative team as witnesses, Vince spent several minutes singing my literary praises, doing his best to convince me that the world did indeed need another volume of Mick Foley memoirs. Hey, if Winston Churchill could put out three, why not me? Who did Churchill ever beat? I told Vince that I would start traveling with a notebook, writing down stories of the road as I thought of them.

Still, until my phone rang a couple of days later, I really felt that Vince was just being nice to me, just trying to score a few points for the inevitable day when I'd be mad about a payoff or some questionable WWE creative decision.

The phone call was from Dean Miller, the lead liaison for WWE in their publishing deal with Pocket Books, a division of Simon & Schuster. "So, I'm told you're going to write another book for us," Dean said.

"Yeah, I guess so," I replied.

I didn't actually have a clue as to what I would write about. Perhaps, I thought, I wouldn't have to write about anything. I'd been writing a weekly Web log for WWE for about two months. Some of it was actually pretty good. At its best, it was thought-provoking stuff. At its worst, it was entertaining filler—things I wrote down an hour or so before deadline.

"Hey, Dean, would it be all right if I included some of my Web entries?" I said, thinking in fact that the book would be *all* Web entries.

"I don't think that will be a problem."

Except there was a problem—my damn conscience. Sure, a book of previously written Web entries would have been easy enough. But I'd taken so much pride in writing my first two books, *Have a Nice Day* and *Foley Is Good*, that any reasonably astute reader would correctly surmise that I'd simply phoned in the third act of this trilogy. What a letdown it would be—kind of like *Porky's III* and the way it undermined the credibility of the first two *Porky's* classics.

So over time, I came to accept that I would write about something else— I just didn't know what.

Around the second week of April, a giant burst of inspiration seemed to crash right into me, leading me to believe that I had an incredible storyline for the upcoming *One Night Stand* Pay-Per-View event.

Unfortunately my editor at Pocket Books, Margaret Clark, called at this most inopportune time. Could I have a manuscript completed by July 4? she wanted to know. July 4? Was she crazy? How would I find the time to write when I had to imagine, visualize, concentrate, travel, wrestle, and even—oh no!—get back in the gym? And what would I even write about?

A second burst of inspiration hit. That's it, I thought. That's the book. Imagining, visualizing, concentrating, wrestling, even getting back in the gym. The idea would be the book. The book would be the idea. I would simply chart the course of this idea from conception to completion—an intense six-week ride that would allow our fans unprecedented access into the meetings, phone calls, backstage antics, TV tapings, and ultimately the wrestling ring, where the idea would play itself out.

I would get to be like Buzz Bissinger after all. But instead of getting inside the mind of Tony La Russa, I'd have to get inside my own.

Prepare yourself—it's going to be a bumpy ride.

The
Hardcore
Diaries

Dear Hardcore Diary,

Sometimes it's all in the pitch. When it comes to present-ing creative wrestling ideas, I have come to learn that the presentation of the idea is often more important than the idea itself. I have heard terrible ideas pitched magnificently, and magnificent ideas pitched terribly, so believe me when I tell you that it's all in the pitch.

A little less than four weeks ago, I participated in our biggest showcase of the year, *WrestleMania*. Many people thought I had been in the best match on a very good show. Sometimes it's hard for *WrestleMania* to live up to the hype, but in this case, I think fans went away from the arena or their television sets pleasantly surprised and extremely satisfied.

Our match was one of the intangibles of the night. I felt like a major question mark was hanging over me, as if many fans, wrestlers, and WWE office personnel wondered whether I still had what it took to deliver the goods on such a major show. Hell, I wondered myself. My knees are shot, my back is bad, my neck hurts pretty much all the time, and I've had a history of head injuries. To make things worse, I'm three bills and change, about 315 before a big meal, and on certain days, every step taken seems like a major challenge. Still, somehow, with the considerable help of a great oppo-nent, Edge, I was able to pull it off.

But not once during the buildup to *WrestleMania* did I ever truly *feel* the story. I may have done a good job pretend-ing, but deep down, I knew something was missing.

Passion. That's what I lacked. For some reason, I just couldn't tap into that reservoir of passion that had been one of my calling cards for so many years. A passion that allowed a not-so-good-looking guy, with a not-so-good-looking body (a bit of an understatement there), with a limited supply of athleticism, to excel in a world where good looks, athleticism, and aesthetically pleasing bodies are the rule. Or maybe there was simply nothing left to tap into. Maybe the reservoir was dry.

I currently have the dubious distinction of having the easiest contract in the WWE. I owe WWE two Pay-Per-View wrestling matches a year, and a nonwrestling appearance at one more Pay-Per-View. In addition, I am required to show up at whatever number of television tapings it takes to properly promote these appearances. So, I'm basically looking at an approximate workload of fifteen days a year. Nice, right? While I don't feel any outward resentment from the other wrestlers, I can't help but feel that I would be resenting a guy like me if I were in their shoes.

I mean these guys are on the road up to 300 days a year (some will dispute that figure, but including travel and promotional days, it gets pretty close), and most are in some degree of pain around the clock. Some awfully big guys travel an awfully long time in some awfully small coach-class airplane seats, and then do their best to put on an exciting show in a year-round business that spans a good portion of the globe. Then those sore, exhausted wrestlers are asked to step aside so an out-of-shape ghost of wrestling's past can step in and take their spot on a major Pay-Per-View.

Most of the guys on the roster genuinely like me. Some even hold me in high esteem because of what I've accomplished in the past and how much I was willing to sacrifice in order to accomplish it. But for those who may resent me, I don't blame them, especially because I haven't had the decency to show up for my ridiculously light workload with a thimbleful of the passion that's so necessary for success in today's wrestling game.

Where had it all gone? After all, it was only two years since my *Backlash* match with Randy Orton, a match that ended the eight-year reign of "Mind Games" with Shawn Michaels, as my personal career favorite. I'd been overflowing with passion for that match. I had thought about it nonstop, to the point of sleeplessness, to the point of obsession, to the point where every waking moment seemed filled with wild visions of thought-provoking, gutwrenching interviews, images of emotional and extremely physical, maybe even brutal, ring action.

My major challenge at *Backlash 2004* was merely to take those images that were so vivid in my head and make them real in front of a microphone, and later in front of the live crowd in Edmonton and a Pay-Per-View audience around the world.

I met that challenge two years ago. I succeeded. In 2006, however, I just couldn't find the passion. I lucked out at 'Mania, but doubted I'd be so lucky when my number was called again, probably in September.

What had gone wrong in those two years? Maybe I'd just simply fallen out of love with wrestling. That happens in all facets of life, doesn't it? People simply fall out of love. But why, after all these years, had I stopped loving something that had been so good to me, something that had actually loved me back for such a long time?

Maybe it was the Ric Flair book, which had caused me to feel abandoned by WWE, due to their decision not to give me any advance warning of the literary pounding I would have to endure.

Or maybe I felt like I had taken the easy way out, by opting for the WWE contract, instead of taking a gamble with the upstart TNA promotion. My longtime buddy Raven (whose real name is Scott Levy; I actually had to ponder that for a while) had gotten in my ear and convinced me that if I were indeed to jump to TNA, it could literally make the difference between life and death for the promotion. I'll get further into my TNA temptation later in the book, as well as explain an instance where Raven inspired a major point in my novel *Tietam Brown*, but for now I'll just say that for a while, I did feel a certain amount of guilt concerning the decision I ultimately made.

That guilt is now gone. The passion that had been so sorely lacking has come rushing back. A giant lightbulb seemed to go off above my head, as one simple idea seemed to flush whatever creative and emotional block I had been suffering from right out of my system.

I know of several writers who create ideas simply by asking, "What if?" What if aliens came down from outer space? What if a shy, socially repressed girl had telekinetic powers? What if a bumbling fool who'd never accomplished anything became U.S. president? All very scary scenarios, right? The idea that rekindled the fire underneath my creative ass was just as frightening, perhaps more so. What if I became the first voluntary member of the Vince McMahon "Kiss My Ass Club"?

With that one simple, repugnant thought, my long estrangement ended. I went back to the one who loved me. As it turned out, she'd never really left; she'd been waiting all along. Once reunited, the pieces all seemed to fall together, like a giant mental puzzle that I was just dying to shake up and reconstruct, only this time not just in my mind, but in front of millions around the world.

I sat on the idea for a few days, partially to let it ripen and mature in my mind, like a fine vintage wine, and partially to figure out if I was really willing to kiss another man's ass. I mean, *literally* kiss another man's ass. Sure, I'd been kissing the same guy's ass figuratively for a decade. But this was different. Did I really have the testicular fortitude required for such a task? On international television? In front of millions? Including my wife and kids? I checked my testicles . . . just as I'd hoped—full of fortitude.

I made the call.

Dear Hardcore Diary,

Vince liked it! He really liked it! Everybody did. In the past, when I'd pitched ideas, it was usually to an audience of two—Vince and someone else. Over the years, that someone else had been a variety of people: from former heads of talent relations J. J. Dillon and Jim Ross, to former head of the creative team, Bruce Prichard, to current head of talent relations, John Laurinaitis, to *Raw* head writer Brian Gewirtz. For this occasion, however, Vince had asked if I would mind pitching the idea to the entire creative team.

Why not? The more the merrier, right? Besides, for an idea like this, that I wholeheartedly believed in, it would be in my best interest for as many people as possible to hear it directly from me, limiting the possibility of a loss somewhere in the translation process.

WWE is always good about offering me transportation, usually a town car, from my home on Long Island, New York, to their office in Stamford, Connecticut. And I'm always good about declining it. Unless, of course, I'm doing work for them in New York City, in which case I gladly accept the ride, so as not to get frustrated with the one-way streets, massive traffic, thirty-dollar parking lots, and general insanity of the city that never sleeps.

But for the most part, I'm much happier in my used Chevy minivan, playing my own tunes as loud as I want, throwing fast-food wrappers onto ever-growing piles of their brethren, and focusing my mind on whatever task is at hand. And this task should be easy. I simply have to sell the creative team an idea that, in all honesty, should sell itself. But in the unlikely event that this idea doesn't sell itself, I'll be ready. Because as I mentioned earlier, sometimes it's all in the pitch. I've even taken great care *not* to look like the casual slob I usually am. No more flannels and sweats for the hardcore legend. At least not for a few hours. No, for this meeting, I've got my pitcher's uniform on: ill-fitting blue sports coat, wrinkled dress shirt, a tie I bummed off Regis Philbin at *Who Wants to Be a Millionaire*, black jeans, and Red Wing work boots.

I was summoned into the booking meeting and immediately seated next to Vince, who, I surmised, wanted to be the first to sample the nuggets of wisdom that were sure to spew from my mouth. Seated around the table were Dusty Rhodes, a certifiable wrestling legend and former booker in WCW; Greg Gagne, a longtime fixture in his father's former AWA promotion, who was fairly new to the creative team; Michael Hayes, one of the great attractions in the business in the 1980s and a mainstay on the creative team for the last decade or so; Ed Koskey, the assistant writer on *Raw*; Stephanie McMahon, the boss's daughter and senior VP of creative writing; Dave Lagana, the head writer on *SmackDown!*; and Brian Gewirtz, *Raw* head writer.

Gewirtz is about 6-4, 220, with a ripped bodybuilder's physique. He's well versed in several of the martial arts and could very well have been a force inside WWE rings if not for a predisposition toward . . . wait, I'm sorry, I must be thinking of a different guy. Actually Gewirtz is a classic nerd, albeit a very creative one. Over the years, he has somehow been hit with the unfair rap of being nothing but a pop-culture couch potato, with no background as a wrestling fan. In actuality, Gewirtz has been obsessed with this sports enter- tainment stuff for almost twenty years, even dressing as yours truly at a college Halloween party. Gewirtz is no simple nerd—he's a wrestling nerd, dammit!

Vince gives me a quick introduction, and then offers me the floor, or the table in this case.

"I'd like to start out," I say, "by letting you know that if you like this idea, you can give partial credit to Michael Hayes for doing a pretty good job of convincing me to stick around after *'Mania*."

Michael is all smiles. In some ways, it's tough to go from being one of the business's most flamboyant men in *front* of the camera, to being a driving force *behind* it. I can see that Michael appreciated the acknowledgment.

"And if you don't like this idea, you can probably blame Michael Hayes, for doing a pretty good job of convincing me to stick around after *'Mania*.

"Look," I continued. "Last year you did a really good job of building up the ECW Pay-Per-View around the aura of the name and reputation of

ECW." Everyone nodded in agreement. "I don't think we can get by on just aura and reputation this year. I think we need to create compelling rivalries that the fans will feel strongly enough about to spend money on." More nods. "I think I've got an idea that will create a compelling rivalry," I said. "But it's an idea that really hinges on three important things."

I'm well into the windup, about to release the pitch.

"Number one, we need to firmly believe that Terry Funk can get over as a main-event attraction in a very short time." I turn to Dusty, who knows Terry as well as anyone in the business. "I think the Dream [Dusty's nickname is "The American Dream"] can vouch for me when I say that even at age sixty, Terry does a real convincing job of making fans think he's out of his mind."

"That's because he *is* out of his mind," the Dream says with a laugh, eliciting further laughs from around the table. Vince isn't laughing, but he is smiling, which is a good sign. His relationship with Terry has been a contentious one over the years, dating back to 1993, when Terry walked out on a major Pay-Per-View, leaving only a note that read, "My horse is sick. I think she's going to die. I think I better go."

"Number two, we need to firmly believe that Edge and I can form one of the most unique short-term tag teams in recent history." There is a general feeling that item number two had distinct possibilities.

"And number three, for this angle to work, Vince, you really need to get physically involved."

Uh-oh, I said something wrong. I sense a general uneasiness around the table. Vince breaks the tension, saying, "Actually, I was going to get physically involved with DX."

DX is D-Generation X, Shawn Michaels and Triple H. They were a harbinger to the attitude era of the late 1990s—a boom period for WWE—and their imminent reformation had been one of WWE's best-told stories. I can see Vince's point, but firmly believe that he is a character large enough to place his footprints in the foundation of two simultaneous angles. Especially if I can convince him that our idea can feed into the DX angle—that an incensed Vince McMahon can be more dangerous than ever. Besides, I've got a secret weapon.

"Vince, I want to become the first ever voluntary member of the Vince McMahon 'Kiss My Ass Club.'"

For those of you who don't know, or simply need a brief refresher course, the "Kiss My Ass Club" is Vince McMahon's long-running, incredibly degrading, incredibly entertaining spectacle in which a WWE Superstar or employee will be made, usually through force, to actually plant a smacker on the boss's billionaire buttocks. And no, when I say "boss," I'm not talking about Steinbrenner or Springsteen, I'm talking about Vince.

The secret weapon seemed to work. Vince's attention was all mine.

I quickly laid out a four-week plan that would see the formation of the Edge/Foley team, leading to our two-week mockery/bludgeoning of ECW "legends" who were not exactly legends, leading to a Foley/Vince verbal confrontation. You see, once Vince caught on to the idea that Edge and I were deliberately trying to sink the ECW Pay-Per-View, he would become irate. Such a deliberate sinking, after all, would cost Vince a fortune—he'd be down to seven or eight hundred million in no time.

"A week after that confrontation with you, Vince," I said, "probably at the *Raw* in Las Vegas [May 22], I would summon you into the ring, with the promise of an apology.

"So you'd say, 'I guess you want to apologize for calling me a no-good son of a bitch last week, huh, Mick?'

"But I'd say, 'No, actually, I meant that one.'

"Then you'd say, 'So, I guess you're going to apologize for saying I was a heartless bastard.'

"But I'd say, 'No, actually I meant that, too.'"

I can see that Vince is intrigued. He likes walking this fine line between fact and fiction. For him, it's every bit as comforting as a brisk autumn leaf-peeping, bird-watching stroll would be to nature lovers.

"So, Vince, you'd be kind of losing your patience with me, as I try to explain myself. I'd say, 'No, Vince, I want to apolo-

My favorite billionaire, Vincent K. McMahon.

gize for what I said about you in my book. Do you remember when I wrote that no man I'd ever met had your drive and intellect?'

"Vince, you'd kind of nod, okay, then I'd say, 'Well, I didn't really mean that.'

"Then I'd say, 'You know how I told you on the phone once that I considered you to be on the level of U.S. presidents? Well, I didn't really mean that either.'

"Vince, at this point you'd kind of snap, you'd say, 'Dammit, what's your point?'

"And I'd say, 'Vince, don't you get it? I was saying things I didn't really mean just because you were my boss, just because you signed the checks.'

"'So?' you'd say. 'What's wrong with that?'

"I'd say, 'Vince, don't you get it, I was kissing your ass.'

"'Yeah,' you'd say, 'but everyone does that, that's part of doing business.'

"'But,' I'd say, 'it's not part of being Mick Foley. Being Mick Foley means saying what I mean, and meaning what I say. It's about being a man I can be proud of. And what kind of a man would I be, Vince, if I'm willing to kiss your ass figuratively, but not literally?'

"Vince, you'd get this big smile on your face, because you'd kind of see where I was going with this. You'd say, 'You mean?'

"And I'd say, 'I want to join the club.'

"'The club?'

"'The club. Vince, I want to join the Vince McMahon 'Kiss My Ass Club,' right here in Las Vegas, Nevada.'"

The creative team seemed to love it. As I thought, it was an idea that was pretty much selling itself, but it didn't hurt that I was pitching the thing pretty damn well. I continued to pitch, describing how the inaugural voluntary membership ceremony could be pushed back to the final segment. In the interim, Vince could be making phone calls, procuring a live symphony, hiring showgirls. After all, it would be Vegas.

Then on to the glorious ceremony, where after being regaled with live music and a Vegas production number, I would attempt to plant that kiss . . . but would see my valiant attempt interrupted by that no-good Terry Funk, who would attempt to take me out of this fateful decision by appealing to my pride, my manhood, my legacy—whatever it might take to get my lips out of the general proximity of Vince's ass.

Then, just as Terry is really reaching me, just as he's about to talk me out of this tasteless moment of oral anguish—BAM!—there's Edge, laying out the Funker, snapping me back into reality, making me realize the treacherous act that Funk was about to perpetuate. Then we'd lay the boots into Terry, much to Vince's delight.

"Then, Vince, you'd get on the mike, you'd say, "Dammit, someone's going to kiss my ass tonight. Get Funk over here.'

"And Vince, you'd get this huge smile of satisfaction on your face as human lips meet human ass."

Vince looks like he's in heaven. This is going even better than I expected.

"But in a split second, that smile would turn into a look of abject horror as you realize that . . . Terry Funk is tearing a chunk out of your ass!"

The table erupts. A couple of the writers nearly fall out of their chairs. My summation is just a formality as everyone agrees that this idea is fool-proof.

Vince can come back madder then ever. He can take out his frustration on DX. He can join forces with me and Edge in our attempt to derail the ECW Pay-Per-View. Sure, it might hurt his pocketbook, but something far more valuable has already been hurt—his ass. His pride, too. His ass *and* his pride. And his pride in his ass. That's been hurt as well.

From there it's a short step to Funk and Tommy Dreamer facing me and Edge at ECW's *One Night Stand*.

Brian Gewirtz has one small concern. "Las Vegas is the night that DX is supposed to get to Vince."

My heart momentarily sinks. But thankfully, Gewirtz isn't done.

"I think if we moved it up a week to the fifteenth, it would be even better. We're in Lubbock, Texas, right outside of Terry's hometown."

A rush of enthusiasm goes around the table. I think everyone sees the potential of Terry Funk taking a bite out of Vince McMahon's ass in his West Texas stronghold, where the Funk name is almost synonymous with wrestling.

I say good-bye to the creative team. Stephanie publicly thanks me for dressing up for the meeting, then asks me privately if her comment hurt my feelings. Of course not. My wardrobe, or lack thereof, is a personal choice I made a long time ago. It's more than fair game for innocent teasing.

Vince wraps me up in a big hug. It seems that we've got ourselves a deal. A deal I can't wait to commence. He likes me! He really likes me! And the truth is, I really like him. Again. But it hasn't always been that way.

Falling
into a
Falling-out

It was May 7, 2001, the day the *New York Times* article came out. It should have been a great day. My publicist at Regan Books, Jennifer Suitor, had told me what a big deal making the *Times* was, but I really hadn't a clue to what extent the world revolved around a single newspaper.

People magazine called that same day, after previously declining the idea of a story. The *Today* show called too, even booking me for the very next day in a minor life-changing interview with Katie Couric. *Today* had also been previously uninterested. Judith Regan called, too. Judith was my publisher, a very important person in her industry—hence the name Regan Books—and had been very supportive of my writing. It seems that the *Times* article had mentioned my interest in writing a novel. Not that I was actually writing one—just that I had an interest.

That interest was apparently enough for Judith, who offered me a two-book contract, with or without the participation of WWE. Hey, I thought, even Mick Jagger makes a solo album every now and then before returning to the Stones. Since retiring from wrestling (or so I thought) in February of 2000, I had been looking for something I could do on my own. It wasn't that I didn't love WWE, or appreciate everything we had achieved together. But I just felt like I needed to do something outside my safe little environment. I was like Herbie the dentist—I wanted to be independent. But just like Herbie had Rudolf, I had Judith Regan. We were going to be independent . . . together.

Out of courtesy, I called up Stu Snyder, then WWE president, to let him know I was planning on accepting Judith's very kind offer. In my opinion, WWE could have been a little more understanding.

As I mentioned, it was May 7, 2001. It should have been a great day. But instead, May 7, 2001, became a day of great division concerning my relationship with WWE. Everything before May 7, 2001, was pretty good. Everything after it? Not so good.

Maybe it was the damn XFL's fault. Or maybe it was the fault of little Mick, about four months old at the time. Yeah, I'll blame it on him. Or maybe it was a combination of the two. You see, prior to the formation of the XFL and the birth of Mickey, I had enjoyed a fairly close working relationship with Vince. I was in the loop. I had been fired (a classic on-air Vince McMahon version) in December 2000, simply as a way to give me some time at home for the impending birth of my child. The on-air firing was the one concept the *Times* writer couldn't quite grasp. I guess in the real world (until Donald Trump blatantly stole Vince's gimmick) such things didn't take place.

But I always assumed I'd be back. After all, I'd moved back to Long Island, in part to be closer to the WWE site-based entertainment complex (restaurant) in New York City, which was vital to my on-air role as WWE commissioner.

Had I known that my days as commish were really over, with the exception of a short-lived return later in 2001, I'm not sure I would have moved. It's expensive on Long Island. Cold, too. But at least the cold eventually subsides.

Had I stayed in the loop with Vince, things probably would have been much different. I had been fired with the general understanding that I would come back to battle Vince at *WrestleMania*, probably with my commissioner's job hanging in the balance. Simple premise, right? Had I been in touch, I simply could have heard their idea, told them it didn't make sense, proposed a better one, had that shot down, reached a compromise, and come back to vanquish Vince at *Mania*.

Instead, I heard the idea about a day before its scheduled shooting, got cold feet, and called up Vince, saying something about "never wrestling again," blaming it on fear of one final devastating head injury.

WrestleMania was salvaged. In fact, it may have been the greatest *WrestleMania* of them all. I even refereed Vince's match with Shane, and aside from considering the possibility that Vince nailing me in the back of the head with a chair (it was supposed to be the upper back) was not entirely unintentional, I thought all was again well in our relationship.

But in retrospect, I will always look at my decision to bow out of *WrestleMania* (a decision that probably cost me a few bucks, too) as the reason I would come to feel like "the boy who cried wolf" in Vince's eyes.

I had been a wrestler, I had been the commissioner, and I just felt like I was drying up, dying on the vine. There were other things I wanted to try in life, without a WWE contract hanging over my head.

It was in July of 2001 that I asked for a meeting with Vince. I showed up in Stamford with a list of grievances, but the moment I sat down, I just went for broke and asked for my release from the company. What ensued was fairly ugly, a shouting match that echoed through the halls of Titan Towers and shook the very foundation of our business and personal relationship.

No, I didn't get the release, at least not at that time. But I did get something else—confidence. Vince McMahon was a superhero (or supervillain) of sorts, a larger-than-life billionaire I had been watching on television since childhood. Yelling at Vince had been very therapeutic. I had stood my ground, made my points, knocked away many of his contentions, and, in the process, gained a new belief in myself.

I mean, after this, life was easy. What was there to fear? I felt like I could do anything. Debate foreign policy with the president? Easy. Stand up for causes I believed in? No problem. Get in the gym and shed some of those pounds I'd piled on? Well, let's not be ridiculous.

I specifically remember the outcome of one of those verbal volleys with Vince. He was contending that the WWE machine had made me who I was, and that it therefore wouldn't be fair for me to just walk away from it.

I said, "Vince, if that is true, how come my most popular character was actually Commissioner Foley, which was just me dressed in my regular clothes, acting like myself?"

"That's not true," Vince said. Although he damn sure knew it was. For although my commissioner character didn't sell merchandise (I didn't even have a shirt) or drive Pay-Per-Views, in terms of recognition and response, none of the other characters I'd played came close.

"It is true, Vince," I said.

"No, that would be . . . Dude Love." I'd done it! Point Foley. By opting for such a ludicrous joke, Vince had conceded that particular round of the great July shouting match.

I finally did get that release in November, with the help of my friend Katie Couric. Apparently, I'd made a decent impression on Katie during our first interview in May, as I was invited back for Halloween, in conjunction with my children's book *Halloween Hijinx*. I'd actually received the invite mere days after that first Katie interview, prompting me to ask a mature question of my publicist: "Does that mean Katie likes me?" Yes, it was asked in the same tone as a sixth-grader in the throes of his very first crush.

"Well," she said, "it means *somebody* likes you, because they just booked you five months in advance."

Thinking about that interview was actually a great source of comforting anticipation to me. It was like the anticipation of a Disney trip or the promise of Christmas morning: it was going to be just me and Katie, and my wife, and kids, and Matt, and Al Roker, and Anne, and . . . well, you know what I mean.

Suffice it to say, it was going to be a big deal, and I didn't want WWE screwing it up.

In my opinion, WWE made the whole Halloween book experience a lot harder than it should have been. It was their book, and I understood that WWE did business in a way that was not conventional. Which was fine with me. But not paying my artist, who was a friend, was not fine. Sure I knew that she'd eventually get paid, but that knowledge was of little comfort to my friend, who hadn't received a dime for work that had been completed several months earlier.

Jennifer Suitor had worked with me on three previous books. We'd spent

literally hundreds of hours together, and during that time, I don't think she'd heard me raise my voice, let alone yell. But, oh, that came to an end the day before *Today*, when I let loose during a phone call from WWE.

"This is not a WWE event," I yelled. "This is *my* event. They didn't ask for me because I was a WWE guy. They asked for me because they liked me. WWE has taken a book that should have been nothing but fun, and they've taken all the fun out of it! You haven't even paid my artist! The *Today* show invited my family, and it's going to be a special day for me. And I don't want WWE there for it!"

Jennifer was impressed. She knew I'd been feeling the strain of this failing relationship I had with WWE, and she knew how much this *Today* show appearance meant to me. Hell, I even wrote a bonus chapter, "Reflections on Katie" for the paperback version of *Foley Is Good.*

So, it was with some trepidation that Jennifer later told me that WWE had asked for four passes to the show. It was at that point in the proceedings that I called a producer at *Today* and effectively had WWE banned from the building.

The show was great. Katie was great, treating my whole family as if we were honored guests. It's been so common in my experiences with journalists and television personalities to be on the receiving end of cheap shots or to be treated condescendingly. Katie did neither, which is probably why she's Katie . . . and they're not. She also flattered me by signing her children's book *The Brand New Kid* to me in a nice way. And in a moment I have publicly claimed was the highlight of my career (much to the chagrin of fans who thought having a tooth sticking out of my nose in Hell in a Cell should have won the honors), Katie even held eight-month-old little Mick in her arms to end the show.

To top it all off, Katie Couric, unbeknownst to her, helped me get my release from WWE.

It was November 5, 2001—just a few days after my Halloween hobnobbing with Katie. WWE was at the Nassau Coliseum, about thirty minutes from my house, but upon arriving at the arena, I was told I wasn't booked on the show. I guess it would have made too much sense. I was told, however, that J.R. wanted to see me.

J.R. is Jim Ross, *Raw* announcer extraordinaire and, at that time, head of WWE talent relations. Basically, J.R. was the liaison between the talent (wrestlers, etc.) and Vince—possibly one of the world's most stressful jobs. J.R. probably won't play much of a role in this book, unlike my other two WWE books, and after this little story, his name might not even resurface. So I will take this time to point out how instrumental he has been in my career. He helped get me my job at WCW, was almost solely responsible for doing likewise at WWE, where over Vince's consistently unenthusiastic response he waged a steady campaign of support on my behalf for many years.

It seems that every few years, J.R. gets taken for granted and is sent out to pasture. And every time, he comes back with a renewed, albeit temporary sense of respect from WWE. I sincerely hope that respect will at some time become permanent.

While I'm on the subject of J.R., let me take the time to send a personal message to Vince concerning his 2005 treatment of J.R., which I'm sure WWE employees will be hustling to have edited, and which, no doubt, Vince will read and respond to with, "If that's the way he feels, print it."

Vince, colon surgery is serious. Not only that, it's a sensitive issue. It's not funny. Exploiting it and humiliating a loyal employee because of it is not only in poor taste but downright baffling to me. As far as I know, only one person found it funny—you.

Back to November 2001. I walked into J.R.'s office at the Nassau Coliseum. He looked up at me, that ubiquitous black cowboy hat on his head, a concession on his part to a time when Vince thought plain old Jim Ross wasn't entertaining enough.

"I heard about that *Today* show deal," J.R. said.

"I guess no one's ever had WWE banned from an appearance before, huh."

"No, can't say they have." J.R. then got serious, leaning forward in his chair. He said, "Mick, we think we're at a pivotal point in our relationship with you here."

I nodded in agreement.

"Vince and I feel that if we were to keep you here, it might very well prevent us from doing business together in the future."

"I think you're right," I said.

"But if we were to let you go, now, we might be able to do business in the future."

"You mean?"

"Mick, we're going to let you out of your contract."

Yes, free at last, free at last, thank . . . never mind. Sure, it was important, but not quite worthy of ripping off Dr. King's famous speech. But for now, it was good to be free. So, with the exception of one final *Raw*, where I was infamously flown out to Charlotte, North Carolina, just to be fired aboard the WWE private jet, I was free.

Free to pursue my own projects. Free to fail at them. Free to come back, of my own volition, with my tail tucked between my legs. But that was all off in the future. It would be eighteen months before I would see Vince McMahon again.

Dear Hardcore Diary,

Who knows when inspiration will hit, or why? Some of the world's greatest songs have been written on napkins or matchbook covers when inspiration struck at unlikely moments.

I do know that I've just become inspired in a fairly unlikely place—a small commuter plane en route from Columbus, Ohio, to New York's LaGuardia Airport. Luckily, I have my trusty notebook on hand, so no napkins or matchbooks will be required to document my extraordinary burst of brainpower.

I once heard Julie Miller, one of my favorite singers, repeat a line that she'd grown up hearing—that there was no such thing as problems, only solutions. Well, the road to wrestling immortality is littered with these types of problems, bumps, and potholes blocking the creative process—bumps and potholes requiring immediate solutions. Because without those immediate solutions, that ultimate destination, wrestling immortality, can be an impossible place to reach.

I know "wrestling immortality" sounds like a pretty pompous phrase. Wrestling fans are an extremely loyal group, but man, they can be a little fickle, too. Which I guess they should be. After all, they are constantly bombarded with spectacular images, dramatic storylines, and an ever-increasing array of physical maneuvers. During the late 1990s the stakes got incredibly high, and the Monday Night Wars between WWE and Ted Turner's WCW upped the physical and creative ante to an unprecedented degree. Wrestling fans have seen so much, so often, that they have indeed become a little jaded.

Yet even within this overcrowded context, it remains possible to capture a special magic, to catch lightning in our own twenty-by-twenty-foot bottle, to etch an indelible sports entertainment memory into the heart of even the most jaded of our fans. It's those types of memories that made me love this stuff as a kid. It's the very possibility of creating those types of memories for others that keeps me loving it today.

And it was that type of indelible memory that seemed to be in jeopardy when I was given the news in Columbus that some unnamed person had taken issue with one of my ideas. Hell, it wasn't just any idea—it was my *best* idea. It was the idea that made me call up Vince in the first place to request our historic meeting. It was the idea that had people falling out of their chairs in laughter at the damn meeting. It was the idea that was going to make millions of fans sit up, take notice, and realize in the course of just a few minutes that Terry Funk was someone to take seriously enough to tune in for next week's *Raw.* Seriously enough to pay to see him at the ECW Pay-Per-View on June 11.

Terry Funk is the greatest wrestler I've ever seen. I'm not saying he is the greatest wrestler ever, only the greatest that I have ever personally witnessed. No one made an impact quicker than Terry Funk, and there has never been a more believable wildman in the history of the game. Maybe Bruiser Brody was just as wild in the ring, but in my mind, when it came to a combination of ring work, promos, and antics that made even grizzled veterans suspend disbelief, no one could beat my friend and mentor Terry Funk.

I still marvel at old tapes of the Funker in action, still wonder how he could just seemingly take over a wrestling show in a few short weeks. Whether it was building toward a bloody climax in the 1970s with Dusty Rhodes in the old Florida territory, or building intense heat in anticipation for the return of an injured Ric Flair in WCW in 1989, no one got over quicker, or was more authentic in their madness, than Terry Funk.

He claimed to be "middle-age crazy" during that classic Flair feud. He was forty-two then, and yet it took him only a few weeks to make that whole show his own. But now, at sixty, he's no longer middle age, he's just damn old, and he no longer has a few weeks to make his presence felt, he has only a few precious minutes.

So just how exactly can a sixty-year-old man, who hasn't been seen in WWE rings in eight years, who is a virtual unknown to a large majority of our fans, be expected to become a main-event star in just a few short minutes of natural television exposure? After all, getting over with the fans isn't easy—if it was, everyone would be doing it. There's no scientific formula, no magic wand to wave, even if Ric Flair did once insinuate that Vince McMahon had worked some type of special magic to turn a loser like me into a WWE champion.

No, there's no magic formula, but when it came to the WWE return of Terry Funk, I believed I had the next best thing. Terry Funk was going to bite a chunk out of Vince McMahon's ass.

Only, if a person on the creative team had their way, there would be no ass-biting, no instantaneous star-making, no reason to tune in next week, no reason to pay for the privilege of seeing an all-time great like Terry Funk.

Why? They were worried. "How will it look if someone who isn't even on our roster is the downfall of the 'Kiss My Ass Club'?"

I pleaded my case to Brian Gewirtz. He and I have always gotten along, possibly because he was a huge fan of mine during his formative years, and possibly because we each considered Professor Bob Thompson to be our favorite teacher in our respective college years. I had Thompson at SUNY Cortland, where he concluded that my senior film project (which consisted in part of a deranged doctor using human testicles as deadly projectile weapons) was an expression of a hidden longing to be a woman.

Gewirtz had him several years later at Syracuse, thirty miles north and about twenty grand a year more expensive than my alma mater. To the best of my knowledge, Professor Thompson (who will actually love being in this book, as it will no doubt endear him to a whole new generation of communications nerds) made no such repressed-gender-jumping conclusion in regards to Brian Gewirtz.

Professor Thompson and I still talk about once a year, and even discussed our fond mutual recollections of our respective *Today* show appearances with Katie Couric. We both agreed that making Katie laugh was one of life's great moments. "It's just such an honor to give her any type of pleasure," Bob said. I agreed with the professor, and suggested maybe one day, the three of us, me, Bob, and former presidential candidate Bob Dole, could all get together to swap warm, fuzzy stories of our good times with Katie.

Where was I? Oh yeah, Gewirtz. Yeah, I was pleading my case to him, even pointing out that the mere suggestion of the "Kiss My Ass Club" closing up due to a mere chunk out of an ass was ludicrous. "Why would it have to be the end?" I said. "Why couldn't Vince just reinstate the club a few months later? He could do it with a whole new intensity, a sense of vengeance."

Gewirtz knows my passion for good storytelling and knows that in my mind, leaving the bite out of the ass of Vince McMahon would be like leaving the bite out of the apple in *Snow White and the Seven Dwarfs*. Sure, you'd still have some funny gags and some likable characters, but no heat on the heel and a big hole in the storyline.

"I'm not saying that it won't get done," Gewirtz said.

"Only that it might not get done, right?"

"Right."

Damn, I couldn't take that chance. Not if I wanted this idea of mine to have a fighting chance at attaining immortality. From time to time, I've been accused of doing things only for the paycheck. And from time to time that's true. Hey, not every idea is a great one, and sometimes a paycheck is our only solace. I even found out last night that a guy I considered a good friend had referred to me as a "whore" at a creative meeting a few years earlier— as a guy who did things only for the money. Again, I'll admit to being guilty of that occasionally, even if "whore" is probably a little rougher term than I deserve.

I should have been more pumped up following last night's *Raw*. Man, we'd really laid down a hell of a foundation on which to build our program. But that conversation with Gewirtz was gnawing at me, taking little bites out of my confidence like a tufted titmouse on the suet feeder hanging from the dead Japanese maple outside my kitchen window. (I'm trying to make this book somewhere in the PG-13 range, so I've got to work in words like *titmouse* where I can.)

I just couldn't take the chance. I had to come up with a new twist, a way to persuade Vince and the whole creative team that we could not only have Terry Funk take a chunk out of his ass, but create a long-term storyline that would see the eventual reformation of a "Kiss My Ass Club" that was bigger, better, and badder than ever.

My answer? Melina. For most people reading this book, the name Melina is self-explanatory. But as I am occasionally reminded by mothers who picked up their son's copy of *Have a Nice Day*, or *Foley Is Good* (and to a much, much lesser extent, my novels *Tietam Brown* and *Scooter*) and couldn't put them down, the idea of a reader not being familiar with the

name Melina is not inconceivable. Unlikely, yes. Unfortunate, definitely. But not inconceivable.

So for those moms and others not familiar with her, I will simply describe Melina as a beautiful young lady that I have come to feel almost like a big brother to. Assuming, of course, that my sister would be Latina, exotic, voluptuous, and possess the single greatest ring entrance in the history of sports entertainment. Possibly in the history of *all* entertainment. As I write this, I'm willing to bet that in the process of transforming my writing from handwritten notebook paper to towering best seller, someone will see fit to put a photograph in the book right about now, thereby relieving me of the responsibility of painting any real descriptive written portrait of the lovely Melina. Turn back a page; there she is. Beautiful, right? Take a good look, because that's the girl who is going to save my idea, the girl who will clear the road to wrestling immortality.

Dear Hardcore Diary,

I may have neglected a very important point in my last journal entry. You see, none of this stuff actually happens unless Vince McMahon says it does. Like President Bush, Vince ultimately is "the decider"; what he says goes. Unlike our president, Vince is a brilliant man, and although that brilliance doesn't always take the form of good taste and decent judgments, he is open to good ideas that may cause him not to "stay the course" if indeed he can be convinced that the current course is not the most prudent one. That's where I come in. Vince may be "the decider," but I'm "the persuader." I need to persuade Vince that my way is the better way, and because I feel very strongly about my idea, and the urgent need for Terry Funk to take a chunk out of Vince's ass, I'm willing to give up something very important to get my way. What exactly am I willing to give up to get my way?

My dignity.

I want to be really honest about the development of this whole ECW story. But my idea involves the sacrifice of my dignity at a later date, to get what I want now. I don't want to get into details about that later date, but I can assure all of you that it will be compelling TV. I hope it will result in that rare wrestling phenomenon—the story that actually makes people think and ask hard questions of themselves. Don't get me wrong, I love what we do, and have come to really value the importance of the escapist entertainment we provide. I also accept that for an awful lot of hardworking people, WWE television programming is a welcome oasis of big, bold, over-the-top fun amid a desert of dreariness. A lot of our fans like to check their worries at the door and enjoy the show on its own unique merits.

But I firmly believe that once they arrive at our location, we can occasionally hit them with images, incidents, words, or actions that make them take notice. Occasionally we can make them feel that genuine emotion—real anger, fear, or concern. Who knows how many goose bumps are raised cumulatively around the world on those special occasions?

If this willing loss of dignity idea goes as planned, it will involve a few of those rare moments, and in the process create sympathy for one character, and considerable heat for two others.

I did have one slight concern—I wanted to make sure that Melina, on whom this whole plot revolves, liked the idea. Either that, or I was looking for a cheap excuse to call her.

I met Melina only a few months ago, and was immediately touched by her warmth and kindness, which served as a sharp contrast to the "she-witch" character I had become a big fan of on WWE television. It had never even crossed my mind that the cruel young lady on my TV screen might be someone I would like to know, let alone become so immediately protective and fond of.

But if you think that fondness involves romantic visions or thoughts that are anything but of the utmost respect, you'd be absolutely right! No, wait, I didn't mean that. You'd be wrong, dead wrong. Honestly. I swear. For reasons that I can't quite explain, talking to her brings about only feelings of childhood innocence. Hey, there's a lot of things I can't explain about myself. Why exactly am I listening to classical Christmas music as I write this, over eight months before Christmas? Why am I writing it in a year-round Christmas room, for that matter? Why do I leave drawings my kids made nine years ago up on my wall, as if the oak paneling was some sort of giant refrigerator, meant for little children's artwork?

As some of you who saw *Beyond the Mat* might remember, my daughter Noelle went through a stretch of time where she had a rather unusual favorite word. Well, the drawing I'm looking at now was obviously created during that "nipple" phase, as every Foley member in this family portrait features a prominent set of them.

I can't explain exactly why I keep them taped to the wall, or why I have the Christmas fixation, except for a very uneducated guess that all this stuff helps me reclaim the innocence of youth, and that every good thing in my life somehow leads me back to Jefferson, New Hampshire, and the trip to Santa's Village my parents took me on when I was only three years old.

Don't get me wrong, I get improper thoughts all the time. As a matter of fact, in about three weeks, I will be doing a radio interview with Christy Canyon, the former adult film star that I used to have improper thoughts about quite regularly. Occasionally, I even acted on them. So, yeah, I get improper thoughts, just like everyone else. But Melina is not responsible for them. As a matter of fact, with the exception of a couple of borderline Candice Michelle thoughts, and a momentary Stacy Keibler exception, I have had nothing but proper thoughts about the whole Diva crew.

But that doesn't necessarily mean I'm dying to do storylines with all the girls, especially storylines that involve me completely sacrificing my dignity. I'm willing to do this one with Melina for three very good reasons:

1. She's very talented and will be able to pull off this difficult role;
2. It will ensure that I do get my way in the "Terry Funk takes a chunk out of Vince's ass" idea;
3. It does indeed give me a cheap excuse to call her.

Which is exactly what I did.

I was at a great place called Abilities, formerly known as the National Center for Disabilities, when I made the call. I was a guest for the media day, which precedes their fortieth annual "Sports Night," a gala fund-raising event that regularly includes some of the biggest names in sports history. This year's guests for the May 18 event include Jack Nicklaus, Jim Brown, Gayle Sayers, Mike Schmidt, Frank Gifford, and me. Jeez, what the hell am I doing in there?

Actually, my role is vital to the success of the fund-raiser. You see, while Sports Night might feature a bonanza of bona fide sports heroes, very few are actually willing to participate in the cornerstone of the gala—the annual play, in which former Olympic skater (as well as former wife of NFL Hall of Famer Terry Bradshaw) Jo Jo Starbuck choreographs an amazing spectacular in which the students at Abilities and any willing athletes sing, dance, and act their hearts out for the entertainment of a very appreciative high-dollar crowd. Oh, and one group of people is made to look like complete fools in the process. And believe me, it's not the kids.

I grew up idolizing people like Willis Reed and Walt "Clyde" Frazier of the New York Knicks. I always hoped that I would one day get to meet them.

Now I see them every year. I guess in some ways, it's like a dream come true. But for some reason, in my dreams, I was not singing or dressing in women's clothing while making their acquaintance.

As a result of the unique demands of this play, not to mention the six hours of rehearsal needed to perform, Jo Jo pretty much has the same list of willing participants every year. With slight year-to-year variations, it's usually '69 Met Buddy Harrelson, an Olympic bobsledder whose name I can't remember, former Islander Steve Webb, U.S. karate coach Tokie Hill, Olympic gold medalist Sarah Hughes, and me. Sarah has actually been doing the show since she was a twelve-year-old unknown, and as a result of our mutual willingness to make fools out of ourselves, we have become good friends. This year we'll see the acting and singing debut of her sister Emily, who represented the United States in the Olympic Winter Games earlier this year. I have known Emily since she was just a kid, and look forward to her inaugural appearance at the event.

At last year's event, I attempted something new, a brave and bold exper-

With my favorite Olympians, Emily (left) and Sarah.

iment in male bonding that met with mixed results. During the grand finale, a genuinely emotional number that saw the kids and athletes turn "The Impossible Dream" into "The Possible Dream," I turned to former hockey tough guy Webb, whose face is every bit as scarred and beaten as mine, and said, "Watch this, during the chorus, I'm going to put my arm around every major-league baseball player on this stage."

The experiment started off well enough—with a firm embrace of Harrelson, a great guy I've met at literally dozens of functions over the years. A Long Island radio personality once mentioned, "If you live on Long Island and you haven't gotten Mick Foley or Bud Harrelson's autograph, then you haven't tried very hard." I think there's a compliment in there somewhere.

It was then on to Harrelson's '69 Met teammate, Ed Charles. Charles had been in an earlier skit with me (where I was, of course, dressed like a woman), so I felt that he'd be responsive to a hug from the hardcore legend. He was.

Now it was on to the Yankees. Jim Abbott once pitched a no-hitter for the Bronx Bombers, with the benefit of only one hand. The other one wasn't just injured, it had been missing since birth. Abbott had seemed genuinely thrilled to serve as a role model for so many of the great kids at Abilities, so I didn't think he'd have a problem with a friendly arm around his shoulders. He didn't.

Only one man stood between failure and completion of this mission. Unfortunately, that one man was one of the most respected and feared pitchers to ever take to the hill—Hall of Fame fireballer Rich "Goose" Gossage. I remember Gossage beaning my idol, Yankee catcher Thurman Munson, only a year before becoming a Yankee himself. Man, he'd seemed pretty intimidating back then. Plus, he'd seemed a little hammered at the cocktail party an hour earlier.

I felt a wave of apprehension wash over me. The chorus was nearing its end. I had to make my move. I took a deep breath, gathering all the testicular fortitude I could muster. Would it be enough? Only seconds to go. Hey, I'd been through worse than this—Japanese Death matches with Terry Funk, Hell in a Cell with Undertaker, traveling with Al Snow. How bad could this be?

I made my move, shuffling over to Gossage, preparing for this record-breaking bit of human contact. I reached out and put my arm around "the Goose"—who quite honestly didn't seem to care for the whole male bonding thing. If looks could kill, I'd have been history. If he'd had a couple baseballs in his hand, I'd have been served a healthy dose of chin music immediately. Not since the glory days of Fire Island's Cherry Grove would a man have taken two balls to the chin with such velocity. (Well, so much for my PG-13 book.)

Yeah, I made it back to my spot by the time the chorus ended, but it was as a beaten man. "You did it," Webb said, but deep down, I think he knew I'd failed. Aside from the kids on stage and the great supporters in the audience, the big winner of the night was Gossage. He'd done what had once been thought impossible—he'd taught the hardcore legend the meaning of the word *fear.*

I think I'll stick to the Hughes girls this year—at least I know they like me.

Okay, back to the Melina phone call. The media day went pretty much as I'd expected—lots of attention from the kids, none from the media. That's usually the drill at these things, a little something I've learned from constant repetition.

I was at the Muscular Dystrophy Association's Muscle Team event last year, the annual fund-raising extravaganza that brings together members of the Jets, Giants, Yankees, Mets, and Nets, when a reporter tapped me on the shoulder and said, "Can I ask you a question?"

"Sure."

"Well, I've been standing here watching you interact with the kids, and I was wondering why all the reporters ignore you when you seem to be the kids' favorite?"

I said, "We all play a role here. The other athletes do a great job attracting the media and the sponsors. They bring in the money. My job is to spend time with the kids."

Once upon a time, things like that used to bother me. It didn't seem fair. But over time, I've learned to heed The Rock's advice from long ago. I know my role, and I shut my mouth.

But wait, Katie Couric's in the media, and she likes me, right? She even wrote it in a book. But damn, now that she's jumping ship from *Today* to the *CBS Evening News,* I'd say my days as a guest of Couric's are over. Yes, it's sad to say, but I believe Katie Couric has touched my knee for the very last time.

At one point in the media day, the guest celebrities went into designated areas to teach the kids a little more about the skills of their respective sports.

Ed Charles taught baseball basics. Steve Webb demonstrated stick-handling, even if his main skill as an Islander was beating people senseless. The Hughes sisters demonstrated Olympic skating skills, albeit on roller skates.

And as for me, I . . . Wait, what did I do? What *could* I do? Hit a kid with a chair? Get thrown off a tall structure? I mean, teaching physically challenged kids the basics of professional wrestling might not even be appropriate, and as a long list of WWE Superstars would be willing to verify, I don't really know the basics all that well anyway.

So I decided to take some questions. At first I handled the usual ones. "Yes, it did hurt when Undertaker threw me off the cell. Yes, I did enjoy teaming with The Rock at *WrestleMania*. Yes, I do think the current administration misled the American public during the buildup to the war." Then I heard another one, slightly different, a little more interesting. "Are you friends with the Divas?"

"As a matter of fact, I am," I said, beaming, proud of my friendship with so many of the girls.

"No, you're not," one kid said.

"Am too!" I shot back.

"Are not!"

"Am too!"

"Prove it," another kid said, prompting snickers from his buddies.

In such a situation, there's really only one way to prove that such a friendship between really beautiful girls and a dumpy, hairy guy exists—speed dial.

Up until this year's *WrestleMania* I had only a couple of names in my speed dial—after all, I barely knew how to turn one of these damn phones on, let alone enter names and numbers into it. My wife was on there, as was my son Dewey and my friend Jill Thompson, who illustrated two of my children's books. Oh, and Test was on there, too. Which of course makes perfect sense. Stacy Keibler put his number in there, back when, frighteningly enough, they were a real couple. I've been trying to get the damn number out ever since. But no matter how many ways I try to delete him, Test keeps coming back. I swear, Michael Myers and Freddy Krueger have nothing on that guy.

But following *WrestleMania*, I had two new names on the speed dial. Good ones, too. Trish Stratus, a great wrestler and a good friend for many years, was one. Melina was the other.

I'd utilized the Trish Stratus button a few days earlier, while watching the *Backlash* Pay-Per-View at my buddy Chris Giordano's house. I actually met Chris at my first-ever Sports Night, and have probably watched about twenty Pay-Per-Views at his house since then. I went the first time because Chris, a huge WWE fan, was a young man with cerebral palsy. I continue to go, five years later, because Chris is a great guy, my kids love going, his mom and dad treat us like part of the family, and well, I get to eat a lot of free food while I'm over there.

While watching *Backlash* we noticed that Trish had fallen awkwardly from the ring and that her match had ended shortly after, in an unceremonious manner. It just kind of stopped. I looked at Chris's wall, noticed a huge poster of Trish, and combining a desire to find out if she was okay with a desire to show off in front of Chris, gave the old speed dial a try. Trish didn't answer, but Chris went absolutely crazy when he heard her on the voice mail.

It was now Melina's turn to make me look good. I hit speed dial. "Hi, it's Melina." Again, just the voice mail, but the kids went crazy, nonetheless.

I waited for the beep. "Hi, its Mick Foley, and I'm hanging out with some really great kids, and they just wanted to say hello." The kids all yelled their greetings. "Also, I've got what I think is a really good idea, and I really want to tell you about it. So, I'll call you back in a couple of days, or you can call me back if you want. I'll talk to you later."

Keep in mind that writing a book by hand takes an enormous amount of time, especially when a completed manuscript is expected in two months. Because of the four kids running around the house, I do most of my writing at night, and subsequently spend much of the day exhausted.

I desperately need a good night's sleep every few days, or else I just won't have the energy to take command of the written page. In other words, the writing will start sucking. Not that it's Pulitzer material anyway, but hey, at least it's got energy. Right?

To ensure that good night's sleep, I do occasionally take a sleeping pill. I may have made a tactical error in taking that pill right before checking my messages. Hey, a message from Melina. She would love to hear my idea. Cool! What a great voice, too. All right, I'll give her a quick call, run down my idea, and be in bed in ten minutes.

I looked at the phone right before I hung up with her. Two hours and forty minutes! Damn. My longest phone call since I was in college and had a secret admirer, who used to call me at all hours of the evening and tantalize me with tales of forbidden lust that I had previously only read about. She would torture my innocent ears (I had both of them back then) for hours, while she simultaneously participated in solitary sex acts, which she described in great detail. It was a great relationship—not necessarily one that evoked childhood memories of Santa's Village, but great nonetheless. Then, unfortunately, we met.

Jeez, how was I going to explain this near-three-hour call to my wife? "You spoke to who? For how long?" My wife knows me pretty well, and she knows I possess a couple of odd but charming quirks, but I'm not sure even she would believe that I talk to this exotic, beautiful, voluptuous woman because she makes me feel like an innocent kid.

Besides, as I try to piece the conversation together, I realize I started fading in the latter stages, somewhere around the two-hour mark. I know she loved the idea, or else did a really good idea of pretending she did. She also seemed genuinely flattered that I would put so much faith in her, and that I would willingly sacrifice my dignity on her behalf.

Which seemed like a perfect time to repeat the words Terry Funk spoke to me right before putting me over in the King of the Deathmatch tournament in Yokohama, Japan, in 1995: "You know, I wouldn't do this for many people."

A Novel
Idea

I finally did write that novel. But I didn't take Judith Regan's offer, although it turned out to be the highest one. As a matter of fact, I took the lowest offer, which also involved the promise of the most rewriting and editing.

Let me assure you, *Hardcore Diaries* is primarily a wrestling book. Sure, I explore some other themes, but I will try to tie them all back in, somehow, to WWE. I am not going to make you suffer through a chapter about the creation of a novel you have probably previously chosen not to read. It's okay, you can admit it.

But as you will find out, *Tietam Brown* is what eventually brought me back to my WWE family. My second adventure in fiction, *Scooter*, is what led to an actual return to in-ring competition. So think of the novels as an extension

Steph dreaming of Honey Bunny.

of my wrestling career (albeit not a very financially successful one) and then suffer through a few pages about the origin of *Tietam Brown*.

I had actually thought about this book for close to a year. The idea had been on my mind for several months before the *New York Times* article actually came out. As far back as September of 2000, I remember sitting with Stephanie McMahon and Kurt Angle at lunch, regaling them with one of the two visions that made me think I could actually do one of these novel things.

I should probably point out that it was in June of 2000 that I wrote *Tales from Wrescal Lane,* a children's book that was eventually released in 2004, following a struggle with political red tape and my eighteen-month estrangement from the company. One of the two "tales" concerned little Steph's attempt to raise money at a yard sale for "Honey Bunny," the doll of her dreams. Along the way, her yard-sale stuff is destroyed, and the kids from Wrescal Lane (WWE Superstars as children) learn a valuable lesson about treating people with respect and kindness.

Vince had been very enthusiastic about the idea, so I sent in the Steph story, along with some prototype "Wrescals" (part wrestlers, part rascal) that my friend Jill Thompson, the artist who did the Halloween book with me, had illustrated.

A few days later, I was on the phone with Vince when he told me Steph wanted to say hello. What followed was one of my favorite conversations; one that, even without *Hardcore Diaries* to document it, would be hard for me to forget.

"Hi, Mick."

"Yeah, hi Steph."

"I can't tell you how much I like your story."

"Oh, thanks. I appreciate it."

"You know, up until I read it, I never thought that you liked me."

"You?" I said in disbelief. "Why?"

Now, I'm going to double-check with Steph to see if it's all right to say this, but my recollection is that she was pretty close to tears, so unless I'm overruled by Steph or if WWE doesn't want her to seem sympathetic, try to picture this moment as a tearful one.

She said, "Well, I always got the feeling that you didn't respect me, because I hadn't paid my dues. That you thought I was only here because I was Vince's daughter."

I didn't really know what to say. I mean, her thoughts, which she had actually shared with Vince, were actually a long way from the truth. As it turned out, I was wrestling Triple H, who was managed by Stephanie at the time when WWE first started scripting interviews. Because I was new to this scripting process and because, to this day, I don't completely believe in it, I was very likely to stray from the script, leaving Stephanie to interpret my actions as a personal sign of distaste for her.

"Steph. That's really strange, because you've always been one of my favorite people."

"Really?"

"Yeah, really."

And with that one conversation, Stephanie McMahon and I became good friends, which I consider us to be to this day. In September of 2001, she took on some more responsibility, assuming the role of one of the show's writers. But prior to that, for a few months after I returned to WWE as commissioner in June of 2000, Steph and I would talk and hang out frequently. So it was not unusual that we would be hanging out with our frequent lunch mate and good friend Kurt Angle when I first spoke of my initial vision for *Tietam*.

"I've got an idea for a book." I told them. "Not really a book yet, just an idea for a scene."

"Let's hear it," Steph said.

"Well, it's about this shy kid, Andy, who was given up for adoption when he was a baby. He's had a kind of tough life, been kicked around in foster care, done a few years in a juvenile center, when his dad comes back into his life."

"Sounds good," Kurt said. Since Kurt probably won't be a big part of *Diaries*, I'll just state that he's a great guy, an absolutely phenomenal wrestler, and someone I'm proud to call a friend.

All right, with that out of the way, let's get a little weird. "Well, Andy comes to find that his dad has some strange habits, including participating in some really loud sex in the bedroom next door. Sometimes he encourages his son to listen with his ear next to a glass against the wall."

Steph and Kurt were both nodding. I mean, let's face it, this father is a great character. Even some critics who didn't care for the book as a whole had to admit the dad was memorable.

"Well, the night is Christmas Eve, and Tietam hires actors to re-create the Nativity scene on his front lawn." Which I thought was completely original until I saw the same idea on *Curb Your Enthusiasm* a year or so later, before *Tietam* was actually out.

"On this night, Andy has fallen asleep, using his Nat King Cole cassette to drown out the sex next door. He awakes to find that something weird is going on, you know, under the sheets. He's startled and he sits up, causing the girl, who had been, you know, doing something to him under there, to retreat from the bed. Andy sees that it's the Virgin Mary, or at least the girl who's dressed like her."

Steph and Kurt were transfixed. I think Kurt was even turned on. He was touching his gold medal in a suspicious way.

"But Andy's dad is not about to let either one of them off so easy. He more or less orders her to finish the job (you can imagine what kind of job it is), and Andy's too scared to say no. So you simultaneously have this kid experiencing both the worst and best feelings of his life. He tries to escape the reality of his situation by turning on his cassette player, so you have this really traumatic episode juxtaposed with the beauty of Nat King Cole's 'Oh Holy Night.' . . . Well . . . that's it. What do you think?"

Steph claps her hands. "I think it's awesome, Mick."

Kurt just stares, then says, "I think you've got some serious problems."

But it was all a ruse by Angle, a way to deny the vague sexual tension that had existed between us for months. Without thinking, I lunged for the former Olympic champion, drawing him into my warm embrace, not caring how many WWE Superstars were witnesses to our forbidden . . . What the hell! Yes, I'm kidding.

I think that lunchroom loquaciousness was actually my first public expression of my ideas. Before that, it had just been a seed in my brain, which over the course of the next year or so seemed to flower and grow, until all that remained was to take all the visions and inspirations that had kept me awake on so many occasions, and put it down in words.

Quite frankly, I was scared. Exaggerating to wrestling stars was one thing. Creating characters, plots, and dialogue was something altogether new. If I'd taken Judith Regan's offer, I guess I would have been forced to. But without a contract to bind me, I bided my time, never quite finding the courage to enter the bold new world of fiction.

If not for the events of September 11, 2001, I may very well have chosen not to enter that world at all. But after mourning the loss of lives, the loss of humanity, and the loss of our country's sense of safety for a month, I felt the need to sit down and write. Really, it was an act of escapism. Because for six weeks I retreated from the world (although much of *Tietam* was written on the road), finding great comfort in my long hours of solitude, telling the upbeat, optimistic tale of redemption that was *Tietam Brown*.

Unfortunately, I was about the only person who saw it as optimistic or upbeat. The word most used to describe it was *dark*. Another common adjective was *disturbing*. I remember checking my messages while I was in England, filming *Robot Wars* for Spike TV, and hearing Barry Blaustein's voice. Blaustein was the director of *Beyond the Mat*, the acclaimed wrestling documentary that wasn't all that popular with Mr. McMahon. But Barry and I have remained friends—I'm even staying with him when I go out to California next week—and he was one of the first people to read the original *Tietam* manuscript. Barry is a well-known Hollywood scriptwriter, so I trusted his opinion, and looked forward to his feedback. What I heard was a little surprising.

"Hi, this is Barry. I just finished your book. And it's really good, but it's really dark. I've been having trouble sleeping. Okay, bye."

Dark? Was he crazy? Didn't he see the hope?

But as it turned out, he wasn't crazy. It *was* dark. But I've come to see the book as a microcosm for my worldview at the time: a pretty bleak place with just a little light shining through.

My literary agent, Luke Janklow, had sent the book out to several publishers, many of whom were enthusiastic, but all of whom had the sense to comment, "The girl's got to live." At first I fought it, saying some pretentious artist thing about "sticking to my vision," but the more I thought about it, the more I came to see the enormous power such a change afforded me. I was bringing someone back from the dead. I was like James Caan in *Misery*, Dr. Frankenstein in—um, what was the name of that movie?—like Vince McMahon resurrecting Mark Henry's career.

Besides, I really liked the girl in the story—maybe even had a crush on her. As far as I can tell (and I have asked for some female opinions on this), even as a married man, it does seem to be permissible to have a crush on another woman, as long as the woman is fictitious, and you are the guy creating her. Pretty cool, huh?

One morning, I received a phone call from Luke, who had sent out the revised manuscript (the one where the girl lives) and had gotten a couple of firm, respectable offers. Neither were quite as high as Judith Regan's original, sight-unseen offer, but they were nonetheless pretty substantial.

"You're going to think I'm crazy," Luke said.

"Okay, what is it?"

"I mean, you're going to think I've lost my mind."

"What is it, Luke?"

"I sent the manuscript to Knopf."

"So?"

I had no idea of Alfred A. Knopf's lofty status in the book business. It was the home of John Updike, V. S. Naipaul, and a lot of other writers whose work I'd never read. I went into my office, which houses a pretty impressive library. Hundreds of volumes, and not a single Knopf among them. Wow, they must be prestigious if I don't read them.

By the time I spoke to the Knopf editor, Victoria Wilson, I was fully aware of what Alfred A. Knopf represented, and how prestigious writing for them would be. I was also fully aware of Ms. Wilson's reputation. "She's not a back-slapper," Luke told me. "She's not going to feed your ego and tell you how great you are. But she will challenge you and make you a better writer."

I dreaded that call. I was terrified of her. Until meeting Melina, it was the most frightened I'd ever been to talk to a woman. I was like Ebenezer Scrooge meeting the Ghost of Christmas Yet to Come. And not the Reginald Owen Scrooge either. Not the George C. Scott, not the Bill Murray in *Scrooged*, not Michael Caine in *A Muppet's Christmas Carol*, not Scrooge McDuck in *Mickey Mouse's Christmas Carol*, and certainly not Henry Winkler in *An American Christmas Carol*. I'm talking about the Alastair Sim, down on his knees, shaking in fear, saying, "Spirit, I fear you most of all" *Christmas Carol*, which is sometimes called *Scrooge*. That's how scared I was.

"I like it," Ms. Wilson said. "You're a natural storyteller. But it's got problems, major problems. I'm not talking about a few edits, either. I'm talking about major structural problems requiring considerable rewriting."

Although Victoria Wilson neither looks nor sounds anything like her, I was actually picturing Margaret Hamilton as Ms. Gulch in *The Wizard of Oz* as I was writing that. Probably not much of a compliment until my admission that I always found the Wicked Witch to be quite sexy. Hamilton, as you know, also played the Wicked Witch in *Oz*. Because as you remember, the whole trip to Oz was a dream, and therefore all the characters played dual roles. Ray Bolger, for example, played both the Scarecrow and Huck. Bert Lahr was both the Cowardly Lion and Zeke. Jack Haley was both the Tin Man and Hickory. And though it took me a while to figure it out, Frank Morgan, an old vaudeville performer, was both the Wizard and Professor Marvel (and the Emerald City doorman, the carriage driver, and the Wizard's guard), which I guess I should have guessed, because of the mystical nature of both characters. Wait, what the hell was I talking about anyway? Oh yeah, Knopf.

With pen in hand, I headed for the spare room above my detached garage about thirty yards away from my house, where I had done the bulk of the *Tietam* writing while sitting in an orange padded chair that super fan Andy Wong of Kowloon's Chinese Restaurant in Saugus, Massachusetts, procured for me from the Worcester Centrum. Why the Centrum? Because that's the building I won my first WWE title in, from The Rock on December 28, 1998. Did the seat hold any emotional value for me? None whatsoever. But it was still a nice gesture, and it sure beat paying a small fortune for one of those ergonomically designed chairs.

Before heading to the spare room, I had given my wife explicit instructions not to bother me under any circumstances. "I don't know how long I'll be in there, "I said. "It might be ten hours, it might be eighteen. But I've got a lot of work to do."

No more than two hours later, I heard my daughter Noelle's voice outside. "Dad, Dad." I feared it was an emergency, the only explanation for an interruption at such a critical time in my writing career.

With my staunchest literary supporter, my wife, Colette.

So away to the window, I flew like a flash, tore open the shutter and threw up the . . . Wait a minute, I think I just spoke through the window screen.

"What is it, honey?"

"Mom says you have to help unload the groceries."

"Tell Mom I'm working."

A few minutes later, I heard her come again. "Dad, Dad."

"Yes, Noelle."

"Mom says she needs your help with the groceries."

"Did you tell her I was working, honey?"

"She says she doesn't care."

With that, I stormed down the stairs and charged the house, ready to fight for my artistic rights.

"Colette, I told you I had to work all day."

"Yeah, I know," she said. "You can go back to work after you unload the car."

"But this is my job. I'm a writer."

"Yeah, sure, Mick."

"I'm not joking," I pleaded, sounding like Donald Sutherland's feeble professor in *Animal House,* the one who finally confesses that his novel in progress is a "piece of shit."

Colette just looked at me, and despite one last protest of "I've written four best sellers," I headed for the car, realizing that convincing my wife, let alone the literary world, that I was really a writer was going to be more of a challenge than I thought.

"Darling."

"Yes, Vicky."

"You cannot rewrite a book in five days."

I was terrified. I should have just said, "Yes, ma'am," but I had put about seventy hours of work into those five days, and I thought my rewriting was pretty good. So I asked what I felt was obvious. "Why not?"

"Because I've been doing this for thirty years, and I know it's not possible."

"But have you read it?"

Victoria let out a frustrated sigh. "Listen, Mick, I have a fifteen-hundred-page manuscript and a thousand-page manuscript to edit. When I am

through with those, I will read your changes. I don't know how long it will take."

Man, I loved writing that novel, but I missed the breakneck creative pace of WWE, where I'd get an idea while barreling down the freeway at 3:00 A.M., and it would come to life in front of millions the very next evening. I think Tom Petty was right. The waiting really *is* the hardest part.

It was about two weeks later when I got the fateful call.

"Darling, how are you?"

My heart was pounding. "Well, that depends on you, Vicky."

"Well, there are a few problems."

"Are they big problems?" I asked.

"One of them is," she said.

"Okay, let me have it."

So, she let me have it. But it really wasn't that bad. She was proposing a big change, but one that basically involved deleting some religious passages. No real rewriting. Vicky felt that my past as a wrestler was going to make me an easy target for critics, and she didn't want unnecessary religious controversy to overshadow the characters and the story. The other change was fairly minor.

"Is that it?" I asked, almost unable to believe my luck. "So, we're ready to print it?"

"I must admit," Vicky said slowly, "I am impressed not only with the work you did but the speed in which you did it."

I was shocked. "Is that a compliment?"

"It's as close as you're going to get from me," she responded. Despite the fact that she was a stern taskmaster, I have often been told how highly she thinks of me, and despite the fact that I'm still terrified of her intellect, I like her very much as well.

"Don't worry," I said. "We'll keep this a secret between you and I."

"That's you and *me*."

"Damn."

But first, here's another exclusive. The next part—where I name the wrestler—actually took place many months before the previous part, where I rewrite the book in five days. If this was a Knopf book, Victoria Wilson would unleash her powers of intimidation on me, forcing me to go back to

the spare room over the garage to toil for hours, making late-night changes in the discomfort of that stupid orange Worcester chair. I'm hoping Margaret Clark, my editor at Pocket Books, will be willing to be a little more charitable. So what do you say we just leave it as it is?

All right, back to October 2001, during the writing-in-notebooks stage. Concerned about my legal safety, I asked a famous wrestler to take a walk with me. Accompanied by Edge and Christian, my favorite two eyewitnesses, the famous wrestler and I sat in a fairly secluded part of a forgotten arena, where I proceeded to read him a few paragraphs of *Tietam Brown*. It is not meant to be an exact reenactment of my conversation with this wrestler, but at times it's pretty damn close. As you read, think of me as poor, shocked Andy, and the wrestler in question as Andy's father, Tietam.

"Dad, I'm having girl problems."

He resumed his dinner-table *Thinker* pose and stroked his chin. He squinted a little and then closed one eye, a study in concentration. Surely he was weighing all the options, drawing inevitable conclusions, and would momentarily come bubbling forth with a sparkling nugget of knowledge that could transform my life in an instant. Then again, this was the same guy who'd used the term "bald-headed champion" only a few hours earlier. What had I been thinking?

His initial analysis of the situation surprised me.

"Well Andy, taking into account that all women are by nature different, and taking into account that you have yet to introduce me to your friend Terri, I would have to first warn you that forming a specific game plan for your specific situation could prove somewhat difficult."

He sounded smart. My dad sounded smart! I could almost feel those clouds dispersing.

"With that in mind, there are some generalities, some strategies if you will, that do appear to be effective with most woman I've encountered."

The anticipation was killing me. Sure my dad had his share of somewhat off idiosyncrasies, and yeah, maybe he didn't do things that other dads did, but women did like the guy, and there had to be a reason. And I was pretty sure it wasn't the fuzzy dice. He opened his mouth. "Well, Andy, whenever possible, get them to lick your ass."

The clouds in my mind that had seemed to disperse accumulated en masse and rained all over my parade. I waited for a big laugh, and then a pat on the back to let me know that I'd been had. We would share a good chuckle over the whole thing, and then he'd tutor me on the lessons of love.

Except he wasn't laughing. Or smiling. Not even a little. As a matter of fact, I'd never seen him quite this intense, not even when talking about the Suglings' scarecrow.

"That way, Andy, no matter what happens after that, you've always got something over them."

With that last line, I closed the book, took a deep breath, smiled, and said, "What do you think?"

Raven, aka Scotty the Body, aka Scotty Flamingo, aka Johnny Polo, looked every bit like a proud father. He was beaming. For a moment, I thought he might actually shed a tear. His first response consisted of two simple words.

"That's fabulous," he said before getting up and walking off in a strut more subtle, but every bit as proud, as the John Travolta paint-carrying Brooklyn bop of *Saturday Night Fever*.

Dear Hardcore Diary,

My son Mickey is a rock-and-roller. He's been that way since about the age of two. But he's also very particular about what he considers to be rock and roll. He's not much of a harmony guy, and definitely not a mellow rocker or light rocker. Just a basic three-chord guitar guy, who happens to make world-class rock-and-roll faces, although truth be told, he brandishes his air guitar a little high—almost like Tiny Tim on a ukulele solo.

It's not as if I'm some king of heavy metal dad either, the type of guy who forces the hard stuff on his kids at the expense of the classics. My musical tastes are kind of éclectic, running the spectrum from Christmas tunes to Emmylou Harris to Springsteen to Drive-By Truckers. Of course, as I mentioned in an earlier book, my definition of eclectic is many people's definition of rotten, and as a result, word spread among my fellow wrestler that the hardcore legend has the worst musical taste in the business.

Fortunately, little Mickey, now five, disagrees. He likes his dad's music just fine, but he can be just a little on the compulsive side when he finds a tune he truly loves. So over the course of the last few years, Foley family vacations have tended to become dominated by one particular song played continuously for days on end. Hershey, Pennsylvania, 2004 was the "We Will Rock You" vacation. Santa's Village 2005 was Tom T. Hall's "Sneaky Snake" and "Everybody Loves to Hear a Bird Sing." But for everyday usage, for sheer frequency over an extended time, nothing could come close to AC/DC's "Stiff Upper Lip." Until, of course, the little guy happened to hear "We're Not Gonna Take It," and his dad made the decision to put the *Stay Hungry* CD into the car stereo, a place it would remain without pause for several months.

I'll get to Twisted Sister in a few moments, but for now, let's get back to "Stiff Upper Lip." Sure, it was a good song, maybe even great. Rugged Angus Young guitar riff, typical over-the-top Brian Johnson braggadocio on the mike. But come on, hundreds of plays over the course of the years? "Play it again, Dad." Over and over? It just lacked that certain something that turns a great song into a classic. It wasn't the top-down, feel-good adrenaline rush of "You Shook Me All Night Long" or the spine-tingling slow build of "Hells Bells." Although I guess I should count my blessings—at least my little guy wasn't happily crooning along to "Big Balls" or "Given the Dog a Bone."

Hey, I just ran to my stereo to find that the *Back in Black* album was actually still on the turntable, a part of a failed experiment in my *WrestleMania* conditioning program, where I came to realize that no music, no matter how cool or how loud, was going to disguise the fact that the Foley knees just can't tolerate Hindu squats anymore.

But, hell, it will make for great writing music. So last night it was Tschaikovsky, tonight Angus Young. How's that for versatility?

Come to think of it, Angus was the main reason I wanted to TiVo AC/DC's performance on the 2000 *Saturday Night Live* hosted by The Rock. Sure, it was the show that helped launch The Rock into the stratosphere, but for me, it seemed like my only chance to capture "Stiff Upper Lip" live, thereby showing little Mick and new "Lip" fan Hughie what true Angus rock-and-roll faces look like. Sure, the image of a fifty-year-old man dressed in a schoolboy outfit might be a little frightening, but not necessarily any more so than the sight of Don Zimmer in a spandex baseball outfit. Or his dad (Hughie's dad, not Zimmer's) in tights and brown leather mask, for that matter.

I entered AC/DC into my TiVo wish list about a month ago, a move that was bearing no musical fruit until one fateful day, when the 2000 *Saturday Night Live* popped up under "Upcoming Programs." I hit record and waited for May 3, the scheduled air date, to arrive.

I watched the show this morning with my children, and found it did more than live up to my fond remembrance of it. The Rock was spectacular, and very much deserving of the attention Hollywood lavished on him as a result of it. Cheri Oteri was every bit as beautiful as I remembered her, and seeing her made me think back to how nice I was to her nephew, so that Cheri would think I was cool.

As for AC/DC—they rocked. Little Mick seemed transfixed by the classic Angus mannerisms, and Hughie happily belted out the same few words over

and over. "Stiff lip, stiff lip, oh stiff lip, oh stiff lip." Granted, the lyrics in their entirety are not likely to be confused with Bob Dylan's best from the sixties, but come on, a song with only three words in it would be a little ridiculous, right? Wait a second, my "Dude Love" theme music had only three words in it: "Dude Love, Dude Love, Dude Love baby, Dude Love."

Unfortunately, watching "Stiff Upper Lip" also brought back some bad memories, long-repressed images of horror that had seemingly been brushed from my conscious thoughts. But as I watched my little guys rocking out in the Foley Christmas room, those distant visions come flooding back, putting me face-to-face with two truths I could no longer deny.

It all started as a great bonding experience. Although The Rock was clearly the star of the show, Vince had done a little maneuvering that allowed me, Triple H, and Big Show to appear as well, a move that we hoped would create interest in our upcoming four-way main event at the 2000 *WrestleMania*. The Rock, of course, was the other entrant. At first, we all kind of felt like dogs trying to pick scraps off Rock's plate. There just seemed to be no reason for us to be there.

Fortunately, one of WWE's writers, Tommy Blotcha, who came from a background as one of Conan O'Brien's writers, was able to make some changes that gave us all a little more to do on the show. It all came off well, did monster ratings, helped The Rock immensely, and for a short time made Big Show look like a potential breakout comedy performer. I still think Show should give Hollywood a real shot one of these days.

Yeah, it all worked out well in the end, but during that interim period, the three of us scrap-pickers all stuck together, passing the time by exaggerating our in-ring abilities, waiting for the AC/DC sound check that we hoped would be the highlight of the day.

The boys didn't disappoint, tearing through not only their two scheduled songs on the show but three others as well for the benefit of the couple dozen cast and crew members who enjoyed the hell out of their own little mini-concert. They even dedicated "Highway to Hell" to us sports entertainers, probably because they'd earned a small fortune lending the tune to WWE for its *SummerSlam* Austin vs. Undertaker showdown.

We were all rocking out when Triple H made the first shocking discovery. I know I've expressed my desire to write a PG-13 book, and it seems like I've danced on the border of R-rated territory a couple of times. Something tells me I'm about to bust right over that border now. But, damn, there's really no other way to put it. I've really got no other alternative but to quote Triple H directly on this one. And Triple H's direct quote was pretty much, "Holy shit, look at the cock on Brian Johnson!"

Of course we all looked. We simply had to. It wasn't like he had it out and was waving it around. It was more subtle than that. But only slightly so. Because, I swear (and you can ask Hunter and Show about this), the damn thing ran about a third of the way down his thigh. It looked like an armadillo was resting in there. Like he was harvesting zucchinis or something. No wonder half the songs in his repertoire are thinly veiled tributes to his penis. I'd write songs about mine too, if it took up that type of room in my trousers.

As I write this, I can almost see the legal red flags being raised. "You can't print this," I'll be told. "It's slanderous." They tried the same stuff when I wrote *Have a Nice Day* and the zucchini farmer in question was Too Cold

Scorpio. I'll tell these lawyers the same thing I told the other ones—men don't consider accusations of possessing a giant penis to be slanderous. They consider it a compliment. (Not that I've ever gotten one.) Besides, if Johnson decides to play rough, I'll forewarn him—I've got witnesses. And they saw the same damn thing I did.

We all did our best to enjoy the rest of the song, but found our effort to be in vain when Big Show unearthed an equally shocking image. "Oh, my God," he said, in a voice befitting a seven-foot, 450-pound monster. "Look at Vince!"

For the second time during the course of the same song, we turned our eyes to a hideous sight. And no, Vince wasn't hiding animals in his shorts, or growing vegetables in his trousers. He was quite simply putting on one of the worst displays of dance moves ever witnessed by man or in this case, Mankind. This is where my limitations as a writer are obvious, because words alone simply cannot do justice to how bad Vince was. You have to use your imagination here. Think of Kenny Mayne on *Dancing with the Stars*, and multiply it by ten. No, it was worse than that. Think of Elaine Benes with the "thumbs-up" dance on *Seinfeld*. Then add a pompadour and shades of Elmore "crazy legs" Hirsch. You're now in the general neighborhood.

In the unlikely event that Brian Johnson does indeed find my contention that he had a massive member to be slanderous, I think I may indeed have a solution, albeit a slightly erroneous one. I'll simply do a little literary sleight of hand—pulling a slight switcheroo. In the new telling of the story, Johnson will have the bad dance moves, and Vince will have the produce department in his pants. Something tells me Vince wouldn't mind that change at all.

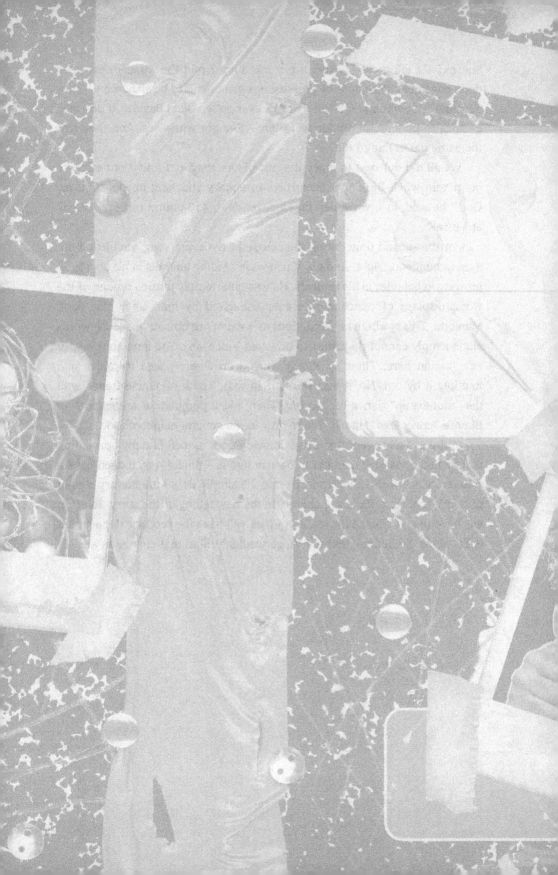

Dear Hardcore Diary,

My weight could pose a problem. I weighed in at 315 about ten days ago, when I started training in earnest for the ECW show. I realized that I'd dodged a bullet at *WrestleMania,* as my weight and conditioning wasn't much of a factor. But that match had incorporated several strategic moments of rest following brutal action, which allowed me to catch my breath. I didn't want to take any chances on this Pay-Per-View. I know the lead-up (unless the execution will be extremely screwed up) will be captivating, but unlike *WrestleMania,* this matchup is not just an "intangible"—it will be the foundation of the whole show.

Sure, the title match (at this point looking to be John Cena vs. Rob Van Dam), will have great heat, and other matches will shock and awe, but I firmly believe our match will be the one on which success hinges.

In all likelihood, I could get away with being 315. I mean with all the bells and whistles that the match will certainly entail, and with a tremendous partner like Edge to carry our team's workload, I will probably be okay. I am still capable of short bursts of great energy, and as a guy who took Clint Eastwood's *Magnum Force* advice—"A man's got to know his limitations"—to heart a long time ago, I do have a knack for working to my strengths and avoiding my weaknesses.

All the same, I'd really like to put "endurance" on the "strengths" list, which will require a couple of definite sacrifices. I need to work my ass off (or at least a good portion of it) in the gym, and I have to learn to just say no to all the candy, cakes, pies, chips, and especially ice cream that have been the staples of the Mick Foley diet for quite a while.

Actually, I eat a sensible, balanced diet for about twenty-three and a half hours a day. That other thirty minutes, however, can get a little ugly. That refrigerator (or freezer) door opens, and common sense just seems to disappear. I've made some pretty startling rationalizations while assuming that late-night/early-morning refrigerator stance. I have convinced myself that the rice in rice pudding is a mainstay of many Asian diets, and that the milk in the pudding is helpful in building strong bones. I have also noted that a portion of the proceeds from Ben & Jerry's Rain Forest Crunch is used to protect the environment. Hey, what more reason do I need? I'm a tree hugger of sorts. Two thousand late-night calories down the hatch.

But I've been fairly good these last ten days. Sure, I've authorized the consumption of some questionable items that most WWE performers wouldn't touch, but at least I've hit the gym on about eight of those days. Surely I would be able to chart my progress on the Gold's Gym scale. I'm mentioning their name because they comp me a membership, and I plan to point to this book, upon its publication, as reason they should continue to do so.

I stepped up on that scale and watched those numbers fly north: 297, 307, 312, and rising. Oh, no, 317. I'd actually gained two pounds. And something told me it wasn't muscle tissue.

I think back to 2004, when I was able to drop sixty pounds in six months, and I remember how stubborn my body seemed to be about giving up any more weight once I hit this 315 territory. I just had to blast through it. Train harder, eat smarter, avoid those late-night sojourns to the fridge.

I was in the middle of a sensible eating day when I foolishly said yes to the in-flight meal en route from New York to Los Angeles. So now I'm counting on my hardcore diary to take my mind off the guilt I feel on account of my decision.

This is my first time writing on a plane in several years. Wait, that's not exactly true. It's not even mostly true. I did quite a bit of writing on our trip home from Afghanistan this past December. This is, however, the first time I've worked on an actual book while flying in about five years. I actually did about ten hours of writing on that trip, about a young Afghan child who had been severely burned in a kerosene fire, whose image wouldn't allow my body or conscience to rest. I'll include that writing a little later in the book, but I don't think the time is quite right for something so heavy.

Because if I'm right, you are so caught up in my creative struggles, weight battles, and deep-rooted psychological issues that heavy talk about a sad child ten thousand miles away might throw us all off course.

I also wrote some letters on that trip, one of them to Candice Michelle. I know I've teased her name before, so I'm going ahead and giving you a little taste of Candice. No, this is not my "dream come true" story, but a cute little anecdote about a very kind, charming young lady, who also happens to have big boobs. And knowing Candice, I don't think she'll find that last comment insulting.

We were several hours into a flight that took forever, onboard an Air Force transport plane, not designed for asses like mine. Unlike other wiser wrestlers and crew members, I did not have the foresight to pack a DVD player, nor do I have the technological prowess to operate a computer. So it was basically me and a yellow legal pad with which to pass the time.

So, I withdrew my Pilot rolling ball pen like an ancient warrior's mighty broadsword and set about catching up with kids I sponsor around the world. I'll talk in greater detail about one of these children in particular a little later, but for now I'll just mention that sponsoring kids through Christian Children's Fund over the last fourteen years has come to be one of the most important parts of my life.

Let's see, how do I segue from sponsoring children to Candice Michelle? How about casually dropping the name of John Irving, possibly America's greatest novelist.

I had written to Irving, along with eight or nine other authors whose work I enjoyed, before the publication of *Scooter*, my latest novel, hoping to get a treasured "blurb," words of praise from fellow authors to slap on the cover of the upcoming book.

My editor at Alfred A. Knopf, Victoria Wilson, had sent out several letters to critically acclaimed authors prior to the publication of my first novel, *Tietam Brown*, and had gotten exactly zero responses in return. I figured I would send out handwritten letters to authors that I personally enjoyed, figuring that they might actually enjoy my stuff, as well. So I was basically asking complete strangers to take ten or twelve hours our of their lives to peruse the literary ramblings of a one-eared pro wrestler and then say something nice about it—for free. Ms. Wilson let me know that my prospects were fairly bleak. "I've read your letters," she said. "And they're very charming, but don't expect anything to happen." I didn't.

But, to my surprise, I received a call from esteemed novelist Richard Price about a week later. Price has been nominated for both an Academy Award and a National Book Award, and is universally respected in the literary world. Cinematic adaptations of Price novels include *The Wanderers,* the Spike Lee film *Clockers,* and *Freedomland,* starring Samuel L. Jackson, Julianne Moore, and Edie Falco.

"I'm really enjoying the book," Price said. "I'm going to give you a quote after I'm done."

"Wow, thanks, Mr. Price," I said in meek, non-hardcore fashion. This was kind of like a Little Leaguer receiving a phone call from Roger Clemens, saying, "You got some good heat on that fastball, kid."

"It really brought back memories," said Price, a born and raised Bronxite, who apparently found my depiction of the borough in its mid-1960s upheaval to be fairly authentic. "Maybe we could get together sometime and trade stories."

"Sure," I said, a little puzzled. "Stories about what?"

"About growing up in the Bronx."

I let out a little laugh. "I didn't grow up in the Bronx."

"You didn't?" Price said, surprised. "Wow, you must have really done your homework." It was the greatest compliment of my literary life.

A week later Price called me up and read me his quote, which was better written then anything appearing in any of my books.

In turns ashcan realist and operatic, lurid and heartfelt, sentimental and hard-nosed, Scooter *is an absorbing tale of one kid's growth into young manhood via sports; sports as an instrument of love, of revenge, of celebration and of destruction. It also, most compellingly, offers an athlete's contemplation of pain, and the unique brand of salvation that can come of its forbearance.*

—RICHARD PRICE

To my editor's great surprise, the blurbs kept coming—well, at least two of them did. Jonathan Kellerman, my favorite crime novelist, e-mailed me a good quote (which of course my son Dewey had to retrieve for me), and I also received a humorous one from Dave Barry, the beloved and hilarious columnist, memoirist, and novelist.

Most surprising of all was a call I received from my publicist at Knopf, Gabrielle Brooks, wanting to know if I had a problem with her giving John Irving my address. Problem? No, I didn't have any problem with that.

A few weeks later, *it* arrived in the Foley mailbox. The letter. Now I know how it felt when that kid received that bedside visit from Babe Ruth so many years ago. Or how Charlie felt when he got Willie Wonka's last golden ticket. Or how Test felt just about every night of his unfathomable relationship with Stacy Keibler.

He hadn't been able to read the book. He thought the first few pages were convoluted, poorly written, and unrealistic and then threw the damn thing out. No, he didn't say that, but he had been working on both a novel and screenplay and just couldn't find the time for *Scooter*. He did say, however, that he had read *Tietam Brown* and enjoyed it immensely. All right, I added that one word, "immensely." But the fact that he read it, liked it, and took the time to write (a full-page letter, no less) meant a great deal to me.

So, of course, out of respect, I wrote him back, thanking him. Now, how many people can say they got a letter from American's greatest novelist? Well, I guess anyone could *say* it, but how many had the proof in hand? I sure was thankful for the one John Irving letter.

Except Irving wasn't done with me. A week later, there was another one in the mailbox, encouraging me to keep writing, telling me not to worry about the opinions of critics.

It was while writing back to Irving, onboard that Air Force transport plane, that Candice asked her innocent question. "What are you writing?"

Candice had been seated in the row in front of me, so that the possibility of conversation required her to turn around in her seat to face me. I guess she also felt it required her to lean over slightly, allowing her two greatest assets to acquire a position of prominence in the general vicinity of my really wide-open eyes. Again, I could attempt to use my Knopf-honed writing skills to paint a portrait of Ms. Michelle, but will instead turn that responsibility over to our WWE photographers.

At that point in the letter-writing process, I had only written a paragraph or two, starting out with the words, "Somewhere in New York, Katie Couric is breathing a deep sigh of relief."

I once told Katie Couric that she had changed my life. She seemed quite surprised, maybe even a little scared. "Really?" she said.

"Yes, before I met you, I wasn't a name-dropper."

I was in the process of telling Irving that after a long run on top, Katie Couric had been supplanted on my name-dropping list, when Candice made her inquiry.

I thought about giving Candice the longest answer possible, so as to

Here's Candice in all her glory.
I'm sure my wife will love this photo.

ensure maximum viewing pleasure. Kind of like a voyeur's version of a Senate filibuster. Just keep on talking. Instead I gave her a short, bumbling answer, the type that had been my trademark throughout high school, college, and well into my mid-twenties.

"Um, I'm, you know, writing some letters."

"Oh, really," she said, seemingly oblivious to the precarious predicament her two assets had worked me into. "Who are you writing to?"

Yes! Yes! This was going to be awesome! I was going to look really smart in front of an absolutely gorgeous woman. I was going to drop my new favorite name, and impress the hell out a very impressive young lady. "Excuse me," I said. "What did you say?" Although obviously I had heard quite well the first time. I guess I was just prolonging my boasting time, as once I mentioned my correspondence with Irving, Candice would be all over me for more info on the origins of our acquaintance.

"Who are you writing to?"

"Oh, just a few kids I sponsor overseas." Good start. Candice smiled and let out a small sympathetic sigh. Obviously, she was impressed with my sensitivity. "And . . . John Irving." Yes, sensitivity and intelligence. I was indeed the total package. No, not the "total package," the wrestler who went to jail for nonsupport and blew the fortune he'd made in the ring.

I waited for her reply. Probably disbelief at first, followed by acceptance, joy, and finally, a long discussion about our favorite Irving novels.

But I guess it doesn't take a genius to figure out what she actually said. If you were voting for "Who's John Irving?" you'd win the prize.

I tried to jog her memory by listing Irving favorites that had gotten the Hollywood treatment—*The Cider House Rules, The World According to Garp, A Prayer for Owen Meaney*—but Candice wasn't biting. She really did think it was nice that I wrote to children overseas. Somehow, I ended up asking if she would like me to write her a letter. She nodded enthusiastically before turning back around, leaving me to finish my Irving letter without Candice's world-class distractions.

"I have come to realize," I wrote to Irving, "that the importance of the name dropped depends in great part on the company it is dropped in."

I actually did write that letter to Candice, and gave it to her as we boarded the plane for the return trip home. About an hour later, I felt a tap on my shoulder. It was Candice Michelle, with tears in her eyes. She leaned over and gave me a kiss on the cheek. "I love your letter," she said. "It's beautiful."

For all her beauty and physical assets, it is actually Candice's gentle nature and free spirit that have made the greatest impression on me. She reminds me of some otherworldly creature, like a fairy or an elf—floating around, flapping her wings, dropping in occasionally to dispense liberal doses of warm hugs and infectious laughter.

For all my fawning over the Divas, I actually have made it my policy not to look at any of the sexy stuff they do. I won't watch the videos, or look at their special magazines. It just seems like a breach of trust. Sure, sometimes I get curious, and wonder what harm a little peek at Torrie Wilson or Candice Michelle's *Playboy* edition would really cause. Probably none. Looking at naked picture of my friends would just feel a little wrong.

Besides, just knowing that I know bona fide *Playboy* cover girls, and knowing that they like me, is good enough for me.

Super Bowl champion Pittsburgh
Steeler James Farrior.

A Blurb from Batman

It's amazing how easily a WWE performer can function in so many cross-sections of society. For all the talk about demographics, I find our presence is accepted and appreciated in so many circles of entertainment.

Pro athletes are a standard front-row presence on *Raw* and *SmackDown!* and I'm always interested to see which famous actors are hanging out backstage at our L.A. shows. So I always seethe a little when I hear or read a news show or article that takes a potshot at what lousy athletes and actors we are. Oh, yeah, why don't you ask the certifiable athletes like Shaquille O'Neal, Ben Roethlisberger, or Charles Barkley who stop by our shows? Or award-winning actors and directors like Nicholas Cage, Michael Clarke Duncan, Arnold Schwarzenegger, Rob Reiner, and Jenna Jameson—okay, maybe the last award Schwarzenegger won was Mr. Olympia, and Ms. Jameson's performances won't send tingles of envy down Meryl Streep's spine, but I think you get the point. Other entertainers really seem to like what we do.

WWE just seems to fit in everywhere. I think about the places I've done autograph signings over the last few years. Wrestling conventions? That's easy. Monster truck shows? Yep. Muscle car shows? Same thing. A wrestler at a horror convention? Yeah, that seems to work. A comic book or science fiction show? No problem. Minor-league baseball, basketball, and hockey games? Sure. It all seems to work. Card shows, libraries, universities, even the Carnegie Museum of Natural History. Okay, so maybe that last one wasn't all that well attended.

I enjoy meeting the stars from all these different walks of life, and have compiled quite an autograph collection along the way. Whether it's talking with "Incredible Hulk" Lou Ferrigno, telling Hall of Fame pitcher Jim Palmer how nice he was to me when I was a ten-year-old kid, or getting to meet Barbara Eden, it's one of the small perks of WWE fame. I even got to meet Sybil Danning on a recent UK sci-fi exposition. Sybil is something of a B-movie queen, who made quite an impact on me with her 1983 *Playboy*. I even had a poster of her on my wall as a college freshman. Obviously, things had changed significantly by the time I met her. No longer an awestruck eighteen-year-old, I was now an awestruck forty-year-old. The girl on my wall, live, in front of me.

Reggie Jackson made quite an impact on me. I'll say this for Reggie—he still draws quite a crowd. I'll say something else for Reggie—his line of questioning can be a little inappropriate. Following a signing in northern Virginia, which consisted of seven Hall of Fame baseball players, beloved Redskin lineman Joe Jacoby, boxing great Joe Frazier, and me (yeah, I felt a little out of place), I found myself sitting in front of Reggie on our flight out of Washington, D.C.

I felt a tap on my shoulder. It was Reggie, the man whose three mighty blasts in game six of the '77 World Series made him a legend for the ages. "Hey, how much you weigh?" he asked.

I was a little surprised by the question, but felt, due to his Hall of Fame status, that a reply was in order. "Around three-ten, three-fifteen," I said.

Reggie nodded his head, and I went back to reading. I turned back around. Momentarily. Tap tap. I turned back around. "How much you make today?"

Hey, it was Mr. October, I had to be honest. Even if I felt a little strange about telling. But back then, right after retiring, I was commanding pretty big bucks. Reggie raised an eyebrow, obviously impressed, although I doubt my fee was even in Reggie's league.

"Watch this," he said as he got up from his seat and approached the flight attendant. Reggie asked a quick question, and then *appeared,* and I do stress the word *appeared,* to be blatantly looking down the young lady's blouse. He even turned and winked at me during the process.

But I got the better of Reggie Jackson on that day. During the course of the trip, his agent or manager set up an odd trade, the kind that a big-league manager would get fired for—a dozen signed Reggie Jackson baseballs for a dozen signed Mick Foley baseballs. Even up. A few days later, I received two dozen baseballs in the mail. The Reggie Jackson baseballs were beautiful; each in its own collector's box, each signature accompanied by Reggie's most prominent stat, his 563 home runs. It was known as the stat ball. Street value of maybe $75 each.

I signed my twelve balls and sent them back. No collector's box, no stat— although, come to think of it, I may have written "300 stitches" on one and "Missing right ear" on another. Street value of maybe $10 each.

Obviously I got the better of that deal. But what the hell was I going to do with twelve balls? I know what Al Snow would do with them, but these are baseballs I'm talking about. So I started giving them out to my friends. One of my buddies would come over to watch a game, and he'd walk away with a Reggie Jackson stat ball.

Apparently, my son Dewey mistook my gestures of friendship and deduced that the Reggie balls were appropriate for giveaways of all varieties. At his eighth birthday party, I couldn't help but notice that the goody bags the kids were leaving with seemed a little bulky. Care to guess what was in there? You got it. In addition to the 18-cent pontoozlers, the 9-cent lollipops, and the absolutely worthless Test trading cards, these particular third-graders were going home with a $75 Reggie Jackson stat ball.

No matter how old I get, there's nothing like the feeling of catching a foul ball for your kid at a major-league game. I remember when my dad snagged a Bob Oliver foul back in '71 when the Yanks played the Royals at the original Yankee Stadium—the house that Ruth built. I was the happiest kid in the world.

Man, how I love being able to do the same thing for my kids. Except I never quite have. Sure, I've brought balls home for them. But those have been given to me, I didn't really earn them. I did catch a foul ball at the World Baseball Classic, though, an opening-round game at Disney's Wide World of Sports in Orlando, which saw Venezuela take on the Dominican Republic.

What an incredible atmosphere, like a huge springtime party for fifteen thousand eager revelers, with flags of both countries being waved with great pride. Some of these people, I knew, had traveled great distances to support their team. I imagined great sacrifices had been made by many of the fans. So when I snagged my first-ever foul ball, I found myself in a dilemma. What should I do?

Okay, first things first—I didn't really snag the foul ball. Unless "snag" means picking up a foul ball that has bounced, rolled, and come almost to a dead stop right by my feet. I didn't trample over a kid to get it either, like that inconsiderate S.O.B. who practically clotheslined a six-year-old in order to secure the prized booty for his horrified girlfriend. I still remember the call of the announcer, "Congratulations . . . you JERK."

No, this one was mine, fair and square, and my kids were going to love me for it. But I wasn't sure I would love myself. After all, my kids already had quite a few baseballs, including one signed by George Steinbrenner. I looked into the crowd and saw thousands of children who would never know the thrill of going home with an official foul ball. I looked into the eyes of an adorable child, five, maybe six, big smile—a child who would cherish such a gift. Then I looked into my heart, before walking across the aisle, ball in hand, saying, "Would you like this?" Unfortunately the boy, who was nestled on his grandmother's lap, spoke no English, nor did she. "Presente?" I said, and the woman said, "Gracias," prompting the child to take the ball from my hand.

I returned to my seat, proud of myself, as I watched the young boy roll the magnificent prize in his tiny hands.

"That was really nice of you," the man next to me said.

"Thanks a lot," I said. "Just trying to do the right thing."

The guy nodded appreciatively, then said, "Do you know who that kid is?"

"No, who is he?"

The guy laughed. "You just gave your baseball to Miguel Tejada's son."

"Really?" I said. "Wow, he's probably already got a few."

At least he should. Miguel Tejada is a former American League MVP, and at over $11 million a year, he's one of the highest-paid players in the game. Yeah, I've got to believe his son's got a few baseballs laying around the house. His dad can probably afford to pack Reggie Jackson stat balls in his son's goody bags.

Early last spring, I was walking around my backyard, cleaning up branches, trying to get the Foley place looking its best. Each year we do some work on the house and think about selling it, moving to some part of the country or world where the dollar goes a bit further. Then each year we admit that we love it, and decide to stay for a while.

At the edge of our woods, I saw a distinctive shape peeking out of last autumn's fallen leaves. A baseball. Which was really no big deal, as we routinely lose a couple dozen or so over the course of a year. Sure, times have changed since my youth, where each kid on the block only had one or two, meaning every lost ball would prompt a massive search through the woods in pursuit of the sphere. I'm sure many a bad case of poison ivy was caught on these lost baseball quests.

But hell, the balls are cheap now; I can get a bag of a dozen for about fifteen bucks. Sure, they're crappy; vinyl cover, not leather, but when they head into the woods, we don't sweat it—we just reach for another. Actually, I still give chase, and occasionally admonish my kids for not bothering to conduct even the most rudimentary of searches.

Besides, this ball was easy. How could they lose this, no matter how cheap it was? Except this ball wasn't cheap. As I got closer, I could see the distinctive markings of a major-league ball. A major-league ball? My kids knew better than this. These were six, seven dollars a pop. I used to sleep in motel rooms costing less. That was a week's meal money back in Memphis.

But as I picked up the ball, I realized it was worse than I thought. It wasn't just any major-league ball. It was signed. Slowly, sadly, I deciphered the smudged words. "Dewey and Noelle, all the best, George Steinbrenner." How could they play with the Steinbrenner ball? How could they? Do you think they admitted doing the deed? No way. In an act that seemed to me to be every bit as clumsily orchestrated as a rare Al Snow TV win, both kids blamed Mickey. When in doubt, blame the four-year-old.

So over the years, I've been excited, alternately surprised, shy, and slightly dissapointed to meet some of the stars of my youth and present. But I've rarely been nervous. But that all changed at last spring's Super Mega show in New Jersey, when I found out who was on the card: Batman and Robin—Adam West and Burt Ward in what was billed as a "rare appearance together." That struck me as a little weird. Why would a combined appearance be rare? Didn't they belong together? How could they be apart? That would be like the Captain without Tennille, Zuko without Sandy, K.C. without the Sunshine band, Billy Gunn without the Road Dogg.

I looked over at the line. Big. Batman and Robin, it seemed, were the star attractions on this show. My line was respectable, but nothing like the mass of humanity stretched out to meet the Dynamic Duo. Actually, there were two lines. Two separate lines to greet the duo. One for Adam, one for Burt. And truth be told, they weren't actually "together." Indeed, there was a barrier between them, both physical and emotional. The physical barrier was a small partition between them, meaning there wasn't even any actual eye contact between the two aging crime fighters.

Why? As it turns out, West and Ward can't stand each other (or maybe it would be more accurate to say, West can't stand Ward), a hatred stemming from the Boy Wonder's not-so-fond recollection of his time spent with West in his tell-all memoir, *Boy Wonder: My Life in Tights*. After reading the memoir, I could see why. Actually, I read both memoirs, West's and Ward's, putting me high up on the list of all-time superhero-loving losers. West's offering, *Back to the Batcave*, was more of a standard, nostalgic look back on his career, focusing on his time under the cape and cowl. Sure, he wrote of his post-Batman career slump and subsequent depression, and he seemed to be a little on the psychologically delusional side when he made his case for still being Batman in the 1989 Tim Burton film. But most of it was a good-natured stroll down memory lane.

Burt's book wasn't so much autobiography as full-fledged sexposé, with Ward playing the role of one-man cheering section for his own performances, sexual or otherwise. Whether he was talking about fighting Bruce Lee to a draw during a sparring session, his ability to speed-read thirty thousand words a minute, or the challenge the *Batman* costuming department faced in trying to make his massive member less threatening to the television audience, the Boy Wonder didn't pass on any opportunity to toot his own horn. But, judging by the words, he wasn't the only one tooting it. Holy love machine, Batman! The guy had stats that blew Reggie Jackson's away. He had, like, Wilt Chamberlain stats. No, I'm not talking about the hundred points at the old Hershey Arena either.

He didn't exactly do West any favors in the book, either. I guess it wasn't that bad. Aside from being portrayed as a philandering, adulterous, pompous windbag, West actually came off quite well. But that's not the way Batman saw it. After all of those near-death experiences, those "Same Bat-time, same Bat-channel" cliff-hanging predicaments, I guess West thought he deserved better. After all those occasions where Robin had slid so gracefully down his batpole, there should have been a stronger bond. After all the times Robin had played so enthusiastically in the dark confines of West's batcave . . . oh, never mind. Suffice to say, Adam West had every right to be angry, even if that anger played itself out in the form of crushing the illusion of crime-fighting camaraderie that so many longtime fans had lined up to see.

The fans were really disappointed. One by one, they'd walk past my table, head down, dejected, clearly disillusioned, after their ultra-quick encounter with the caped crusader.

"What's wrong?" I asked one particularly battered-looking batfan.

"Oh, man," the poor guy said. "Batman's a dick."

A dick? Batman? Did this guy realize his accusation of penile impersonation bordered on blasphemous? But then I thought back to some interviews I'd seen of West over the years, where he had occasionally seemed arrogant. Perhaps a dicklike demeanor was not beyond the scope of imagination.

I said, "Really? What do you mean?"

"Well, he won't sign anything Burt has signed. And he charges like twice as much if it's even a picture that Burt is in."

By this point, a few other disappointed fans who shared this man's bat-pain had gathered by my table, sensing they had an understanding shoulder to lean on, a way to vent their sadness and frustration.

"He won't even make eye contact," one such sad soul said.

"No eye contact?" I said in disbelief.

"None."

Another bystander summed it up well, using a now-familiar phallic phrase: "Batman's a dick."

Oh, no, this wasn't good for the hardcore legend. Why? Because little Mick was a huge Batman fan, and I had planned on surprising him with an autographed photo of the duo, who seemingly before my very eyes had gone from dynamic to demonic.

Well, actually, Robin didn't seem too bad. Fans leaving his table seemed to be genuinely pleased.

It was a heck of a dilemma for me, reminding me of the mid-1980s Clash tune, "Should I Stay or Should I Go." Should I stay at my table, where it was safe, forever wondering what results a quick meeting with Batman would have yielded? Or should I go over to West's table, a copy of *Have a Nice Day* in my hand, opened to the page of my touching tribute to the role West and Ward had played in my life?

What the hell? I decided to go . . . to Burt Ward's table. I showed Ward the passage in the book, and he seemed genuinely flattered. Granted, with his speed-reading prowess, the paragraph took him only a sixteenth of a second to read, but it was an emotionally fulfilling sixteenth of a second. I paid for a cool autographed picture featuring both Batman and Robin, and bought the memoir as well. Then, slowly, with great trepidation, I snuck over to West's table.

What if he really was a dick? Would it ruin my ability to enjoy the old shows with little Mick? Would it be like trying to watch *Hogan's Heroes*, knowing Bob Crane was a porn addict, or a Knicks game knowing Marv Albert had a women's clothing fetish? Would it be like watching Bing Crosby movies, knowing Bing used to beat the pulp out of his kids, or watching *Dancing with the Stars*, knowing Stacy used to date Test? I took the chance anyway.

It was fairly late in the day, so the West line had subsided, meaning I had only a few minutes' wait time until my moment of reckoning. Two more people, one more person, my turn. As I started to speak, West's manager looked up and, recognizing me, said, "Hey, you sold quite a few copies of that book, didn't you?"

"Yeah, I guess I did."

"Adam, this is Mick Foley," the manager said. "He wrote a best-selling book."

West's eyes were upon me. "Yes, sir, Mr. West," I said. "And there's a part in here where I talk about what a big role you played in our family over the generations."

West took the book from my hand and read it. Aloud. No Burt Ward speed-read either. No, Adam West read it slowly, mellifluously, with his rich, resonant baritone making my sophomoric scrawlings sound like the word-play of Updike.

My kids could not, under any circumstances, look like doofuses on Halloween. I consider myself a pretty lenient parent, but sometimes a dad had to take a stand. Dewey was a huge Batman fan, and

**Batman rules!
Hanging out with
Adam West.**

exactly as my mom had twenty-five years earlier, I would be summoned
into the room to call the action as Adam West and Burt Ward laid the
smack down on all the villains' candy asses. *"Bam! Pow! Biff! Kapuff!"* I'd
yell as my kids both threw kicks at imaginary bad guys. Dewey wanted
to be Batman and Noelle wanted to be Batgirl, which was a dilemma,
because I knew that half of West Babylon would be wearing the cowl
and cape. I was determined that my kids would have the best of all the
costumes, so I special-ordered some outfits from the lady who made my
wrestling tights. Sure enough, my kids were the best-looking Batman and
Batgirl in town. And they weren't wearing the trendy new black outfit
with the built-in muscles either. No, my kids were wearing the classic
Adam West blue and gray—the way it was meant to be damnit!

With the paragraph done, I looked toward West for some type of reaction. A sign, any sign, that my heartfelt words had touched him somehow. But I got nothing. Instead, West started thumbing through pages, studying photos, before turning to page one and reading the opening sentence aloud.

As I've already expressed, I'm trying to keep this book somewhere in the neighborhood of PG-13. Sure, the AC/DC story was kind of risqué, but I pondered the possibility of using verbiage slightly less graphic and just couldn't substitute a more innocent euphemism in place of the real deal. Besides, it was a direct quote.

Likewise, what follows is a direct quote from Batman, reading the works of Mick Foley. Please try to hear his voice as you read it.

"I can't believe I lost my fucking ear."

West looked up at me. "You've got a very dynamic writing style," he said. "You capture the reader right away."

With that, West took my ten-by-fourteen glossy of the Dynamic Duo in action and, no questions asked, signed his name. Then he picked up a copy of *Back to the Batcave* and signed that one, too. I had a fifty in my hand, but the Crusader ignored it, saying, "No charge," in the same definitive style in which he'd just mentioned my fucking ear.

I was stunned. I walked back to my table feeling alive, almost weightless, as if floating on a fluffy white cloud of Adam West's making. I had been so full of doubts just minutes ago, but all those bad thoughts had been replaced by a much brighter one—Batman rules!

Then I laughed as I thought of Adam West's voice as it praised my book's words. And I said to myself, "Who needs a quote from John Irving when I've got a blurb from Batman?"

Dear Hardcore Diary,

Yesterday was *Raw*—live TV—always a hectic day, but particularly so yesterday, as I found myself in the unenviable position of finding out that my grand vision was about to go whistling down the drain.

I showed up early to the Pond (the arena) in Anaheim, around eleven A.M., early enough, I thought, to sit in on the television production meeting, just to make sure that my visions of hardcore grandeur were on the same page as the writing staff. They weren't. Not on the same page, barely even on the same book.

As it turned out, the production meeting had started nearly an hour earlier, and was drawing to a close as I sat down. However, Vince asked me to stick around, which did not immediately set off any ideas in my brain that something was amiss. But amiss it was.

There would be, I was told, no "Kiss My Ass Club" segment on the May 15 *Raw* from Lubbock. Doing so would infringe on Vince's ongoing saga with Shawn Michaels, the Spirit Squad, and the imminent reformation of DX. Apparently, Terry Funk taking a chunk out of Vince's ass would intrude on Shawn and Triple H's sole dominion over Vince's ass, or any other body part. Sure, I understood the importance of some Vince physicality in completing Triple H's babyface turn, but unless I'm mistaken, both of those guys have had a little bit of TV time dedicated to them over the last decade or so.* Terry Funk would have a few short minutes to be made into a main-event attraction, and as I've

* Although I know I will probably regret publicly criticizing Shawn or Hunter, two of WWE's top stars, I would be less than forthright if I didn't explain my frustration at feeling that their issue was being pushed at the expense of mine.

mentioned before, to truly maximize that short time, he really needed to take a chunk out of Vince's ass.

No chunk out of Vince's ass meant no instant star-making, which meant no marketable match, which meant watered-down Pay-Per-View, which meant reduced buy rates, which meant crappy payoff, which meant, Why the hell am I even here?

Now, let me get back to the money issue—the whore issue. I did not volunteer for this ECW Pay-Per-View because of the payoff. Yes, in the end, I hope to be well compensated, but that compensation would be deserved due to my idea being a successful one—an idea that people would find captivating enough to plunk down their hard-earned money.

To me, that idea would be made almost unrecognizable without the storyline presence of Vince McMahon.

As I was about to vent my frustration, Vince received a message that a road agent had just been informed of a very serious family matter. Although I'm in the middle of criticizing him here, and will undoubtedly continue to do so over the course of *Hardcore Diaries,* Vince does possess a big heart (I'm not kidding), and he and his daughter Stephanie rushed out immediately to console his distraught employee.

As a result, Brian Gewirtz caught my initial verbal onslaught. "Goddammit, Brian," I said. I very rarely take God's name in vain, or curse at all, for that matter, but I did indeed begin this particular conversation by breaking one of the Ten Commandments, Commandment Number Two, to be exact. "If I'd known you guys were going to water this thing down, I wouldn't have volunteered. You were at the meeting [the one in Stamford]. You know the 'Kiss My Ass Club' was the centerpiece of the whole damn thing. Otherwise, it's just another angle, and I didn't volunteer to turn heel and sacrifice seven years of goodwill with the fans to turn heel for a second-rate show."

"Second-rate show" might seem a little harsh, but I truly felt that without the angle being done properly, the show would indeed be second-rate.

Would I sacrifice seven years of goodwill for a huge show, a *WrestleMania,* with the potential for considerable compensation? Maybe. But for the ECW show? Not likely. Especially because I would be turning on a segment of our audience that had followed me the longest, and supported me the most.

Thankfully, Vince came back in before I could berate Gewirtz any longer.

I should probably also give thanks for the returning presence of Stephanie McMahon. You see, while I have no problem yelling at Vince, I would indeed have a problem yelling in front of Stephanie. First of all, she's seven months pregnant. Secondly, she's just really, really . . . nice. And she's my friend. Several years ago, before she took on much more responsibility in WWE, she was someone I spoke to all the time. Someone I felt pretty close to. Even though we've drifted a little over the years, I have occasionally found my day brightened by a card or call from Steph. No business mentions, just genuine small acts of kindness.

One of my most treasured gifts was a small replica of the WWE hardcore title belt that Steph had put together for the occasion of little Mick's birth in 2001. As many of you know, the original hardcore belt was rather unsightly. Its collection of broken, jagged pieces of metal held together with duct tape represented a genuine case of beauty being in the eye of the beholder, because to those who earned the right to hold the belt, it truly was a thing of beauty.

I realize I'm talking about a championship belt that was held by Test and various members of the Mean Street Posse, but try to work with me a little here.

Apparently, little Mick was not aware of either the origin of the belt or the origin of the gift a couple months ago when he approached me with a gleam in his bright blue eyes. "Daddy, I fixed it," he said, holding out his little hand to reveal . . . oh no, that he had taken off every piece of duct tape and broken metal, leaving only a tiny, clean piece of black leather.

Okay, okay, I'll get back to Vince, but let me just state my genuine belief that my whole ECW adventure was salvaged by two women and a book.

Vince sat down, ready to tackle the monumental importance of my concerns, which were apparently not as monumental as the importance of the protein bar he was in the process of opening.

"Vince, you know how passionate I was about this angle, right?"

Vince took a bite of the bar. "Uh-huh," he mumbled.

"I remember how Steph said she was so glad to see me thinking of ideas again because my heart wasn't into *WrestleMania*."

"Uh-huh." Another bite. This time he wasn't even looking at me. Holy crap! I have had a long history with Vince, much of it smooth, some of it great, some of it a bit tumultuous, but I'd never before been made to feel second best to a protein bar.

It was at this point in the proceedings that I first thought of taking my ball and going home. Just saying, "This isn't what I came back for," and leaving. Sure, it wasn't a very mature thought, but as you can surely tell by reading this book, not all of my thoughts are. But Vince with his damn protein bar was really getting to me.

I tried to plead my case for Vince's involvement in our angle. He understood my concerns, but didn't agree with them, stating the need for him to not spread himself too thin by getting physically involved in two angles.

I went for broke. "Vince, you know this whole thing hinged on your willingness to get physically involved. Without you, and without the 'Kiss My Ass Club,' there's no angle. I don't want to go out there and give tough-guy promos. I'm not that guy anymore. I wanted to create something great. I don't want to come back and give up all the credibility I've earned with the fans, just to get involved in something half-assed. Hell, maybe you guys should just do this show without me."

I was officially in the process of taking my ball and going home, when I thought about my book, this book, *The Hardcore Diaries*, and how badly the book would suck if it just kind of ended here. I went home. The end. Not very captivating, right? Not to mention it would be the shortest book since *The Wit and Wisdom of Test*.

It did cross my mind that a plot twist such as this, however damaging to my visions of wrestling immortality it might be, could make for good reading. For some reason I thought immediately of the Bob Dylan line, "You'd better start swimming, or you'll sink like a stone." Did I really want to sink? Was this book really reason enough to participate in something half-assed, something that had just been ordered to take a detour on the road to wrestling immortality? A detour, or a dead end? Was it possible to still get there, albeit in a roundabout way, with the estimated arrival time pushed months into the future?

By the time you read this book, all of the events that I am documenting will have unfolded. Hopefully, it will have been responsible for great, if not immortal, wrestling memories. If so, thank Melina.

Up until that moment, I had not had a single guilty thought about Melina. After all, I'd had no need to—she's like a little sister to me. I know it doesn't make sense, but I swear I have never had a single indecent thought about her. I just can't see her that way.

But as I contemplated leaving, a tidal wave of guilt crashed into me. I just imagined her little voice on the phone, and how excited she was about the idea. This angle would be a big deal for her, probably the biggest break of her WWE career. It would give me great happiness to be responsible for such a break occurring. Likewise, it would cause me a great deal of sadness and guilt to be responsible for such a potential career break not occurring.

"Oh, that's awesome," my mind heard her say. "Thank you so much for thinking of me."

What was I going to tell her? "Oh, that idea I spent three hours telling you about? Yeah, that's not going to happen. Why? Oh, because I walked out on WWE when I didn't get my way on the ECW program. Sorry to get your hopes up. Talk to you soon. Okay, bye."

I couldn't do it. I just wouldn't be able to live with the guilt.

So I did my best to invoke the spirit of Monte Hall. "Vince, let's make a deal."

Thankfully, Vince was done with his damn protein bar. And in truth, somewhere in the proceedings he offered me one, which I graciously accepted.

"A deal," Vince said, his businessman's instincts showing signs of perking up. "What kind of deal?"

I thought back to Dylan, and realized it was time for me to start swimming. It was time for me to make the emergency pitch of a lifetime, like Mitch "Wild Thing" Williams of the Phillies, coming to save the day in the sixth game of the '93 World Series. Wait, Williams gave up a towering home run to lose the game, had his house repeatedly pegged by the farm-fresh eggs of furious fans, lost his confidence, could no longer throw strikes, and was subsequently forced into early retirement. Probably not the greatest analogy.

It was do-or-die time for the hardcore legend. Time for me to dig into the batter's box and take my cuts. I intended to swing for the fences, and knock this baby out of the park.

Yeah, I know I just talked about making a perfect pitch, right before talking about hitting a home run. So what? Why can't I write conflicting sports analogies? Because in a way, I was attempting to save my ECW idea by simultaneously scoring runs for my future project. The one involving Melina. The one involving the total humiliation of Mick Foley.

I know I wrote earlier about not fully spelling out this second idea, about trying to keep some of the mystique alive. But hell, I think our fans will find this stuff captivating. And its not as if we haven't revealed as much or more on our own television shows, Web sites, and outside media projects. Besides, it's not as if I'll be revealing an upcoming storyline. By the time the book's out, it will be part of wrestling history. So here it is—a *Hardcore Diaries* exclusive—the Foley/McMahon conversation that salvaged it all.

Back to Vince, saying, "A deal, what type of deal?"

Come on, Monte. Make this deal work. "I'll agree to do the ECW show, if you will do my angle with Melina."

"Okay, let's hear it," Vince said.

"Well, when I initially heard that there were some reservations about Terry Funk taking a chunk out of your ass, because it would destroy the 'Kiss My Ass Club,' I did my best to think of a way it could come back stronger than ever."

Vince nodded. He was actually looking at me, not a protein bar in sight.

I continued. "Now, what if we found a way for us to do the voluntary ass-kissing segment at a later time, when it wouldn't conflict with your deal with DX? As long as we can establish that I volunteered to do it, and then establish a reason why it doesn't get done, we could always go back to it, right?"

"I guess that's true," Vince said.

"So maybe after a couple weeks or months, you can call me out to the ring and say, 'You know, Mick Foley, you claim to be a man of your word, and as far as I'm concerned, you broke your word.'

"So I would act like I have no idea what you're talking about, prompting you to say, 'You came out here and volunteered to kiss my ass, and dammit, I expect you to keep your word.'"

Vince seemed intrigued.

"At which point, Vince, I would say that I wouldn't kiss your ass in a million years, and launch into a promo about why that was so."

"Okay," Vince said. "I like it so far."

"Then you would say, 'Either you kiss my ass, or *someone's* going to get fired,' which would cause me to go off on a diatribe about how I didn't need your job, look at me, I wear fifteen-dollar sweatpants, drive a used minivan, and haven't paid for a haircut in years. So you want to fire me, go ahead. Do it. Do it!"

Vince was all smiles. I could tell he really liked it.

"But then you'd say, 'Mick, you misunderstood me. I didn't say if you don't kiss my ass, *you're* getting fired. I said, if you don't kiss my ass, *someone's* getting fired.' Then up on the big screen we see Melina. Then you'd say,

'Look at her, Mick, she's like a sister to you. You'd do anything for her, wouldn't you? Well, you'd better figure out just how far you're willing to go, because if you don't kiss my ass on *Raw* next week, right here in the middle of this ring, then she's . . . FIIIIRED!'"

I knew this point of the idea would be subject to doubt, and I was ready for the inevitable questions.

"I'm not sure this fits into any storyline," Vince said.

"Yeah," Steph added. "How do we explain a *SmackDown!* talent suddenly showing on *Raw* for no apparent reason?"

"We give them a reason," I said. "I mean, that's what we do, we're story-tellers. So let's start dropping little clues over the next few months, so that when her picture goes up on the screen, it makes perfect sense."

"What kind of clues?" Gewirtz asked.

"Well, we've got the history of her showing up on my Web site. Have Michael Cole [*SmackDown!* announcer] bring it up every once in a while during an MNM [Melina's tag team] match. Like, you know, saying, 'What is the deal with Melina constantly showing up on Mick Foley's Web site?' And then Tazz [color commentator] would say, like, 'Hey, Cole, they happen to be friends, Mick Foley has good taste, unlike you!'"

"We can do that," Vince said.

"Okay, great." Man, I was starting to see light at the end of this creative tunnel. The tunnel leading to . . . wrestling immortality? "And like tonight," I continued. "At Kane's movie premiere, get a shot of me and Melina hanging out on the red carpet, for no apparent reason. But if we do things like this a handful of times over the next few months, it will make perfect sense to our fans when her picture goes up on the screen."

"Okay," Vince said. "Where do we go from there?"

"Well, say, we do this at the beginning of *Raw*—that way we have almost two hours to create interest. Then we go to *SmackDown!*, where we make it a big deal. Get comments from *SmackDown!* guys. A few guys understand. Maybe Batista warns me that she's not worth it. Then you do a pretaped sit-down interview with Melina. I'm telling you, Vince, you wouldn't even have to give her any lines. Just let her say what she really feels about me." I was half-joking here, but I do firmly believe that she'll need only to tell the truth to make our fans think that she really likes me.

"So when we get to *Raw*, assuming this segment is at the end of the show, we've got almost another two hours to really get people into it. Meanwhile,

Vince, you're in the middle of putting together an incredible spectacular to complement the spectacle of me possibly kissing your ass in the ring. Dancing girls, maybe a choir."

Vince seemed to like it, he really seemed to like it.

"So when it's time for the ceremony, you come on out to your music, doing the walk."

If you are not familiar with "the walk," look it up under the definition "ludicrous," where there should be a photo of Vince doing it. Or think back to my AC/DC journal entry, and try to think of that same dance only slightly modified, done on an entrance ramp in front of millions of people.

"I come out to my music, obviously concerned about the decision I've got to make. Maybe have J.R. make a *Sophie's Choice* reference. Then, maybe you bring out the Spirit Squad to do a 'Kiss My Ass' cheer. Finally you play Melina's music, but she's not doing the sexy walk, she certainly doesn't do the sexy entrance. Maybe she gets on the mike and tells me how sad she is, how terrible she feels, how she never meant for our friendship to cause this type of pain. Maybe she's even crying.

"But I would say, 'Hey, listen, Melina, I've had my time. Things worked out for me better than I ever dreamed. But your time is now. You're on your way to being one of the biggest Superstars the world has ever seen. I can't deprive you of that, and I can't deprive our fans of watching you do just that.'

"But when I kneel down, and my face gets perilously close to your ass, she's going to grab that mike and literally scream, 'No, don't do it, please don't do it.' Tears and all.

"So I get up and go over to her. She's sobbing her eyes out. I lift her chin and gently say, 'Listen, Melina, this is what's going to happen. I'm going to go over there, get down on my knees, and for about one full second, I'm going to kiss that miserable son of a bitch's ass. Then I'm going to walk out here with my head held high, go home and watch as you show everyone every Friday night on *SmackDown!* why you are the top Diva in WWE.'

"And then, Vince, I'm actually going to kiss your ass."

Vince liked this. I've seen him smile when he was showing off pictures of his grandson. This was the exact same smile. He was really, really proud. Proud of his club, proud of me, proud of his ass.

But I wasn't through yet. I was almost done with my massive home-run swing. I just needed to follow through.

"Vince, it would seem like the time to gloat. But you wouldn't. You would be almost befuddled. Like you couldn't believe the lengths that someone would go to help out a friend. You'd slowly pull up your pants. You'd shake your head. You'd say, 'You know, I never really understood platonic friendship. Quite frankly, I couldn't understand why it would even be necessary. What good it could do. But now, as I look at you, I have to say, I respect the incredible sacrifice you made on behalf of your friend Melina. And I bet Melina has a few words for you.'

"At this point, Melina would be sobbing, barely able to speak. She'd try, but fail after only a couple of garbled words. Finally, she'd gather herself together enough to say, 'Mick, I just want to say . . . I just want to say . . . I just want to say . . .'

"And then she'd get this devious, wicked smile on her face and say, 'I just want to say . . . you're FIIIIRED.'"

Vince let out a yell. I knew he loved it. I saw that idea sailing back, back, back, back. It was . . . outta here. A home run for Foley. Now I merely had to recap the advantages of my idea, savoring the moment like a ballplayer taking his celebratory jog around the bases.

"Look at the heat it will put on you, Vince. It will make you the biggest S.O.B. you've ever been—and that's saying something. It will shine a huge light on Melina, one I'm sure you will take full advantage of. And it will make me incredibly sympathetic, and give me a ready-made angle when I return."

Vince was still beaming. He laughed and said, "And it will give us a chance to finally have that match together."

"You're damn right it will, Vince, you're damn right it will!" Now, actually, the thought of working a big match with Vince is absolutely terrifying, as it could be a major fiasco. Shawn Michaels pulled it off, but I'm not exactly Shawn Michaels. Cactus Jack could have pulled it off eight years ago, but I'm not exactly Cactus Jack anymore, either. But I wasn't about to ruin the mood with a little thing like honesty. Not while my idea was still soaring majestically through a purple twilight sky, hit so incredibly well that it might well continue its flight until landing firmly in a land called . . . wrestling immortality.

Dear Hardcore Diary,

I should probably mention what actually happened at *Raw,* as it was a very eventful program for me. A week earlier, Edge and I had set up a hardcore *WrestleMania* rematch. In our promo, which was done under the guise of a "Cutting Edge" interview segment, we had both continued with our practice of referring to our match as "the greatest hardcore match of all time." Sure, it was a little bit of a stretch, but not a complete whopper. Maybe like a whopper of a different sort, the fast-food sort, as it was a claim that would be readily consumed by our fans around the world. Hey, if the president can make the public think he is a great leader just because he continually says it's so, then certainly we can take a really good match and claim it was the all-time best.

In the interview, I said that I wondered where I had gone wrong in the *'Mania* match, but upon further examination, I realized that my one mistake lay in not realizing that on that one night, April 2, 2006, I would be face-to-face with the toughest S.O.B. in wrestling.

I don't like when WWE Superstars publicly run down each other's in-ring skills. To me, it cheapens the product, making our fans feel like they're watching a cavalcade of no-talent stiffs, instead of world-class sports entertainers.

For example, in the buildup to *'Mania,* Triple H voiced his opinion that John Cena was "not a very good wrestler." Then why exactly is Cena our world champion? And how did that comment make Triple H look when he lost to someone who wasn't very good? Like someone who was a little worse than not very good? Which would be what . . . lousy? Or even if he'd won, who would he have beaten? A guy who was "not a very good wrestler," which would make Triple H what—a little better than not very good? Or average?

Not me. No, if someone is going to beat me, he'd better

be damn good, or at the very least someone I can claim is damn good. Which reminds me of one of the all-time great wrestling boasts, one which I've utilized occasionally over the years. "It takes a good man to beat me, but it doesn't take him very long."

During the buildup to that match, Edge had continually pointed to the fact that I'd never really stolen the show at *WrestleMania,* never had that "defining *WrestleMania* moment." Which was actually true. I have somehow managed to be seen as a legend in pro wrestling without ever truly stealing the show at the biggest showcase in our industry—*WrestleMania.*

So here's the *Raw* promo where I refute Edge's charge, and set up the *WrestleMania* rematch (or at least the promise of one) that will get our ECW ball rolling.

> **MICK FOLEY:** Don't get me wrong, just because I lost the match doesn't mean that I didn't get that defining *WrestleMania* moment that you spoke so often of, because I did. Let's take a look at it right now . . . [*We see an image of a bloodied Edge, seemingly in shock.*]

> **MICK FOLEY:** There, there it is, ladies and gentlemen, my defining *WrestleMania* moment. Looking at your eyes and knowing you'd never be the same again. Looking in your eyes and knowing that you knew from then on it was all downhill for Edge, knowing that I had taken years off your life, knowing that you would never want to go thru that type of hell again. And you see, that's where you and I differ, Edge, because I do want to go through that type of hell again, and I want to go through it tonight. So what I'm saying, it's you and me, *WrestleMania* rematch, right here in Columbus, Ohio.

> **EDGE:** You're on crack. I'm not wrestling you in a match, I'm not fighting you tonight, no way, not gonna happen. But I tell you what, because you were stupid enough to come in here and challenge me, next week, just out of principle, I'll take you on in any match that you want.

I felt like there was a great deal of interest in this rematch, just based on the feedback I received from our fans over the course of the past week. Everyone seemed to know about the match, and everyone seemed excited. Maybe they were already buying into our "greatest hardcore match of all time" collaborative conspiracy, because they all seemed to be under the impression that they were in for a hell of a match. Boy, were they going to be disappointed.

With my production room meeting home run still in flight, I felt free to enjoy the five hours before going live at 6:00 P.M. Pacific Time. Going live on the West Coast always seems a little strange, as like most actors or athletes, WWE performers are creatures of habit, each one with their own way of getting motivated or physically prepared for the unique experience that is live television. The earlier start time just feels a little . . . different.

I was introduced to Rick Rubin, a legend in the music production business, who has helped shape the sounds of legendary albums by a who's-who of rap and heavy metal royalty, including Run-D.M.C., Limp Bizkit, and the Red Hot Chili Peppers. But the man I was interested in talking about was Johnny Cash. Rubin had been largely responsible for engineering Cash's unlikely comeback in the 1990s, helping endear "the man in black" to a whole new generation, and putting a final emphatic exclamation point on Cash's phenomenal career.

I had to ask him about "Hurt," the Nine Inch Nails song that an ailing Cash somehow made his own; a haunting, unforgettable hunk of raw emotion that gives me goose bumps every time I hear it—even now as I write this, I see and hear it in my mind.

"No," Rubin said. "We didn't know it would have the type of effect it had. We knew it was special as we were doing it. But we had no idea how special until the music video was done."

I agreed. It's not often that a video can actually enhance a song—it often takes away from it. But it would take a tougher man than me not to feel something while watching that one.

My mother is absolutely crazy about Johnny Cash, and will probably love to hear my story about meeting Rubin.

I also met a legend of another type, a certain hardcore legend in his own right—longtime porno mainstay Ed Powers. Powers, who apparently specializes in a variety of acts that are not in most people's sexual repertoires, is a huge wrestling fan, and seemed genuinely sad upon finding out that I was not familiar with his work.

But my father is absolutely crazy about Ed Powers and will probably love to hear my story about . . . What the hell? Yes, I am just kidding.

I did want to ask for a couple pointers for my upcoming Christy Canyon

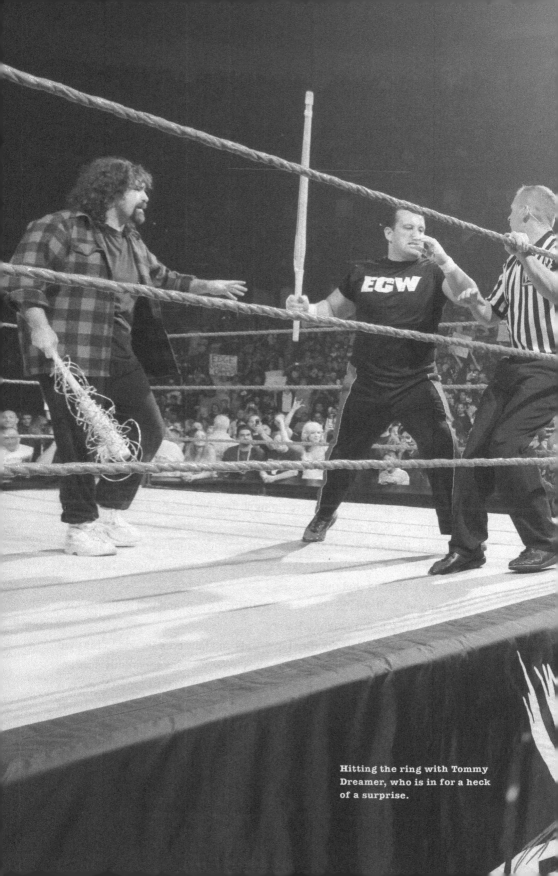

Hitting the ring with Tommy Dreamer, who is in for a heck of a surprise.

interview, but alas, Ted DiBiase, a WWE legend/road agent/ordained minister, was nearby, and I feared insulting him should he find out that I was indeed somewhat familiar with Ms. Canyon's body of work.

Match time. Another piece in the puzzle. Although I'm still not happy about the absence of the ass chunk in my life, I'm still savoring that talk with Vince. I've also heard a rumor that I might wrestle John Cena for the WWE Championship at *SummerSlam*. I'm not sure if my body will ever be up for a singles match of that caliber, but I'll sure as hell try. I'll tell you one thing though—win or lose, I won't be entering that ring with a guy who's "not a very good wrestler." He'll be a warrior, a gladiator, a god. Now if I only have Triple H's talent once I actually get in there.

Edge and I have talked, and we can both see the positive side of the creative shake-up. It will give us a chance to really tell our story in Lubbock, as opposed to creating a huge spectacle with the Ass Club segment. Both of us are swimmers. We'll keep our heads above water in a way that would make Bob Dylan proud.

Edge heads to the ring with Lita in tow. I may have felt bad about the real-life soap opera involving Edge, Lita, and Matt Hardy, but there's no denying that the two of them (Lita and Edge) have been box office and ratings magic ever since.

They cut a little promo on me—just a way to draw up a little last-second interest. I hear the telltale car-crash sound, followed by the three-chord guitar riff that sends me through the curtain, onto the entrance ramp, barbed-wire bat held aloft, taking in the unmistakable sound of 15,000 fans giving me a . . . surprisingly lackluster response. Hey, I don't know why—I could have sworn I was popular with the fans. Sure, the audience had seemed slightly subdued through the show—California fans can be that way—but I thought that surely I'd be the guy to change all that.

With mike in hand, I started the swerve in motion.

MICK FOLEY: "You know something, Edge? What you just said was
   exactly right. We did have the greatest hardcore match in
   wrestling history . . . at *WrestleMania*. Which means the winner
   of tonight's match could rightly claim the right to be considered
   the greatest Hardcore Champion alive today! But the more I

thought about that, the more I realized we couldn't crown the greatest Hardcore Champion without also including the initials E-C-W. I thought back, Edge . . . *Raw* last week . . . do you remember it? You said, 'Any match you want, Mick.' So I'm about to make the match I want: hardcore, triple threat. Edge! Foley! And the Innovator of Violence, ECW's Tommy Dreamer.

Sure, not everyone knew Tommy Dreamer, and maybe some that knew him only from his WWE tenure as the guy who drank water from the urinal were a little less than thrilled, but I don't care about Tommy's May 8 reaction—I'm looking at Tommy's June 11 reaction, and I bet it will be dynamite.

Dreamer and I head to the ring, as if we're a tag team. I've got the bat, he's got the kendo stick. I'm covering up my horrible physique with a trademark red and black flannel. Dreamer's physique hider of choice is his trusty black ECW T-shirt. Even in the midst of absorbing some of the worst beatings ever seen by man (or Mankind), Dreamer has often found the intestinal fortitude to pull that damn shirt down over his protruding love handles. Together, our asses are the size of some small countries.

We slide into the ring together. Edge bails out. I'm fully aware that I'm drifting back and forth between past and present verb tenses, but I don't care. This is the way I see the action. I urge Dreamer forward, so he can get to that no-good bastard (still a PG-13 word, I hope) Edge. And when he does— wham!—I nail him in the back with a mighty swing of the barbed-wire bat. It's a hell of a swing, a home run swing, a Bonds-on-BALCO's-best swing. I proposed an idea of Dreamer's—that he get in some impressive offense before being destroyed—but the idea had been turned down in no uncertain terms by the big guy, Vince McMahon, himself.

And then it gets ugly. Or beautiful, depending on whether or not you're Tommy Dreamer. Actually, it's just four more simple moves. A bat to the head, busting Tommy open. A modified elbow/bat drop to the head. A legdrop onto the bat, which is conveniently placed in Tommy's testicular region. Followed by Mr. Socko, and a hokey double pin, the video of which I hope to take full advantage of in Lubbock.

The audience is confused, as I hoped they would be. Jim Ross is busy posing some very good questions for the fans. Hopefully they will contemplate my actions and give me a chance to explain myself before jumping to the premature conclusion that I'm now a heel, or a bad guy. Because in my

mind, I'm not. I'm just protecting what's mine: my legacy. Keeping it safe from the prying hands of ECW.

Edge and I shake hands. I grab Lita's hand and kiss it gently. I'm determined to be the antithesis of every "ho"-shouting fan. I will treat Lita like she's a proper lady. The three of us walk up the ramp, victorious, leaving a battered and very bloody Tommy Dreamer (who has been excellent in his role as a symbol for everything ECW stands for) vanquished in the ring. We pause so that Lita can raise the hands of both me and Edge.

A few hours later, I step off a tour bus onto the red carpet at the premiere of Kane's movie, *See No Evil*. I'm immediately approached by a WWE television producer who tells me she's been told to get an interview with me and Melina as soon as she gets to the theater. It's really going to happen! We will start telling the story right away.

What a day it's been. I've battled with Vince, hit a home run, gotten a possible *SummerSlam* title match, ruined seven years of goodwill with the fans, and willingly agreed to be publicly humiliated. And now I get to go to the movies with Melina. Not a bad day. Not a bad day at all.

At the See No Evil premiere with Melina.

You Can
Go Home
Again

I was in New York City in June of 2003, on *Tietam Brown* promotional duties, making my way to Penn Station, when a WWE fan told me that Triple H and Kevin Nash were scheduled to face off in a Hell in a Cell match at the *Badd Blood* Pay-Per-View on June 15, 2003. I caught the train into Huntington, something of a halfway point for me, then drove the rest of the way home. Those long rush-hour commutes are kind of overwhelming for me, and always leave me with a renewed respect for the sacrifices working men and women make every single day. Give me 400 miles of open roadway any day. A few good CDs, and I'm gone. But four hours or more of rush-hour traffic or train rides with the asses of strangers pressed against mine? Hopefully not, unless, you know, the stranger is pretty good looking.

Once I was behind the wheel, my mind began wandering as I followed a steady parade of cars eastward, hoping to get ahold of some renewed energy by the time I got home, so my kids could see Superdad and not some 300-pound slug pulling up the drive. And it just kind of hit me. Hell in a Cell. Mick Foley. Special referee. It was a natural. After all, Hell in a Cell was the match that ninety-nine percent of our fans knew me for. Who better to maintain order than the guy who'd gotten the ever-living crap kicked out of him in, on, and around the structure? A single call to J.R. got the ball rolling, and within twenty-four hours, it was a done deal.

About nine days later, I was in my Miami hotel room, having second, third, and fourth thoughts, realizing I was about to reenter a world I had long presumed was part of my past. One o'clock rolled around, the scheduled arrival time. I lay in bed, watching the clock, wondering about the ramifications of not showing up. Everything had seemed so easy on the phone. Vince had even called me, telling me how much he was looking forward to my return. WWE had even been kind enough to put my upcoming book signings on their Web site, and had offered to mention the book on their *Raw* and *SmackDown!* shows. To no-show my first WWE appearance in eighteen months would be a big mistake.

I pulled into the parking lot around three, then walked to the double doors leading to the back of the arena, realizing on some level that the doors were symbolic of the world of wrestling I'd left behind. Once they opened, life was going to be different. I took a deep breath and swung a door open, stepping inside.

"Mick, Mick!" A woman's voice—there she was, Stacy Keibler, running toward me, the world's most beautiful welcoming committee member. As she jumped into my arms, I realized that coming back was not as difficult as I thought it might be. Then I saw Test, all six foot six of him, glowering behind her, his front teeth looming large, impossibly so. "Hey, Mick, good to see you," he said.

"Hey, it's good to see you too, Test," I said, realizing how odd those words sounded when they weren't told as a lie.

It *was* good to see him. It was good to see everybody. Gerald Briscoe was right there. Pat Patterson, Triple H, even the Texas Rattlesnake himself—Stone Cold Steve Austin. It was good to see Vince, too. He wrapped me up in a big hug, and we spoke for quite a while. I told him that I felt like I needed to go off on my own for a while, but that there wasn't any reason we couldn't do more in the future, including the publication of *Tales from Wrescal Lane*, which had been on the literary disabled list since 2000.

We managed to do a really good job of making a guest referee seem as important as possible during a single two-hour episode. Triple H had warned me against getting involved, and didn't take well to my decision to follow through on my intention to do so. He caught me with a few blows and sent me hard into the steel steps, my momentum hurtling my substantial bulk through the air, over the steps. He then walked out, assuming of course that his work in Miami was through.

Not so fast, Triple H. As he walked up the ramp, I crawled into the ring and pounded the mat three times, as if making a count. At first the crowd didn't get it, but as with so many situations in wrestling, it's all in the sell. I held three fingers aloft as Triple H looked in amazement, before heading back down to finish the job—this time with his trademark move, the pedigree. Surely no one would get up from this, unless, of course, he was in line for a really big push. But I didn't have to get up—not all the way, at least. I just had to muster the fortitude to raise my hand in the air and come down to the mat with it three times.

"One." The crowd got it now. "Two." They were yelling it out. "Three." There was no question at all that the hardcore legend was back.

Triple H and Nash had a very good match, possibly Nash's best performance until his portrayal of the ruthless prison guard who has his anabolic steroids replaced with estrogen in the *Longest Yard* remake. I guess I was pretty good, too. The second honeymoon was in full swing. I loved WWE, and they loved me.

I was even asked back to *Raw,* simply as a way for WWE to hold a hardcore tribute in my honor at Madison Square Garden, the arena that held so many special memories for me. It was where I'd seen Jimmy "Superfly" Snuka leap from the top of the steel cage, onto a prone Don Muraco, back in October of 1983. It was where I'd seen Sergeant Slaughter battle the Iron Sheik in the classic Boot Camp match in '84. It was where I'd seen six-foot-eight-inch, 300-pound monster Sid Vicious parade around the ring, his arms flapping like a chicken, in a match with Vader, prompting Vince to say in disgust, "I never want to see that again."

The night turned out to be a memorable one indeed, with Stone Cold presenting me with the original hardcore belt, in all its duct-taped, broken-metal

Being honored at Madison Square Garden was a career highlight.

glory, in an in-ring ceremony attended by several of my hardcore contemporaries, such as the Dudley Boys, RVD, and Al Snow. I wish the late Crash Holly had been present for it, as I understand he took the oversight very personally and it made him consider me in an unfavorable light.

I even saw my Knopf editor, Victoria Wilson, in the front row, looking about as out of place as a human being possibly can. But she was happy for me, and proud to see how well thought of I was in my environment.

What an environment it was, too. Following a really well-produced video, set to the Staind song "Right Here," twenty thousand people chanted my name. Okay, maybe it wasn't that many. Maybe, due to the extravagant *Raw* set, it was only fifteen thousand—still an official sellout. And sure, some of those in attendance weren't participating in the chant. But still, there had to have been two, three hundred people mumbling my name out of the corner of their mouths.

In a farewell address worthy of Lou Gehrig, I grabbed the mike, hoping to find an appropriate philosopher, poet, or esteemed scribe whom I could quote. I went with Frosty the Snowman, saying, "So I'll say good-bye, but don't you cry, I'll be back again someday." That someday would turn out to be six months later, in December, for the start of the biggest angle of my wrestling career—an angle that actually started about a half hour after the in-ring ceremony.

But first, after accepting a hug from a very emotional Stephanie McMahon, I asked a brief question of the boss's daughter, the answer to which hung around in the dark, sensitive recesses of my mind, waiting to become the catalyst for my WWE heel turn almost three years later.

"Steph, how come Terry Funk wasn't here?"

"Uh, Mick, Terry wanted too much money to come in."

Next, it was time to leave the wrestling world a slightly better place. I may not have a whole lot of exceptional in-ring talent, but I do consider myself among the best when it comes to advancing people's careers. There is always a lot of talk within the wrestling business about what constitutes a "great worker." Are impressive in-ring skills enough to make someone a "great worker" even if those in-ring skills don't translate into interest, box office, or buy rates? Is a "great worker" someone who draws money, regardless of how his stuff actually looks? Or is he someone who continually helps others out, by either honing their opponents' skills (much as Fit Finlay has done with Bobby Lashley) or increasing their stature in the company? In my opinion, it's a combination of all three, and I've always taken pride in excelling at the third. I'll let fans and other wrestlers debate where I stand on the first two.

Randy Orton was the guy I was hoping to help out on this particular night. I knew Randy's dad, "Cowboy" Bob Orton, aka Bob Orton Jr., aka Bob "Ace" Orton, aka "Boxing" Bob Orton, from my days on the independent scene and from tag-teaming with him in Herb Abram's short-lived UWF back in 1990. I believe Colette and I even conceived Dewey on a wrestling tour of Aruba, on which Bob and I tagged.

I'd seen Randy work enough to know his potential, and thought, "Hey, why not let him throw me down a flight of stairs?" I mean, how bad could it be? I had scoffed at stunt coordinator Ellis Edwards's suggestion that I wear special pads for the wimpy one-flight journey, informing him that I was Mick Foley, and I didn't need pads. Man, I wish I'd had pads. Because not only did Randy split my head open like a ripe melon with a shot from the indestructible hardcore title display case, but the wimpy one-flight fall caused a deep shoulder-blade bruise that kept me in intense pain for weeks.

To make matters worse, the wound was in the back of my head, and although it required five stitches to close, not a single drop of blood was seen on camera, rendering it useless.

Still, I was on a tremendous high when I hopped into my Impala, cranking up tunes of questionable quality as I journeyed back home. I don't question the quality of my tunes—other people do. After all, there's got to be some reason why nobody wants to ride with me. Here, I'll list my current collection of CDs that I'm rocking out to on this eight-day West Coast run. You be the judge.

Loretta Lynn: *Van Lear Rose*. Alan Jackson: *Precious Memories*. Julie Miller: *Broken Things*. Bruce Springsteen: *The Rising*. Bruce Springsteen: *Born to Run*. Dolly Parton: *Those Were the Days*. Drive-By Truckers: *A Blessing or a Curse*. Jethro Tull: *Songs from the Wood*. Tom Petty and the Heartbreakers: *Anthology*. Ray Davies: *Other People's Lives*. Slaid Cleaves: *Broke Down*. The Cowboy Junkies: *The Trinity Session*. Waylon Jennings: *Lonesome, On'ry and Mean*. Patty Loveless: *Mountain Soul*. Neil Young: *Harvest Moon*. Steve Earle and the Dukes: *The Hard Way*. Gillian Welch: *Soul Journey*. The Cult: *Sonic Temple*. The Dixie Chicks: *Home*. John Mellencamp: *Human Wheels*.

What do you think? You should probably just stick to reading the book and watching *Raw*, and run the other way if I ever offer you a ride.

By the time I arrived home, about an hour and a half later, the tremendous high had subsided, seemingly in direct correlation to the pain in my shoulder, which was cringe-inducing. Usually pains like these don't truly surface until morning; I did not interpret this early onset of agony to be a good sign.

I lay down in bed, eager to tell Colette about the big night. Unfortunately listening to tales of my big night was not a high priority on Colette's late-night agenda. The garbage, however, was. "Mick, could you please take out the garbage—the kids forgot to do it."

So I rolled out of bed, clad in red flannel PJs, and took out the garbage.

Upon returning to bed, my wife had another request. The guinea pigs' cage, it seemed, was starting to smell. Was it possible, she asked, for me to clean up the mess? So I went upstairs to their room, where they don't actually have a cage, but one of those plastic kid's pools that allows them some running room. By the smell of things, it had last been cleaned during the Clinton administration. Dutifully, I shoveled the pig poop, using a dustpan and garbage can, while remaining painfully aware of how big a problem this shoulder was going to pose.

My night, however, wasn't quite done. Not according to Colette. "Mick," she said. "Could you check and see if the dog has been fed?"

It was more than even a hardcore legend could take. Dejectedly, I turned to Colette. "You know, two hours ago, twenty thousand people were chanting my name."

Dear Hardcore Diary,

A few hours ago, I was the emcee of a fund-raiser for a young wrestler, John Grill, who had been paralyzed from the chest down during his very first pro wrestling match, which took place around six weeks ago. The move that caused the damage was apparently a German suplex, my least favorite maneuver in the business. Most people reading this book will be familiar with the move, as it is frequently used in today's wrestling game, from the smallest of independents right up to the WWE. Although it's commonplace, it has always struck me as dangerous, as the margin for error seems too damn narrow. Even though a single German suplex doesn't seem to result in many injuries, I firmly believe that the preponderance of serious neck injuries in WWE is caused at least in part by the constant repetition of the move.

I was always known as a guy who took a lot of punishment. Maybe the punishment I took was unprecedented, leaving a dangerous legacy for others to attempt to follow. But for the most part, I was in control of my own destiny. I *took* big bumps in and out of the ring, I wasn't *given* them. There's a huge difference. *Taking* bumps means that I assumed personal responsibility for the outcome of a move. Being *given* one means that safety is someone else's responsibility.

I always knew there would be a price to pay for the style I chose. I pay that price every day. But at least I'm still functional. Slow, but functional.

Chair shots are another matter. I took too many, especially in 1998 and '99, when my body was really wearing down, but I nonetheless wanted to present a physical product. That was pretty much when it became open season for the headshots, which I took full force, without blocking, as if it was some macho rite of passage instead of sports entertainment.

Some fans ask me if I resent current WWE Superstars who dare to have the common sense to actually put their hands up to block heavy metal objects traveling at high speeds, aiming for their heads. No, I don't. I actually wish I'd done a little more of it myself. This book might actually be grammatically correct. Maybe I could even learn how to use a computer.

For those fans out there looking to get into WWE, some other type of pro wrestling, or even looking to mess around in their backyard—please be smart. Be safe. I know I covered some of this same terrain in *Foley Is Good*, but it bears repeating. If you want to be any good, start out as an amateur wrestler. Go to college. Get an education. The chances of making it in wrestling are slim, and the chances of getting badly hurt doing it are very good. Have that education to fall back on. Don't do anything that could potentially compress the spine—piledrivers, Pedigrees, powerbombs, huracanranas, tombstones, German suplexes, etc. And for God's sake, don't use fire.

Yeah, I know I used fire at *WrestleMania* with Edge, but including Lita, our match involved three people with a combined forty-five years in the business, plus a fire marshal who had approved the move, and about ten guys with fire extinguishers hidden in the crowd, ready to put it out the moment anything didn't look right.

Plus, it was *'Mania,* man, a far cry from a couple losers trying to impress their pimply-faced girlfriends in the backyard at Uncle Marty's family bar-b-que.

Look, I don't care if it's in a backyard, a first pro match in an armory, or *WrestleMania*—a wrestler can always say no. As I said earlier, I earned a pretty decent living by knowing my limitations. On many occasions, I simply said, "I don't feel comfortable doing that." Once you've voiced your concern, only a real jerk would insist on making you follow through against your wishes.

Dear Hardcore Diaries,

What am I thinking? Starting a *Hardcore Diary* entry at midnight? Even if it's a short writing night, I won't be in bed until 4:00 A.M. The late-night writing poses a problem because my little guys get up around six. Obviously it would be a little hard to function on two hours' sleep, let alone train for a huge match and write semi-literate stuff. So as a result, I often end up sleeping in the top bunk of Hughie's bed, knowing that the littlest of my little guys has already beaten a path to his mom's room, or will be doing it in the very near future.

So the good news is, I get in a few extra hours' sleep. The bad news: I'm a 319-pound man (although I'm working on the weight) in a child's bed, which, considering my history of lower-back disc problems, is asking for trouble. Well, I asked for it, and I got it—major back pain, bringing back the S-shaped posture that I'd been known to style over the years. What a crummy time for a back injury, with the ECW show only four weeks away, and the deadline for my *Hardcore Diaries* manuscript due only three weeks after that.

And how to explain this injury to my dozens and dozens of fans?

"What did this to you?" they'd ask. "Was it Edge's spear? Kane's chokeslam? Cena's F.U.? Triple H's pedigree?"

"No," I'd say. "It was worse than that. It was Hughie's bunk bed."

It was a good day. Although I had written "write all day" in my calendar, I opted to spend the day with Colette, just hanging out—taking a bath, ordering in, watching a movie in the Christmas room. Hughie and Mickey go to preschool three days a week, so we try to pick one of those days as designated husband-wife day.

I made a couple of calls before heading out to the show. One to Jason Antone, of the J-Rock show, out in West Bloomfield, Michigan. Jason, twenty-four, suffers from Friedrich's ataxia, a rare genetic disorder that can cause muscle weakness, speech problems, loss of tendon reflexes, and loss of sensation in the extremities. But Jason has a great attitude, helped in part by his enthusiasm for his show, which airs monthly on several public-access channels across Michigan.

I keep meaning to send him a taped interview, but keep forgetting. But I told him that when I was next in the area, I would be sure to head over for an interview in his house. I told Jason about *Hardcore Diaries*, and how, due to the nature of the book, he might very well find his name in there.

"Can you really do that?" Jason asked.

"Sure," I said.

"No."

"Yeah."

"No."

"Listen, Jason, it's my book, and I can pretty much do whatever I want with it. So if I say you're in there, you're in there."

"Thanks," he said. "That's awesome."

Next up on the Foley phone list was Stephen Wexler. I met Stephen about five years ago, when I was a special guest at his bar mitzvah. Stephen suffers from a rare neurological disease known as familial dysautonamia and was not supposed to live past the age of five. But he's seventeen now, and still going strong, although some days are better than others for him. Occasionally, when he's a little down, his father will give me a call, to let me know that a phone conversation or visit might help him out. In this case, Stephen had just gotten out of the hospital following a knee surgery. I invited the family over tomorrow night for pizza and *SmackDown!*

I've got to try to get back into my *SmackDown!* groove again. For a few years, *SmackDown!* night was Foley night, as I would regularly visit various kids I had met along the way who had been facing serious illnesses and challenges. It really wasn't that hard, and the kids and families really seemed to love it.

At my friend Stephen Wexler's
bar mitzvah, in 2002.

Come to think of it, I've got to get back to doing a lot of things I did regularly up until a couple years ago. I was really good about visiting schools and libraries, talking to kids about the importance of staying in school, reading, and getting an education. For a while, when I was really into it, I would talk about the dangers of drugs, and the serious ramifications of bullying.

I remember when Dewey first started playing Little League, at age eleven. He started a few years late, mainly due to his obsession with WWE. For years, that's all he wanted to do. Wrestling tapes, wrestling figures, wrestling video games, wrestling trivia, wrestling shirts. With the exception of Stone Cold condoms (I kid you not), he had just about everything on the market. It's too bad there never was a Mick Foley condom—that would have been real effective birth control. "Hey, is that a picture of Mick Foley? On your penis? Oh, gross! Forget it. Just take me home."

I tried to take him to a department store to purchase his first baseball glove when he was about seven. But on the way to Sporting Goods, he passed the WWE action-figure aisle and forgot all about the glove.

"No, Dewey, that's not what we came for."

"But I want it," he said, holding one particular figure aloft.

"No, buddy. I'm sorry, we've got plenty of wrestlers at home."

"But I've got my own money."

"Sorry."

"But I've got my own money."

At that point, he began to sob uncontrollably, and our special father-son baseball bonding moment was over. It would be three years before he got that first glove. The action-figure culprit? Jeff Jarrett. Which in case you forgot, is J-E-ha ha-double F J-A-ha ha-R-ha ha-double R-E-ha ha-double T. Sure, Jeff hasn't said that in about seven years, but I thought it would be good for a nostalgic laugh. I've known Jeff for over eighteen years, and I came very close to working with him at TNA last year, but come on, he's not worth crying over.

I walked out onto the field for Dewey's first game and sat down on the bleachers with the other baseball parents. Sure, I was the only dad with his hair halfway down to his ass, but I did my best to fit in. Realizing that it had been over twenty-five years since I'd been on a Little League field, my mind began to wander, drifting back to that day, so many years ago, when I last played the game.

Back in 1976, I'd been a pitcher, the proud possessor of both the fastest and wildest arm in the league. I was good, but I hated the pressure, and by my last year in Little League, 1978, I was strictly a catcher, like my hero, the Yankee's Thurman Munson. Munson died that next year, in 1979, and it would be about twenty years before I became interested in the game of baseball again.

I don't even remember our team name, but I remember the opposing team, the Exxon Tigers, because of the memory that team's coach etched deep into my subconscious memory.

During the first inning, I tried to throw a runner out who was attempting to steal second. The attempt was successful, largely due to my throw, which may have been a little less than Munsonesque.

"Look at that!" the Tiger coach, an adult male, said. "Blooper arm."

But hey, I'd get my turn at bat, and then it would be my turn to laugh. I did get my turn at bat, but I didn't end up laughing, as I bounced to short and was thrown out at first by several steps. Even before several knee surgeries, I wasn't exactly a merchant of menace on the base paths.

But as I headed back to the dugout, which wasn't actually a dugout, but merely a bench with a wire mesh fence in front of it, I heard the Exxon coach, Mr. Sensitivity, crank up another comment about my limited physical skills. "Look at the way he runs—like he's got a dump in his pants!"

As I caught the warm-up throws at the top of the next inning, the umpire, whose sister Felice was a good friend of mine, heard me crying.

"What's the matter, Mick?" he said.

I continued crying.

"Mick, what's wrong?"

I started one of those long sentences that kids make when they're trying to hide their shame. "The other . . . coach . . . keeps . . . making . . . fun . . . of . . . me."

"Do you want me to say anything?" my friend's brother asked.

"No."

I was twelve years old. Twelve. Being ridiculed by a grown man. For having the audacity to be slow. And there I was, twenty-five years later, sitting in the bleachers, hurting every bit as much as I did the moment the words hit me.

The umpire's name was Ken Erikson. The last time I saw him on television, he was the Olympic softball team's pitching coach, celebrating a gold medal victory with his team.

I went on to wrestle a couple of thousand matches, write a few towering best sellers, and get interviewed a couple of times by Katie Couric.

I don't know what happened to that coach. But I have thought about finding him, so I can pay him a visit. So I can tell him what an inconsiderate prick he was. But also to thank him for making me realize an important truth that I went on to share with thousands of kids over the next few years.

I have a little paperweight on a bookshelf hanging over the desk upon which most of Hardcore Diaries is taking shape. Surrounding the paperweight are framed photos of children I've known who have since passed away. The paperweight reads, "No act of kindness, no matter how small, is ever wasted."

In honor of the Exxon Tiger coach, I added a new phrase: "No act of cruelty, no matter how small, is ever forgotten."

Yeah, I did a lot of talking for a while, but I seem to have lost my drive. Part of it stems from the uphill battle I face every time a school asks me to speak. Almost without fail, I will learn that the school board or some other governing body put up strong resistance to the idea of a wrestler talking to their students.

"You really proved them wrong," I've been told on several occasions. But why should I have to be in the position to constantly prove people wrong? It gets frustrating after a while.

I've had a couple of meetings with my local congressman, Tim Bishop, about setting up some kind of literacy or anti-bullying campaign. I would volunteer to spend one day a week, every week, for free, speaking to kids at different schools across our county. He seemed genuinely interested, but nothing ever came of it. I can't help but think that some well-meaning advisers told him to steer clear of the wrestler, for image purposes.

One evening, I received a phone call from Senator Clinton's office. I was told that Paul Begala (a former advisor to President Clinton, and a top political commentator) had recommended me for a literacy campaign, after meeting me in an airport. Again, I offered to donate one day a week, for free—but this time at a different New York City school every week. I never heard back.

"What do you think happened?" my wife asked.

"They probably Googled me," I said.

Yeah, part of my problem is bureaucratic, but part is personal. You see, I'm just not sure if what I'm saying is actually important, or if I'm even qualified to say it.

I was really good at talking about writing back in the days when people actually bought my books. But when they stopped buying, I stopped writing. Don't get me wrong, I've loved the writing experience. Each book, including this one, has been a pleasure to work on. But I've come to realize that I'm not really a writer. Writers write. It's in their blood. I'm *not* a writer. I'm a *wrestler* who happens to write. There's a difference.

As for bullying? Hell, people might listen to me for a day or two, a week tops, but in the long run, forty-five minutes with Mick Foley isn't likely to change people much. Certainly even an impassioned speech from "the hardcore legend" is no match for a young lifetime of bad habits and peer pressure. For most kids, my visits are simply a cool way to miss math class and ask if it hurt when I was thrown off of the top of the cell by Undertaker.

I think part of the reason I have increased my interest and contributions to children overseas is that, unlike my intangible efforts in schools and libraries, these charitable interests yield concrete results.

When I traveled to China with Operation Smile, I could actually hold a child who had just received a new lease on life due to a single one-hour cleft-lip operation. I could see the joy in his father's face when the child he'd entrusted to our care just an hour earlier came back looking like a new boy.

When I traveled to the Philippines this past winter, I could see the early childhood education center that my proceeds from *Tales from Wrescal Lane* had built. I could see the reports on the hundreds of families who now had access to clean drinking water as a result of my contributions.

As a long-time UNICEF donor, I was very enthusiastic about the prospect of promoting Trick or Treat for UNICEF with WWE. I talked to Vince and Shane McMahon and received their blessing.

"What would it entail?" Vince asked.

"Not much," I said. "An article for the Web site, a mention in the magazine, maybe let me take one of the orange boxes into the ring with me on *Raw* or *SmackDown!*"

I called my contact at UNICEF with the idea and assumed it was a no-brainer.

Well, of course, it wasn't, as I learned while driving to the White Mountains last fall for a weekend Santa's Village sojourn. My wife said it looked like I was being kicked in the stomach when I received the news on my cell phone. It had been decided, I was told, that UNICEF couldn't have anything to do with WWE.

My initial impulse (which I had the good sense to repress) was to start running down their goodwill ambassadors, pointing out the violent or sexual shows they'd appeared in. Hell, if they held movie stars to the same criteria that WWE was apparently being judged by, Angelina Jolie would have been laughed out of the UN offices—the vial of Billy Bob's blood around her neck, making out with her brother at the Oscar's, appearing in *Hackers*.

But she's been a godsend for the United Nations, drawing attention to refugee crises, almost single-handedly raising awareness about international adoption, nailing Brad Pitt. Honestly, I think she should be given some kind of award from God, for making the most out of what she has been given.

I admire people like her, people who take a stand. People who honestly believe that to those to whom much is given, much is expected. People like Bono, who's doing so much to help with the multitude of devastating problems facing the African continent. People like Paul Newman, who with his big heart and his Newman's Own products has not only raised $150 million for children's charities but helped create and inspire a network of camps for children with cancer and other life-threatening illnesses. And people like Julia Roberts, whose volunteer work at Newman's "Hole in the Wall Gang" camp raised her status in my eyes from great actress to great person.

But I guess there has to be a limit to what celebrities should say or do. I mean, I used to be a Dixie Chicks fan before they badmouthed George W. Bush, saying they were embarrassed to be from the same state as the president. Now I'm a *big* Dixie Chicks fan.

I know UNICEF has done some wonderful work around the world for decades, since 1946 to be exact. I just wish they would have let WWE be a part of it.

Following my figurative kick in the gut, I focused most of my international attention on Christian Children's Fund. They seem to like me, even giving me the honor of addressing most of their staff at a luncheon at their home office in Richmond, Virginia. And in one of my biggest personal achievements, I was featured in the Summer 2006 issue of *Child World*, their quarterly donor magazine.

One of the things I'm enjoying about writing this book is that I'm never really sure where a particular entry will take me. I really thought this one would be about the local Ring of Honor (ROH) show, including my talk with Brian Gewirtz, who happened to be there as a fan. Hopefully I'll get to ROH later. But I certainly didn't begin writing tonight with the idea of covering topics of bullying, my own self-doubts, Angelina Jolie, or the Dixie Chicks. All that stuff just kind of came out.

It's about 3:30 A.M., so I've been writing for three and a half hours, during which time I've written about 2,500 words. Which is a pace of about twelve words a minute—pretty brisk, considering I'm doing it by hand. Granted, most of the words are small, maybe even monosyllabic, but you get my point. Don't you? I'm moving quick, kind of going in whatever direction my heart and pen take me.

I hope this entry wasn't a downer. Just in case, I'll try to make the next one a happy one. But as long as I mention Christian Children's Fund, I'd like to insert an entry from my blog, written February 22, 2006, en route to the Philippines, where I would be meeting my sponsored child, Herma Grace, for the very first time. Hope you like it. Now, if you'll excuse me, I've got a child's bunk bed to climb into.

Herma
Grace

Trish Stratus, a longtime WWE Diva, is among my best friends in the wrestling business. So when Trish sat down at my table at the Philippines Air lounge, she seemed like the perfect person to ask a question I had asked myself many times before: "Does it seem weird that one of my biggest inspirations is a little girl in the Philippines whom I have never met or talked to?" I then told her about Herma Grace, who refers to me as "Dad" and who has become a beloved part of the extended Foley family.

Herma Grace is a child I have sponsored through Christian Children's Fund for the past five years. I first began my affiliation with CCF back in 1992, a time when I was too caught up with WCW wrestling and first-time fatherhood to really commit much time to thinking about others, no matter what their situation might be.

I really can't remember why I called CCF. I imagine it was one of those Sally Struthers appeals that I had seen literally hundreds of times, but I'm not sure. A few days later, a letter came in the mail that included a photo of a child, Nida, age nine, who was in need of sponsorship. Well, my life may have revolved around wrestling and family, but I was not completely without a conscience, either. So I wrote that first small check fourteen years ago.

Nida wrote to me almost every month for nine years. I think I wrote to her a total of five times. I didn't realize at the time that the CCF sponsorship program is about so much more than writing monthly checks. It's about establishing relationships with children in need. It's about letting children with very little in their lives—through no fault of their own—know that someone out there cares.

Christian Children's Fund has been caring about these kids since its inception in 1938—now assisting more than 10 million children in thirty-three countries regardless of race, religion, or gender. In addition to monthly sponsorships, CCF's donations support literacy training, vocational training, health and immunization programs, water and sanitation development, early childhood development, and emergency relief.

Unfortunately, they can't force a grown man to write letters. So one day, I received a letter informing me that Nida had turned eighteen and had gradu- ated from the sponsor- ship program. Included in the letter was a photo

The mysterious missing piglet photo.

of another girl, nine years old, from the same part of the Philippines, who was in need of a sponsor.

She was a tiny thing with big brown eyes filled with sadness. Never would I have guessed that the child in the photo would touch my heart, give me such joy, and perhaps most importantly have the deceptive strength needed to unbolt the Foley checkbook and turn those small checks into larger ones.

Herma's first letter to me started a small stir in the family, instigating an event I will call "The Case of the Missing Piglet Photo." The photo in question was Herma, age nine, bathing a piglet. On the back she had written, "Take this photo as a simple remembrance of me." Vowing to be a better sponsor the second time around, I taped the photo to the refrigerator. It was missing a day later. Had it fallen off, or had it been stolen? But who would steal a photo of a tiny child . . . and why?

Maybe I should have been a detective, for when asking my kids if they had seen the photo, I couldn't help but notice a slightly odd look on my daughter Noelle's face; a guilty look. Noelle, it turns out, had taken Herma's photo because she had referred to me as "Dad" in her letter. Noelle, seven at the time, was suffering through her first bout of jealousy. To this day, the Case of the Missing Piglet Photo remains a touchy subject in our home.

Despite having vowed to be a better sponsor, I quickly slid back into my non-letter-writing way. It may surprise people to know that despite writing towering best sellers (as well as a few that didn't loom quite so large on the sales chart), I am a notoriously sluggish letter writer. I don't write often, and when I do, it's not all that good.

Well, over the course of the next several months, Herma Grace made it clear to me that not writing was not an option.

"Dad, why don't you write to me?"

"Dad, it's been four months since I have heard from you!"

"Dad, how could you lose to Tiger Ali Singh in Kuwait?"

Okay, I made that last one up.

So I started writing steadily, and I found that corresponding with this child, who came from so little, was giving me so much. For anyone who hasn't received a letter from a child asking God to "shower you with more blessings, give you better health and a harmonious family life," my next statement might seem unrealistic, like a big exaggeration, but it's not. Because in my life, I have known what it's like to hear twenty thousand people chant my

Little Mick is featured in this photo album, which was created by Herma Grace.

name: "Foley, Foley, Foley, Foley!" I also know what it's like to have a child I've never met draw me a picture of Mickey Mouse and thank me for "being kindhearted and generous to people in need." Please trust me when I say the feelings I get from each are almost identical.

I'm not downplaying the incredible rush that I get from a live crowd; I'm just trying to explain how this child's letters make me feel and how thankful I am that she has been a part of my life.

She is no longer a little child. I received a photo several months ago, and Herma Grace, soon to be fourteen, is turning into a beautiful young lady. About a year ago, I began to look into the possibility of visiting Herma in the Philippines. Unfortunately, her province is home to much conflict, including sporadic violence and the occasional kidnapping of foreign tourists. It is not a place CCF feels comfortable taking their donors for a visit. Instead, they suggested arranging a meeting in Manila.

I had been debating the "sixty hours by plane" for several months when the phone call from WWE came. Keep in mind that I had been more or less retired for six years, and during that time, I had never been asked to participate in an overseas trip. (Okay, I was on a one-day trip to England when I was commissioner, but I'm not counting that one.) Let's just say it was unusual to receive such a call.

"We have a couple of trips you might be interested in," Ann Gordon said. Ann has been working at WWE Talent Relations since sometime before the dawn of history, and she told me the first trip would go to Bangkok, Thailand, and Japan.

"Hmmm," I said, trying to figure out how to put my next thoughts into words befitting a seasoned wordsmith.

"Um, do you think if I went over there that I could, maybe, you know, get my own flight to the Philippines? Because I sponsor a girl there who I would really like to see."

Ann actually started laughing.

"What's so funny?" I asked.

"Well," she said. "The Philippines is the next trip I'm going to ask you about."

So, here I am on Philippines Air Flight 103, an hour before touching down in Manila. I think about this child I never met or spoke to, realizing that fact is about to change. I made sure that her entire family (mom, dad, two brothers, and two sisters) will be there, as I would hate for this special meeting to be a cause for resentment among her siblings.

A month earlier, I had completed an exhausting four-day whirlwind promotional tour of Manila. Before leaving for the tour, I asked Christian Children's Fund if it would be okay to mention the child and the fund, as they were the sole reasons I was going on the trip. I had even pledged to donate the money I made on the two trips to CCF projects in the Philippines.

I don't even pretend to understand how my mind works when it comes to finances and what constitutes acceptable and unacceptable expenditures. Will I spend $70 for a hotel if the wake-up call is less than four hours away? No way. It's off to the airport for me. But will I travel a total of 120 hours and spend several days 10,000 miles from home for free? Yeah, if I feel strongly about the cause. And I do feel strongly about this cause. And to my surprise, CCF felt strongly about letting me tell the story—my story, and theirs.

Philanthropic organizations can be a little funny when it comes to wrestling. Some, such as Make-A-Wish and the Muscular Dystrophy Association, openly embrace us. Some choose to keep their distance or avoid any relationship at all. I will always be grateful to CCF for accepting me and embracing me—even referring to me as an unofficial ambassador in one of our correspondences.

I'm not sure why it took me so long to make that call back in 1992—why it took hundreds of appeals like tiny hammers tapping away at my conscience until I finally picked up that phone. I think perhaps it's because global poverty can seem so intimidating as to appear insurmountable. But for CCF and groups like them, successes are measured one child at a time.

Helping Herma Grace and getting to know her through her letters has been not only a joy, but one of the great honors of my life. And that honor costs less than a dollar a day. I would consider it an honor if anyone reading this would even think about sponsorships as a result of my words.

Here is the contact info:
Christian Children's Fund Official Web site:
www.christianchildrensfund.org/sponsorship
Phone: 1-800-776-6767

Tell them Mick Foley sent you.

Dear Hardcore Diary,

The Wexlers just left, following a successful night of *SmackDown!* and pizza at the Foley house. Mr. Wexler had to actually carry Stephen out of the car and into the house, a fact that has become increasingly necessary over the course of the last year and a half. Despite the tough breaks he has had to endure, I've never seen Stephen when he wasn't smiling, which leaves me feeling like I should be smacked around by a couple of Stone Cold comeback punches the next time I have the nerve to complain about *anything.* Except for people who mess around with my ECW *One Night Stand* ideas. I reserve the right to complain about that.

Increasingly, I feel like I may have been dealt an unlikely favor when the "Kiss My Ass Club" segment was shelved. Sure, it would have been one of the all-time great episodes in *Raw* history and would have instantly made Terry Funk a name to contend with, but with Mr. McMahon involved, the possibility of turning a serious angle into an over-the-top comedy routine was a strong one. Which is not really a knock on Vince so much as a lack of foresight on my part. I can rattle off a long list of Mr. McMahon's best attributes, but a sense of subtlety wouldn't be up there. For this thing to succeed—and there's no guarantee it will—we're going to be dealing with various shades of gray. Had Vince been involved, it very well could have been too black and white.

It's not an easy path by any means. I will need to be vehemently pro-WWE while still remaining vaguely fan-friendly. Edge will be vehemently pro-WWE, while professing an open hatred for the fans. The Funker and Tommy Dreamer may very well find themselves swimming against a tide of apathy for a while, although I can't help but believe that Terry Funk's WWE return on Monday in Lubbock,

Texas, only about eighty miles from his house in Amarillo, will be met with great enthusiasm.

I just hope that they don't try to script us. I understand the concept behind scripting interviews. It helps ensure that time considerations are not abandoned, and it gives the creative team some assurance that storylines are being followed and that the correct points are being made.

At their best, these wrestling interviews, or promos, are a mesmerizing combination of emotion and instinct. The very best can go out to the ring armed only with a microphone, a few basic ideas, and a heartfelt belief in themselves. The words will come naturally if only the situation is right and the emotion is real.

And if the situation isn't right, and the emotion isn't real? Well, then we fake it, depending on experience and a cache of clichés to carry us through. Sometimes they suck. Hence the need for scripting. But on Monday night I'll be in that ring face-to-face with Terry Funk, the greatest wrestler I've ever seen—my mentor and friend. And deep down, I'll want to show him that when I'm in my groove, I'm as good with a mike as anyone. And deep down, he'll want to show not only his Lubbock fans, but millions more around the world, why he's even better than me. We both believe in ourselves, but more importantly, we both believe in each other. We each understand that it's not really about him or me—it's about *us*. We have the same goals—get people talking about *One Night Stand*. The situation will be right. The emotion will be real. We have the genuine ability to create magic on Monday. Please don't hand us a script.

And if they give us a script anyway? I say do what comes naturally and then blame Funk afterward. What are they going to do, fire him?

I may do verbal battle with Paul Heyman the following week in Las Vegas. In which case, I'll just say reread the last two paragraphs and apply all the same principles to Paul E. He's one of the greatest promo men in the history of our business, and better yet, he lives, eats, and breathes ECW. He knows he'll be fighting for ECW's very existence out there, and will have a deep belief in every word he says. And I'll believe in everything I say. And better yet, I'll go out to that ring believing it was Paul E. who called me a whore. Vince, please do yourself and your shareholders a favor—don't hand me a script. Let us make some magic.

I think there is an even bigger long-term danger to the scripting process. It eliminates the need for a wrestler to think for himself. I will admit that some of my best lines have been written for me. Hey, Tom Hanks has a couple of little golden men on his mantel, thanks to saying scripted lines, and I'm pretty sure DeNiro didn't ad lib most of *Raging Bull*. So I'm not ashamed to admit that not all of my material has been my own.

Luckily, most of the scripted lines came later in my career, when Mankind became something of a comedy character, and Commissioner Foley regularly held court in center ring with a cast of thousands. Well, maybe not thousands, but you get my drift.

But that was fourteen years into my career, when I had already been thinking for myself through the course of hundreds of interviews. And it seems like I was always thinking. Much to the chagrin of my wife, I was obsessed with those damn promos. She would see me staring into space, one eye twitching, right hand shaking, and she would know I had just ventured into Promoland. Sure, I'd return once in a while to pay a few bills or conceive a child, but for many years, I was only an occasional inhabitant of the real world.

Many of today's WWE Superstars have never even seen Promoland, let alone taken up residence there. They've had no reason to. It's almost like a defunct mom-and-pop amusement park, made obsolete by the advent of computer technology. But just as there will always be a place for the classic out-and-back wooden roller coaster in today's world of high-tech, big-dollar thrill rides, there will always be a place for the heartfelt promo in today's tightly scripted sports entertainment environment.

I spent quite a bit of time in Promoland today. Physically, I may have been elsewhere—throwing junk from my garage into a rented Dumpster, hitting the gym, buying authentic German cold cuts for Mother's Day. But mentally, I spent most of my day at the old park, hearing lines in my mind, squinting an eye, shaking a hand.

I bounded in my front door around six P.M., soaked in sweat, drenched with excitement.

"Colette, Colette!" I called.

My wife met me at the stairs, rushing to my needs as if I was Hughie with a boo-boo. "What's wrong, Mick?"

"Listen to this promo idea."

"Sure."

"Well, there's this scene in my last book where Scooter is having the gash on his cheek stitched by his mother."

"Okay." I love my wife, but like most people, she doesn't actually read my novels, so I had to kind of spell it out for her.

"Well, while she's stitching him up, he comes to find out that his mother never told him that the girl across the street used to try and visit him when he was injured years earlier. [His father accidentally shot him.] He says 'Mom, did Nina ever come by when I was hurt?' She says, 'Oh, that Spanish girl?' Even though Nina was Puerto Rican.

"Well, when Scooter finds out that his one real friendship was sabotaged by his mother, and that she also hocked his grandfather's engagement ring, he ends up pulling away from his mother before the stitches are done, leaving the needle hanging from its thread, swinging back and forth across his face."

Colette's look of mild uneasiness was vivid proof that my visit to Promoland was time well spent. "What does this have to do with you, Mick?" she said.

"That's how I want to do my promo."

Colette stared at me with a mixture of shock and intrigue.

"I'll have Funk hardway my eye. We'll go to the trainer's room, and I will actually do the promo while I'm being stitched. It's never been done before." Who knows, maybe it has, but I'm on a roll here.

"Then, when I really start getting into it, I'll tell the doctor to leave me the hell alone, pull away from him and do the rest of the promo in close-up, making sure I move my head around a little so that the needle can swing back and forth, like a pendulum. Then, if I feel like it, I'll give the thread a real good tug and undo all those stitches."

With that, Colette jumped into my arms and we made passionate, hardcore love right there on the stairs. Okay, so I made that last part up. Besides, there's no S-E-X allowed in Promoland. It's a family place.

May 14, 2006
Aboard American Airlines Flight #703
en route to Dallas, where I will connect
to Lubbock for tomorrow's <u>Raw</u>

Dear Hardcore Diary,

My son Mickey is a religious zealot. Yeah, I know just last week I called him a rock-and-roller. He still is. But he's a religious zealot, too. I don't mean "zealot" in a bad way, even if I'm not sure it's possible for that particular word to carry a positive connotation. I just mean he has a particularly keen interest in the life and teachings of Jesus—his birth and even more so, his death.

The interest started inauspiciously enough, with a manger scene at Santa's Village last fall—the same trip where I received the verbal smackdown from UNICEF. Until that point, Mickey and I had enjoyed a rather unique relationship when it came to Christmas, and especially Santa Claus. Mickey was that rare child who didn't like Santa. I'm not talking about a kid who cries when placed on Santa's lap—that's a seasonal rite of passage that all my kids have been through. We cherish those photos of our kids bawling their eyes out when forced to sit on the lap of a strange fat guy. And, no, I'm not talking about me.

But Mickey wasn't afraid of Santa—he just didn't like him. Actually, not liking him was less about genuine dislike and more about working an anti–Santa Claus gimmick in order to get a rise out of his Santa-loving dad. Seemingly every night, the little guy and I would perform a ludicrous ritual in which he would approach me slowly, a huge sparkle in his mischievous blue eyes. My heart would tingle every time I saw that look, for though it may have been the single dumbest act of bonding in the history of fathers and sons, it was, nonetheless, one that brought me great joy on a nightly basis.

At first, his whisper would be inaudible, intentionally so. "Pss, pss, psss."

"What, I can't hear you," I'd say.

"Pss, pss, psss." Just a little louder. He would be positively beaming by this point.

"I'm sorry, Mickey. I can't hear you. Can you speak a little louder?"

Without fail, he would fight to suppress his laughter, long enough to whisper, "I don't like Santa Claus."

"What?" I'd say in an over-the-top display of shocked disbelief.

"I don't like Santa Claus." Not even a whisper anymore. Just a genuine attempt to cause his dad deep emotional distress.

"What . . . did . . . you . . . say?"

I wish my writing could do justice to just how happy this routine made him. I'd reach out for him and apply the big tickle, dishing out punishment, demanding an immediate retraction.

"Take it back. Take it back." Occasionally he would take it back, just long enough to catch his breath, so he could start anew with more blasphemous big-guy berating.

"I don't like him! I don't like him! I don't like Santa Claus!"

Obviously, it was all in fun. Mickey never really *disliked* St. Nick. But he honestly didn't see the need for such a guy. After all, as he explained on many occasions, he had enough toys.

"Mickey, what would you like for Christmas?"

"Nothing."

"Nothing?"

"No, I have enough toys."

"I'm sure you must want something."

"No, that's okay. I have enough."

Where had I gone wrong? How could I have raised such an unselfish child? What a poor reflection on me. "Come on, buddy, how about one toy?"

"No, you can give it to someone else. I have enough."

All kidding aside, I was always touched by these little talks. I remember taking Dewey and Noelle to Kmart a few years ago, armed with a fistful of "wishes" of less fortunate families that I'd taken down from the church bulletin board. This was going to be my way of teaching my kids the real meaning of Christmas. Instead, about a half hour into this spiritual shopping experience, my kids both literally fell to the floor in tears, sobbing upon their discovery that the Kmart excursion would yield no personal treasure for them.

In fairness to my two older kids, we tried the experiment a few years later, as volunteers for a great group called Christmas Magic, and this time Dewey and Noelle were more than up to the task, shopping and wrapping their little hearts out for the sake of kids they would never even meet.

I was so proud of both of them. But also a little flabbergasted when, after doing so much work, they both came up to me and said, "Dad?"

"Yeah?"

"What's Santa bringing us?"

Man, my kids were ten and twelve at this point, legitimate contenders for *Ripley's Believe It or Not* as the last kids on Earth to not catch on to the whole Santa deal. Hell, it had been earlier that year, on Easter eve, when exhausted by travel and faced with the prospect of pulling an all-nighter in the role of the Easter Bunny, I called Dewey over.

"Dewey, you're twelve, right?"

"Uh-huh."

"Do you still think a rabbit travels the world, handing out eggs and candy?"

"I guess not."

"Good, I need your help."

But I wasn't going to be quite so quick to give up Santa. Sure, the whole Easter Bunny thing is ludicrous. But this was Santa, man! Santa! I tried to gently explain to my kids that in a way, by helping people out, we were kind of like Santa. We were doing Santa's work.

They just stared at me. "But what's he bringing us?"

I knew it was the right time. After all, I'd already had the talk with Dewey. You know, *the* talk. Birds. Bees. *That* talk. But somehow, an intelligent twelve-year-old who already knew about procreation, pregnancy, and premarital hanky-panky hadn't deduced that reindeer couldn't fly.

So, I did what seemed right. I lied. "I'm sure Santa will think of something," I said.

Let's get back to Santa's Village. As we approached Santa's house, the charming log cabin where Santa meets and greets his guests, I could sense that Mickey was a little apprehensive. We'd assured both him and little Hughie that they didn't have to actually meet Santa—although one can never have too many photos of their children crying their eyes out on the big guy's lap. I told the kids that we would simply walk past it.

Mickey had other plans. Somehow, even at the tender age of four, he gathered the resilience, pride, and intestinal fortitude to make a heroic dash to Santa's door. "I don't like you, Santa Claus!" he yelled, before sprinting to the safety of his hysterically laughing parents.

But Mickey's whole idea of Christmas changed the moment he saw the life-size nativity scene. One by one the questions came.

"What's that?"

"That's the Baby Jesus, buddy. He's the reason we celebrate Christmas."

"Who's that? I thought Jesus was something you said when you dropped something, 'Oh Jesus.'" I swear he actually said that. I suppressed my laughter and said, "No, actually Jesus was God's son.

"That's the Baby Jesus, buddy. He's the reason we celebrate Christmas."

"Who's that?" he said, pointing to a larger figure.

"That's Baby Jesus' mother. Her name is Mary. And that's her husband, Joseph. But he's not Jesus' father. God is Jesus' father."

One after another the questions came. "How come? But why? But how?" Man, I'd been barely able to explain a regular conception to a twelve-year-old, let alone an immaculate one to a four-year-old.

But I must have done okay, because little Mick's interest never waned over the next few months. Eventually, he came to grudgingly accept that Santa was going to bring him a few gifts, although he did demand that Santa leave his stuff outside the front door. He was allowed to bring toys. He just wasn't allowed inside the house. Which actually made the distribution of the gifts a snap. Ready, set, dump. Watch the Alaistair Sim version of *A Christmas Carol*, which is sometimes called *Scrooge*. Wake Colette up, ask if she had a special gift for me. Accept humiliating rejection. Sleep until 3:30 A.M., when the older kids complain that Santa hasn't shown up with the toys yet.

But Santa's act was strictly secondary to little Mick's fascination with Baby Jesus. Unfortunately, I don't think Mickey completely grasped the idea that Jesus, at a certain point, stopped being a baby. Possibly I should have consulted a book or member of the clergy about how best to deal with the

Hughie, Mickey, Colette, me, and Noelle with the big guy, at my favorite place, Santa's Village. (Dewey was working as an elf.)

Santa's Village
2006

subject of the Easter celebration. Had I done so, the ensuing Easter talk may have been a little less confusing.

"Daddy, what happened to Baby Jesus?"

"Well, he died, buddy," I said.

"Why?"

"Well, uh, he, uh, died for our sins." I knew as I said it that this was a little vague. Besides, at this point in his life Mickey's sins had been pretty much limited to a little late-night bed-wetting, some massive fib-telling, and the previously mentioned verbal bombardment of Santa Claus.

"Why?" he asked.

"So that, um, whoever believed in him could have everlasting life." Wow, now I was hitting a four-year-old with gospel teachings that even I don't fully understand.

In truth, this "Easter" talk took place some time in January, giving Mickey over three months to mull over my words. And every day, he wanted to know more—about the cross, the crucifixion, cemeteries, churches, even questioning the rationale of commemorating the death of the Messiah with the distribution of chocolate bunnies. Well, that's not quite the way he put it. I think it was more like, "Why do we get chocolate when Baby Jesus dies? Why? Why are we happy when Baby Jesus dies? Why?"

Mickey wasn't happy about it at all. Colette saw him moping around the house, carrying the cross I'd received as a communion gift in 1984. Yeah, for those of you doing the math, I was a little old for communion; nineteen, to be exact. My dad, who has missed something like two Sunday masses in his life, never forced me to go to church—I started going on my own, and was communed and confirmed under the private instruction of Father Thomas McGlade, an absolutely wonderful man whose death still bothers me because I never told him in life what I'm writing right now.

For a year or so, I even thought about the priesthood, before opting to travel down the pro wrestling road. I think I could have handled the vow of poverty—I took a similar one when I worked for Jerry Jarrett in Memphis— but the whole celibacy thing was another issue. Even in my prime I never had an insatiable sex drive, but damn, forever is a little longer than I was willing to go without.

I considered myself something of a devout Catholic for the next ten years or so, until seeing a photo in *Newsday* (Long Island's main newspaper) of the priest who married me and baptized my first child, underneath the bold headline "Pedophile." I had been reeling a little from a string of problems in the Catholic Church—the denouncing of birth control despite overpopulation and starvation, the failure to allow priests to marry, the failure to deal with the obvious pedophilia problem—and the *Newsday* photo and story seemed to serve as a knockout blow. My churchgoing just kind of stopped. And while my faith in God never ceased, my faith in men acting in his name certainly did.

A few days later, I noticed that Jesus was no longer in an upright position on my crucifix. He was dangling by one hand, like Sly Stallone in the climactic scene of *Cliffhanger*. The culprit was Mickey, who was doing his best to free Jesus from his death, although I thought I'd made it pretty clear that he had to die in order for us to live.

Maybe a few of the books Colette got him cleared things up a little, because as he absorbed the lessons for the tenth, fifteenth, and twentieth time (the kid loves to be read to), he seemed to get the hang of Jesus' life, even asking if we could reenact some of the more well known parts of the New Testament.

So he'd say, "Dad, pretend to be blind, and I'll be Jesus and heal you." So I would stumble around the Christmas room until the little guy healed me in his own unique way, summoning the power of God as if he was Mr. Freeze unleashing a mighty blast of superfrozen molecules. And while I'm not an official biblical scholar (although I am staying at a Holiday Inn right now—I checked in about an hour ago), I'm willing to bet that Jesus' healing miracle sound effects couldn't compete with those of little Mick.

One night, after returning home from the road, I asked the little guy if he'd like to see a movie. "I have a better idea," he said. "How about we'll play Jesus. You be Jesus, and I'll be the bad guy and put you up on the cross."

And that's just what we did. I laid down on our makeshift whiffle-ball bat and Captain Hook sword combination cross, and Mickey pretended to drive nails into my wrists. Yeah, I know that sounds a little morbid, but they were really just crayons placed between my fingers.

Then it was my turn to be the bad guy, and I did my best to put my little guy on the cross, not knowing he intended to come back to life in fulfillment of the Scriptures. But I guess the subtlety of rising on the third day and appearing before his disciples had not been completely explored in his books.

Jesus' resurrection, little Mick style, resembled more of an Undertaker sit-up spot followed by a Hulk Hogan comeback. Yes, in the gospel according to little Mick, Jesus didn't really love the sinners—he beat the bejesus out of them.

Some days when I asked him what he wanted to do, he'd simply say, "Go to church," without a moment's hesitation. And believe me, it wasn't as if we were pushing him into it—this was all of his own free will. When Mickey found out Dee Snider (the Twisted Sister guy) was recovering from throat surgery, he sent him a get-well card decked out with about a hundred crosses.

Colette and I started wondering if God was trying to send us some kind of sign. Maybe our son was meant to answer some kind of calling. Maybe he'd be a great leader or inspirational preacher—if only we would take him to church instead of Chuck E. Cheese.

Colette even suggested a family viewing of *The Passion of the Christ*, but I felt I had to draw the line somewhere. I didn't think it was appropriate for a five-year-old, and said if Mickey really needed to see a bearded man bleeding profusely, being treated in an inhumane fashion, I could probably find a few of my old matches from Japan for him. But we really did feel like we needed to encourage his interest. So one Sunday, after a friend's birthday party, I took him and Hughie on a little local church field trip.

We visited a Presbyterian church that pre-dated the Revolutionary War, and a Methodist church right next to it that was over a hundred years old. We were invited into the Methodist church, and Mickey took it all in like an art enthusiast taking in his first LeRoy Neiman—oh, what a terrible example. We drove a few miles more so he could see the Lutheran church where I had gone to preschool, and even the Catholic church where I had received communion, learned so much, and then been so bitterly disillusioned.

And through the eyes of my five-year-old son, I began to feel my faith being restored. For years I'd felt my conscience pulling at me, leading me into volunteer work, so as not to ignore the gifts that God had given me. As odd as it sounds, I do consider the exposure I've received from WWE, and the instant recognition it affords me, to be a gift from God. A gift that gives me the potential to help—a potential that really has to be used.

I sometimes wonder if God really puts people in our lives for a reason, or if circumstance merely creates the potential to either use or ignore the gifts God gave us to make the most of any given situation.

Since my estrangement from the Catholic Church, I had often thought about finding a church that was more consistent with my beliefs. But how? I'm sure there must be some method of finding a match, some kind of spiritual dating service to set you up with the right place. I remember stopping in on a church in rural Georgia when Dewey was just a baby. It was Sunday, we were new to the area, and we thought, "What the heck, we'll just drop in." At the time I wasn't nearly as aware of the cultural differences that existed within different denominations of Christianity and within our social and moral framework. This was 1992. I didn't know what red and blue states were. I just thought we were all God's children. So we stepped inside.

It was like some kind of science fiction freak show, with the young Foley family playing the part of the aliens from outer space. The choir stopped singing in mid-note. They just stopped and stared. At us. Granted, we were probably an unusual sight. My hair was much longer then, hanging way down past my shoulders. I probably had a black eye and some prominent stitches in my head. Colette's boobs were probably halfway hanging out of her blouse, like the buxom young lady in the "Datapalooza" scene in *The 40 Year Old Virgin*.

We actually felt like we had to give an explanation for why we were there. "Hi, we're new in this area and thought we'd stop by." At which point the service commenced, but just barely. Something was definitely not right with that scene, and that something was us.

I'm not a fire-and-brimstone guy. I just don't see *that* Jesus. I don't *feel* him. I'm more of an "It is the night of the dear Savior's birth" in the Nat King Cole version of "Oh Holy Night" type of believer. I'm a Luke 6:36 Christian believer—a "forgive and you shall be forgiven" type of guy.

So no, I don't go for the heavy stuff, but nonetheless I feel that I'll be dealt with rather harshly if I don't make the most of the gifts I've been given. And by "dealt with kind of harshly," I guess I mean eternal damnation, burning in hell, all that heavy stuff I just said I didn't go for. I really believe God loves me. I just think he expects a lot out of me. "For whom much is given, much is expected." And I've been given an awful lot.

I pass by an old Methodist church quite often (not the same one I just mentioned). And every time Mickey would see it, he'd say, "I want to go there." Especially during the season of Lent, where a cross draped in purple cloth was placed out on the front lawn of the church. And every single day, I'd say, "We'll go tomorrow."

About a month ago, we saw a sign outside the church for an upcoming rummage sale. I had several carloads of things to give away, but was looking for the right place to donate to. We'd had a near emotional disaster on our hands several months earlier, when a charity failed to make the scheduled truck pickup, and as a result Hughie and Mickey saw all their beloved toys (actually it was stuff they'd either outgrown or never used) discarded on the curb like a collection of failed Al Snow character portrayals. So, to avoid scarring their tiny little psyches, Dad had to bring back each undersize garment and every unused toy, lovingly arranging them around the house, where they could be promptly ignored.

But this rummage sale was perfect. Close enough to my house so I could take care of it all in just a few trips. No need for a rental truck, no trusting a charitable group's truck driver to find my house, which is located just a couple blocks off the beaten path.

So, I packed up the used minivan, making sure to fold down the third row of seating to maximize available packing space. My older kids, especially Noelle, are so embarrassed by my van. It's not "cool" like her friends' parents' cars are. I've tried telling her that it's not the car that makes the man, but the man who makes the car, but she doesn't buy it. Then again, she's embarrassed by my hair and clothes, too, but doesn't let it get in the way of telling me she loves me several times every day.

I pulled into the parking lot to drop off the first load. I was met by two volunteers for the sale, church members who didn't have a clue who I was, despite the fact that I was blasting the "Dude Love" theme song when I pulled into the lot.

Despite my rather unconventional appearance, I didn't feel any attitude, didn't have the sneaking suspicion that I was being sized up or prejudged. Just two nice, normal people, helping me unload, thanking me for my time.

Who knows, maybe God really does put things into our lives for a reason. Maybe each yellowjacket is carefully selected for a preordained role, including the one that scared Mickey, prompting him to run to me in overblown fear, just as I was about to make my second trip to the church. "Where are you going, Dad?" he said. So after a month of "tomorrows" I made the best of one today, taking little Mick along to the church he'd inquired about so many times.

He was so excited, like a child on Christmas morning, assuming of course the child in question actually likes Santa, instead of treating the guy like some unwanted intruder. I introduced little Mick to Diane, one of the women

Mickey and
Hughie
outside our
church.

who had been so nice to me. I said, "My son Mickey loves churches. He asks every day if he can visit."

Once inside, little Mick fell in love with the place. I guess I fell in love with it, too. Well maybe not love, exactly. If the church was a girl, I guess I was smitten. But I'd have to get to know her a little better before making a commitment.

But little Mick wasn't so jaded—he really did love it. He jumped at the chance to join Ms. Diane's children's choir, and counted the days until he and

Dad could return. "Today, Dad?" he'd ask, every bit as excited about our upcoming church date as he is on the eve of a Disney World visit. Finally it came. Sunday was church day, and little Mick made the most of it. Singing his heart out in choir practice, though he didn't know a single word. Perusing the Bible in the main church service, looking for hidden meanings in the parables Jesus spoke. But mainly he just took it all in and loved it—just as I did.

The congregation was small, less than fifty, I'd say. The pastor was a little tough to understand at first. He comes from Korea, so he struggles just slightly with some of the words. But his message is peaceful. There's no fire and brimstone. The choir just kept right on singing even though I was there. No explanation was necessary. Nothing seemed wrong with the scene. I wasn't a stranger in a hostile environment. I was a welcome visitor in the house of God. Maybe I was . . . home.

Today was Mother's Day. The whole Foley family, including Grandma and Grandpa, in a rare Methodist appearance, gathered in God's house to hear Mickey sing—his first public appearance. He even had a choir robe just for the occasion, and looked adorable up at the front of the church with all the other children. Yep, it was a wonderful sight—fifteen children in robes . . . and me. You see, Mickey got a little scared, even though he had his colorful stuffed elephant with him, so he insisted that I hold his hand. Then, in a per-formance reminiscent of Cindy Brady pulling the big choke when the red light went on in the quiz show episode, little Mick closed his eyes, held his ears, and began to cry. Maybe it was a little overwhelming for him.

He finally got to put his choir practice skills to use on the way home. "Dad," he said. "I want to hear 'Stiff Upper Lip.'" My son, you see, is a rock-and-roller. He's a religious zealot, too. But maybe he really does have a calling. Maybe he has already encouraged a lost lamb to return to its shepherd.

Dear Hardcore Diary,

We go live in twenty minutes. *Raw* from Lubbock. I haven't written this way before—in a locker room, so close to bell time. I guess I'll actually head to backstage around 9:00 Central, giving me a little time to write and a little time to fire myself up, get my emotions where they need to be, and look a hell of a lot tougher and meaner than I actually am.

7:50 P.M. Just had a quick physical from the WWE doctor, and now I'm back. I'm just hanging out, trying to let the butterflies in my stomach settle down, and can't help overhearing Terry Funk and Carlito talk about the benefits of being second-generation wrestlers. One of the unfortunate aspects of our business is that occasionally guys will attempt to make names for themselves at the expense of other wrestlers. "Liberty takers," we call them. Apparently people didn't like to take too many liberties with second-generation wrestlers, especially when their fathers ran wrestling companies.

I had a couple of run-ins with liberty takers over the years, but nothing that left me too broken or bitter. I guess I had a reputation as a guy who could make others look good, so the whole principle of taking liberties was kind of self-defeating. I know I take great pride in having a reputation as a guy who never takes liberties.

It's kind of do-or-die for me and the Funker. Maybe that's overstating the importance of our first in-ring confrontation just a little, but not by much. You really only get one chance to make a first impression in front of WWE fans. Especially when the big match takes place in less than a month. It's imperative that we leave these fans with a lasting impression.

Look, I know this update was a little brief, but *Raw* has begun, Vince and Triple H are already in the ring, and I've got to take a little trip to Promoland. I'll see you when I get back.

11:10 P.M.—Holiday Inn, Lubbock, TX. To write or not to write? That is the question. I have to leave for the airport at 4:30 A.M. If I opt for sleep, I may get four hours of beauty rest, although I have a history of not being able to sleep when I am anticipating an early wake-up call. If I write until it's time to leave, I will be miserable on the plane, grouchy all day, and unable to do any writing at home. Decisions, decisions.

I just called the front desk to have some coffee sent up, so I guess my decision has been made. I'll just do my best to act happy when I get home. Hey, if I can pretend to be best friends with Al Snow for months for the sake of a lame wrestling angle, then certainly I can do my best Super Dad impression for a few hours upon returning home.

I arrived at the United Spirit Arena today somewhere around 1:00, just in time to find out that much of what I had proposed had been personally shelved by Vince. Brian Gerwitz was on vacation, so writer Ed Kosky had the distinction of being on the receiving end of a hardcore grilling on this certain night.

I looked at the rough outline of our television segment, which offered Terry Funk very little chance to speak.

I pointed out, "Ed, if we don't give Terry a chance on the mike, it's going to be awfully tough to convince people to spend money on him."

"I know," Ed said. "But Vince felt that if he came out of the crowd, he'd be bringing the beating [the one Edge and I would eventually give him] on himself."

"Ed, I have no problem introducing him. That's fine. But once he gets to the ring, he needs to be Terry Funk, or else there's no reason for him to be here."

Ed hemmed and hawed a little bit, before finally getting to the root of the problem. "Vince is a little concerned about giving Terry a live mike."

"Why?" I asked, "because he thinks Terry's out of his mind?"

"Well, kind of."

"Well, of course he is, Ed," I said. "That's what's going to make this whole thing work. But the idea of bringing in one of the greatest promo guys in history and not letting him talk is ridiculous."

It was then that the conspiracy theorist inside me surfaced, causing me to ask a blunt question before I had given my mind a chance to decipher the wisdom of such a choice. "We do want this show to succeed, don't we?"

It was posed as a question, but it was obviously an *accusation*, and not as ridiculous as it might seem. Over the years there have seemed to be Pay-Per-Views that were designed to fail, self-fulfilling prophecies of failure for good wrestlers who were finally given top spots on shows that didn't have a chance. Sure, it seemed to be mostly an old WCW trend, but there have been times when WWE's promotion of certain shows looked so lethargic as to make one wonder.

Kosky knew he was in a no-win situation. "Look," he said. "As of Thursday, it was written your way. Vince changed it on the phone when he became a little worried about Terry. I think he's expecting you to try to talk him out of it. I think he's looking forward to it."

So it was off to Mr. McMahon's office. In a situation like this, I always find it best to prioritize my concerns. I may be "the persuader," but I'm also a realist and understand the precarious nature of attempting to change too many of Vince's decisions, especially on the day of a show. My priority was to get Terry Funk some mike time. I really don't care as much about his entrance, as long as he makes a lasting impression once he's there.

The meeting was a success. I conceded that giving Terry Funk a formal introduction, as opposed to an entrance through the crowd, was probably more effective. But I pressed my point about the importance of showing the world that Terry Funk was a star, a man they would feel good about spending money to see. The concern about the live mike surfaced. As condescending as it sounds toward Terry, I convinced Vince that I would nurture Terry through this thing, even cutting him off verbally if he got carried away on a tangent. In the end, I got my way, but as a concession I had to agree to an in-ring rehearsal, which probably was a career first for a forty-three-year veteran like Terry Funk. Let me just clarify—Terry Funk is not forty-three years old. That's how long he's been involved in the wrestling game.

Before leaving, I told Vince about how well I thought *The Hardcore Diaries*

were progressing (although I guess you guys reading it will be the judge), and how the bumps in the creative road were actually good for the writing of the book.

"That's good," Vince said. "I'll be glad to add some more."

Earlier in the afternoon, I wandered around the arena, reading little snippets of *The Hardcore Diaries* to interested parties. Okay, it was a little more than snippets. Big Show and Triple H got the whole AC/DC story—and loved it. I know I ragged on Triple H a couple times in a few diary entries, but he and I go way back, to around 1992, and over the years have been pretty good friends and even better in-ring opponents.

I don't always agree with his creative direction, but I respect the hell out of what he has accomplished in the ring, and will always be thankful to him for helping me leave my full-time wrestling career on such a high note, by virtue of our two classic Pay-Per-View brawls in early 2000. And I still have a personal photo he inscribed for me during that time, and consider it one of my most valued wrestling keepsakes.

I let Candice hear her little airplane letter story too, and as I expected, she wasn't offended in the least. In fact, she seemed quite touched by the part about the fairy floating around dispensing hugs and laughter. I thought at one point she was wiping away a tear, but she was actually just scratching her nose. She did however share with me her philosophy on hugs—how giving them is her own little way of making the world a better place, and how she instinctively knows whether someone will be receptive to a Candice hug. Shawn Michaels, for example, always struck her as solely a handshake guy. "How about me?" I asked. "What did I strike you as?"

"Oh, I knew I was going to hug you," she said. "I just wanted to jump in your arms and wrap my legs around you . . . and . . ." She then laughed in such a way that I knew there was no way in hell that the last part would ever actually happen.

My
Sandwich
with
Candice

I suppose it all started with the sandwich. You see, it was a very special kind of sandwich. A sandwich to make the happy happier, and the giddy even giddier. A sandwich to make a homecoming homier, and natural enemies . . . friends.

Does that last paragraph seem familiar? No? Not even a little? Okay, go back and substitute the word *snow* for *sandwich* in every sentence. Does it seem familiar now? It should. After all, it's the introduction to *Frosty the Snowman,* the children's animated classic that I just put into my DVD so I could start this unique, heartwarming story out in a unique, heartwarming way.

But to tell you the truth, I'm not sure where the hell the sandwich came from. I mean, I know I was at Landstuhl Air Force Base in Germany. I know we'd just flown the first eight-and-a-half-hour leg of a seventeen-hour flight, and that we were relaxing for a little while before embarking for Afghanistan, where we would try to spread a little holiday cheer, WWE style, for thousands of our service members who would be spending the holiday a long, long way from home.

We had split into two groups at Landstuhl; one group visited with an enthusiastic throng of military families at a large on-base gymnasium. The other group, our group, visited injured or sick service members at the nearby hospital.

It was upon our return from the hospital that the sandwiches appeared, courtesy of WWE Diva Trish Stratus. As you may recall, Trish is someone I like a lot, someone I feel pretty close to. Someone thoughtful enough to make sandwiches for several beautiful women . . . and me. For you see, as odd as it might seem to comprehend the following scenario, as difficult at it might be to digest the following food for thought, I was virtually surrounded by every WWE Diva on the tour.

Trish Stratus? Check. Candice Michelle? Yup. The 2005 Diva Search winner, Ashley? Ditto. Maria? Present. Lilian Garcia, the world's most beautiful announcer? Yes. They were all there. But why?

Why? I could almost see MSNBC host and correspondent Rita Cosby, who was along for the tour, asking herself that very same question. Rita has interviewed many heads of state and various world-class luminaries, but even she seemed baffled as to why exactly all the women would hang around a not particularly handsome guy like me when there was such an abundance of appealing males from which to choose. Not counting Coach, of course.

The answer is actually quite simple, I'm the safety valve. At least, that's what Trish calls me. The guy they feel free to talk around. I guess if it wasn't for my superdeedooper heterosexual lifestyle, which produced four children—count them: one, two, three, four—I'd be kind of like the gay friend.

But that still doesn't explain where the sandwiches came from. Yes, I know that Trish brought them. But from where? Did she make them on the plane? At the hospital? In the lounge? If it wasn't so late, I'd call her and ask. As you might recall, she's on my speed dial. But safety valve or not, that would be kind of a weird question to ask. "Yeah, Trish, it's Mick Foley. Good, thanks, how are you? Oh, that's good. Listen Trish, do you remember where you got those sandwiches in Germany back in December 2005? Hello, Trish? Hello? Hello? Damn!"

So, we'll just have to forget about the origin of the sandwiches, and just accept that they were there. Six of them. Peanut butter and honey. And Trish was dispensing them with great care to the unlikely assemblage of Mick Foley and the Divas.

I wolfed mine down in about a minute, maybe less. The girls were a little less voracious. A little more aware of things like chewing and swallowing.

After several minutes of the tiny bites and polite chewing, I heard it. It?! Candice's voice. Heralding forth an offer that was the stuff of dreams. Or at least a visualization all but realized. "Would anybody like the rest of this sandwich?" she asked.

I turned to see Candice Michelle, the dispenser of hugs, she of the large assets, holding aloft half a sandwich. But it was no ordinary sandwich. It had two bites taken out of it. I let out an audible, yearning, mournful sigh. A sigh loud enough to draw the attention of the Divas, who sensed something might be wrong with their beloved hardcore legend.

"Mick, what's wrong?" Lilian asked.

In truth, I thought it was my heart. It had just done a big flip inside my chest.

I hesitated, trying to figure out how best to explain my odd reaction to a seemingly innocuous question.

"I'm sorry," I said. "It's just that this is almost exactly like a scene out of my last book."

The girls seem transfixed as I told them the story of Scooter Riley, age nine, growing up in the Highbridge section of the Bronx back in 1969, a period of great transition for the neighborhood.

Young Scooter is invited into the home of Nina Vasquez, a beautiful Puerto Rican girl, a few years his senior, new to the United States. Her English is weak, but her manner is warm, and she asks Scooter to watch game three of the World Series with her. Once inside, she makes Scooter a sandwich, peanut butter and banana (not exactly Trish's creation, but close enough), and after allowing Scooter a couple bites, asks a fateful question.

"Can I have a bite?"

Here's a little passage, direct from my novel *Scooter*, which explains just what happens to young Scooter, and how much the incident meant to him.

I handed her the sandwich. I could have sworn her thumb touched mine when the handoff was made. I looked at her mouth as she took her bite. Oh, my God, it was more than I'd dared dream. I had just assumed that she'd bite down on virgin bread, but that was not the case at all. Nina Vasquez chose instead to journey down the road that I'd just traveled. Her mouth clearly touched the bite I'd made—she was almost kissing me by proxy. She knew it too, I could tell—the way those big, dark soulful eyes looked at me as she chewed.

I don't think she knew my life had changed as she swallowed the bite. I wondered if this was one of those moments Grandpa spoke of, where one transcends or whatever. Because I thought I'd just transcended.

I took the sandwich from her hand—the one with two bites missing. I put our special sandwich on the paper plate and placed the plate onto my lap. Where it covered my first erection.

A couple of the Divas had tears in their eyes upon hearing of young Scooter's emotional attachment to the sandwich. Candice Michelle realized she now held more than a simple sandwich in her hands. Indeed, she held the fulfillment of my dreams.

So did I take the sandwich? You're damn right I did. I took it and journeyed directly down the road that Candice had just traveled. And I really enjoyed the trip, too. I'm pretty sure I didn't break any of my marital vows or any of the commandments, either. The girls really seemed to enjoy the unique culinary adventure I'd just taken them on.

"This might sound weird," Ashley said. "But that was kind of hot."

"Wow!" Candice said, in her otherworldly way. "I feel like I just made out with Mick Foley."

Trish Stratus, as kind and thoughtful as she may be, had lacked the foresight to bring along some paper plates. I really could have used one.

Don't try this at home.
Getting burned by Edge
at *WrestleMania 22*.

Oh, my eye, part I, with Mickey, 2004.

COURTESY OF THE FOLEY FAMILY.

Oh, my eye, part II, with Mickey and Hughie, 2006.

COURTESY OF THE FOLEY FAMILY.

Displaying Terry
Funk's handiwork.

"Born to Be Wired"
at *One Night Stand*,
June 11, 2006.

Having a word with Ric Flair during our "I Quit" match.

Vanquishing the **Bad Santa** in Afghanistan, December 2005.

"No, Mick, don't do it."
On the verge of joining
Mr. McMahon's club.

COURTESY OF THE FOLEY FAMILY.

Afghan
Diary

As much as I like that story (and I hope that you did, too), I can't help but think that I would eventually come to regret mentioning Afghanistan only as an interesting side note to my somewhat strange sandwich situation.

When I was originally asked about writing this book, I readily agreed, thinking in truth that it would be fairly effortless. After all, I would simply be putting my *Foley Is Blog* Web entries into book form. As it turned out, I abandoned the prefabricated Web log rehash in favor of *The Hardcore Diaries*. Much as I feared, my enthusiasm for the weekly Web format fizzled quickly, but not before I had a chance to do some work with it that I am very proud of. Perhaps the piece I am proudest of is my December 10, 2005, entry written on the long plane trip home, after a very emotional visit to the Bagram base hospital.

I feel strange, however, about asking readers to dive headlong into such a heavy story immediately after spending such a pleasant pit stop with Mick Foley and the five dazzling Divas. So think of the December 9, 2005, entry as a buffer zone; a way to slowly get your feet wet, before diving headlong into the deep end of the pool.

5:15 A.M., local Afghan time: Let me state for the record that Gene Snitsky can snore louder than any man on this planet. Perhaps somewhere on the plains of Africa there lies a pregnant rhinoceros, making more offensive, guttural sleeping noises than Mr. Snitsky . . . perhaps. But as far as people go, Snitsky gets the nod. He's the loudest there is, the loudest there was, and the loudest there ever will be.*

Several of us are scheduled to appear on Rita Cosby's live MSNBC show this morning. Rita's show airs live at 9:00 P.M. (ET), so due to the fact that Afghanistan is somewhere in the vicinity of way the hell over on the other side of the world, I knew our wake-up call would be coming at a very early hour. I did not know, however, that Gene Snitsky's own, personal alarm clock would see to it that no other wake-up call would be needed.

I think we're all very excited about Rita's show. Not only has she treated us very well, but through adventurous and memorable days, she has become almost like one of the gang. I am truly thankful for her decision to take the trip with us. Most of us in the wrestling business accept that the mainstream news media is either going to ignore us or knock us, and I think most of us understand that Rita's show will allow people back home to see us in a different, far more positive light than the one they've previously viewed us in.

My enthusiasm for this whole Web log thing may fizzle over time, but until that fizzling process begins, I am determined to offer WWE fans not only a different perspective on

* It was so loud that in between the first and second paragraph, I took solace on a doorstep in 30-degree weather in order to evade Snitsky's onslaught.

the big WWE issues of the day but also a perspective on the smaller, sometimes overlooked moments that make the WWE experience so unique. After all, our WWE photographers and film crews do such a great job of capturing actions and emotions that describing them in words seems kind of unnecessary. I mean, fans can see in a heartbeat how excited the troops are about our trip. A vivid Mick Foley description of why the troops are excited probably doesn't add a whole lot to the situation.

But by taking my pen and marble composition tablet behind the scenes of last night's huge autograph extravaganza to reveal the clandestine and heretofore unreported note-passing process that took place between the table of Mick Foley/John Cena and the table of Ashley/Candice Michelle, I truly feel like my Snitsky-induced early wake-up will not have been in vain.

I have another statement for the record. At the time of the autograph session, I was tired. Really tired. Goofy tired. Understandably tired. We were finishing up our second nonstop day of visiting bases and were given the option of either eating at the mess hall or resting in our "hooches," armyspeak for small wooden buildings where several large wrestlers all sleep—separated only by some plywood. Do you know how fatigued WWE wrestlers have to be to all bypass a free meal in favor of a nap?

8:00 A.M. We have just returned from Rita's show, which went really well, with the exception of my having casually mentioned on national television that I was writing a Web log about passing notes to beautiful girls at our autograph session. In other words, my clandestine encounter is not so clandestine anymore. Even worse, my wife will now find out about her husband's note-passing ways and expect a full explanation.

Well, here goes: with more than a thousand members of the U.S. military lined up in the cold to meet their favorite WWE Superstars (and Coach, too), you would surely expect each and every wrestler, Diva, and TV personality to be at their most fired up for the good of the fans. Not this WWE Superstar. For the first half hour of this extravaganza, I yawned, nodded off, and displayed so little charisma that I was mistaken for Al Snow. To make things even worse, I couldn't help but notice that the reaction I was harnessing—even when seated at the same table as WWE Champion John Cena—was not what I was expecting or used to. What was the deal? Gradually, after careful study, I came to realize just exactly what the deal was.

Cena and I were seated at the second table from the entrance, with the other members seated two to a table for a total of ten tables that looped in a semicircle around the building. Now, in my mind, a good autograph session is like a good wrestling card. It should build slowly, travel a trajectory of brilliant peaks and gentle drops, and then climax with a crescendo. Therein lies the problem: Cena and I were basically the second match on the card, following the opening match . . . Candice and Ashley. What a predicament! The fans were going absolutely crazy for the girls, who responded in kind by really lavishing attention on the service members. The crescendo, the climax, was occurring immediately, and Cena and I were left to try to pick the crumbs from the girls' plates. Fearing for my reputation, I fired off an angry note to the Divas. As a Foley Web log exclusive, here is the angry note in its entirety:

> Dear Candice and Ashley,
> The Hardcore Legend and the WWE Champion are sitting together, but by the time fans get to us, they couldn't care less. I was so excited about this autograph session, and now you've ruined it. Thanks a lot; you guys are really great friends.
> Yours truly,
> Mick Foley (The Hardcore Legend) &
> John Cena (The WWE Champion)

Really mature, right? But hey, it seemed to be just what the doctor ordered. Just seeing the two Divas laugh revived me in a way that a Red Bull, a Diet Coke, and a double shot of espresso had failed to do. We even got a note back—meaning that since for the first time since ninth-grade gym class, I was engaged in a full-fledged note-passing session. It was awesome.

So awesome, in fact, that there was only one way to top it: photo defacement. It started innocently enough with the blacking out of a couple of Lilian Garcia's teeth on a "Tribute to the Troops" glossy photo of WWE Superstars and Divas. It graduated to drawing aviator goggles on Vince McMahon (a questionable move at best, considering that he signs the checks) before setting our sights firmly on the image of Coach. Time seemed to fly, as Cena and I directed our considerable artistic talents into as many Coach creations as time would allow. There was Afro Coach; Mohawk Coach; Hasidic Coach; Pinocchio Coach; Kung-Fu Coach; El Coacho (Mexican masked wrestler); Mickey Mouse Coach; and others too ridiculous to mention. We even tried to create "Helluva Announcer" Coach, but we gave up in frustration when we deemed the task impossible. Hell, Vince McMahon has been trying to do the same thing for three years, and even he can't pull it off.

I went back to the hooch in high spirits. Our time in Afghanistan has not only been a time of accomplishment, it has been a time of extreme laughter, bonding, and even note-passing. It was a time to remember, a time to relive, which I was in the process of doing when Gene Snitsky's snores ruined it all.

Afghanistan and our "Tribute to the Troops" tour is behind us, though I think it's safe to say that all of us will bring home memories to last a lifetime. We'll be back in the United States in about twenty hours or so, giving me plenty of time to write, which is nice to know since I feel like I have a lot to write about.

As I look around the plane, I wonder what specific memories will be brought home. I'm sure all of us felt privileged to have been there. Yet I wonder what specific memory each individual wrestler, Diva, or crew member will take with them. I wonder whether there was a moment in a Black Hawk, a conversation with a soldier, or even a real deep look at the bleak landscape of Afghanistan that really registered in the memory banks.

As for me, I'm haunted. And no, it's not just the memory of my Santa vs. Santa match with JBL that's causing this. Sure, the match was really stupid . . . really bad, too! It was also really fun, though, and I hope the ridiculous memory of two Santa Clauses slugging it out with such devastating objects as toy sacks, down pillows, and salad tongs will put a smile on some soldier's face at a time when he can most use one. No, it's far more than Santa vs. Santa doing the haunting. It's the memory of a little boy in a tiny cot in a small hospital on Bagram Air Force Base, and lessons I hope that I learned from having the privilege of being in his company.

I was in Group 3—the laughingstock of this trip. Our wrestling roster was divided into three groups of six or seven people, and over the course of our time in Afghanistan, each group set off for different locations. During last December's trip to Iraq, I was in the "cool" group . . . the "macho" group. We got hit with rocket fire. We wore helmets and bulletproof vests. We crisscrossed the country via Black

Hawk. I even went to the perimeter in Sumarrah. So what if video evidence showed my reaction to enemy gunfire to be slightly less than hardcore? I was there . . . brother.

Not this time. While Shawn Michaels and John Cena camped out with the Special Forces in the mountains, I was watching Chris Masters lose to an airman half his size in an air mattress jousting contest. Yes, an air mattress jousting contest. So, while Vince McMahon, Triple H, and even Candice Michelle visited weary, thankful soldiers at forward operating bases, I was visiting the camp's post office. Yes, if the previous night's autograph session note-passing incident brought back memories of ninth-grade gym class, this special post office visit brought back memories of a fifth-grade field trip. Oh, wait, I did get to do an impromptu meet-and-greet when our bus made an unscheduled stop so that Gene Snitsky could take a dump . . . the results of which he actually took photos of. Which I guess if I posted on this site could give a whole new meaning to the term *Web log*.

We also visited the base hospital, and I've been haunted ever since. I knew I wouldn't be seeing any severely injured servicemen. The badly wounded are usually sent to Lundstuhl Hospital in Germany, where they spend a short transition period before being flown back to the United States. Over the past few years, I've been a pretty regular visitor to the Walter Reid Army Medical Center and the Bethesda Naval Hospital, both in the Washington, D.C., area. I pride myself on being pretty good with the wounded service members. More, I think, because they just feel comfortable with me than because of any special talent I have or any special wisdom I can offer to them.

I cannot claim, however, to being very good with burned children, especially one who has never seen me on his living room television set and who doesn't speak my language.

Our group was understandably weary following our day of jousting, post office visits, and spontaneous Snitsky stops when we arrived at the small hospital. I stopped to sign an autograph and found myself quickly separated from my colleagues. Had it been a larger facility, I would have attempted to catch up, but it was just two hallways intersecting in the middle. Getting lost did not seem like a possible option. So when a chaplain asked if I would like to say hello to wounded Afghan civilians, I allowed my fellow Group 3 members to wonder where I might be and accompanied the chaplain. "There is one child, in particular, who wants to say hello," she said. She then pointed to the rear of the room, which housed about ten or twelve injured Afghans, mostly male, who lay on small green cots that lined both walls in groups of five or six.

I asked the chaplain if the boy was familiar with WWE. "No," she said, "he just knows that you are famous and he's very excited to meet you." I immediately looked at the young boy, who flashed an excited smile. I was then informed that the man in the cot across the aisle from him was a detainee, a status that required the presence of an armed guard at all times. I gave the detainee half a smile, which he chose not to return. At that time, I did not know the nature of his physical condition or the reason for his detention. Had I been aware of the reason, I would not have offered him the smile.

The detainee had apparently been making an improvised explosive device (generally referred to as "IED"), which exploded and blew off both of his hands. The wounded man then showed up at the gates of Bagram asking for help from the same Americans whose lives he would have gladly ended.

I then walked over to a boy who wore a cast on his foot. I never did learn the nature of his injury because I became distracted by another boy, much younger, whose injuries were literally breathtaking. I know the word *breathtaking* usually carries a positive connotation as it is most often applied to incredible views or beauty—human, natural, or other. Yet the extent of this poor child's injuries literally took my breath away. His face thankfully had been spared from the worst of the burns on his body. Most of his body seemed to be one large mass of scar tissue, as if he'd been wrapped up in a bodysuit of angry scars. His hands were the first thing that I noticed, as they lay outside his blanket. One hand contained the vague outline of his former fingers. The other hand, the right one, seemed to be nothing more than a deformed pink and purple circle connected to a wrist. It was this hand that he extended to me when I stepped over to his bedside.

The child, the chaplain told me, was the victim of a kerosene heater explosion, an occurrence far more common to the impoverished in Afghanistan than I could ever comprehend. These explosions, the result of poorly built heaters and cheap kerosene/gasoline mixtures, are an everyday occurrence. I even saw photos of a two-day-old child whose entire tiny body had been engulfed in hideous flames.

I dedicated my 2000 children's book *Christmas Chaos* to a little boy named Antonio Freitas, a burn victim from Massachusetts, who touched my heart in a profound way. A line in the book reads, "What pain this little boy had

Dear Santa Claus,

I write to ask,
Please make my wish come
true.
I do not want a toy this
year—all I want is you!

To pack your bags and
spread good cheer again on
Christmas Eve.
To give all kids around the
world a reason to believe.

known, such suffering for a child, but the thing that touched dear Santa most was the magic of his smile."

Antonio had a magic smile. This poor child, Midikula, did not. Like Antonio, he knew pain and suffering, and his little face reflected it. As I mentioned, his face was almost scar-free, but sadness and despair were etched all over it.

Within seconds of our meeting, the little boy began to weep and shout out anguished words. An interpreter laid out the sad translation. "He says when he leaves the hospital, no one will care for him, He is only happy here." Happy is not a word I would ever associate with that room of ten or twelve patients, including one terrorist. I have been allowed into the hospital rooms of suffering children many times and have been a patient myself on a few occasions. Despite the best intentions of caring staff and the tremendous assortment of board games, video games, DVDs, and televisions, I have never thought of hospitals as places where children are happy. There were no board games, video games, DVDs, and televisions in Midikula's room. There was just a tiny green cot and the love and caring of a few dedicated professionals.

The interpreter spoke again. His words did more than take my breath away. They put tears in my eyes, a lump in my throat, a knot in my gut, and a chill down my spine. "He wants you to take him back to America," he said. I'm not sure if I have ever, in my forty years, felt so helpless or like such a pathetic liar when I simply said, "I can't." "I won't" would have been more truthful. *Can't* is a strong word. In fact, it's not a word that I used or accepted very often during my career.

My wife and I have a half-joking tradition when I am set to leave for developing countries. "Don't be afraid to bring a child home," she always says. She said it when I went to China in 2002 and Iraq in 2004. We used to talk about adopting an Afghan child after the initial U.S. invasion of the country. I shared that thought with a few friends and actually received disapproving feedback, as if the existence of Al Qaeda camps in Afghanistan was the handiwork of orphaned children. Now here was a child begging for a home, and I simply said, "I can't."

The boy was scratching at his scars, lowering his blanket as he did, revealing to me just some of the terrible damage that the explosion had done to his torso and abdomen. The chaplain later told me that one leg needed amputation because the damage was too extensive. His other leg, despite the efforts of physical therapy, had lost all range of motion, becoming permanently fixed in a locked angle. A prosthetic device, I was told, was almost an impossibility. The money just isn't there, and even if it was, the country's rugged rural landscape would render the device almost useless. A wheelchair would fall victim to the environment as well. Ramps and elevators aren't exactly accessible in the Afghan countryside.

I searched my pockets for some kind of gift that I could give to this poor child. I also searched for some soothing words, but even with a translator's help, those were tough to find. I handed him a coin that had been given to me by a base commander. The coins are given out in the military for excellence, and I guess my Santa vs. Santa match qualified as such. The translator asked for one, but I told him I was out—the second lie I had told while standing at this child's bedside.

As I prepared to leave, I told Midikula that I would send him a box of toys when I got back home. Through the translator he told me that he would like two large white stuffed animals, a dog and a cat. I then touched the boy's head and, with the best smile that I could manage, I exited the room.

I returned minutes later, bearing gifts. When I told the chaplain that my good-intentions-to-good-deeds ratio was low and that I'd be much more likely to follow through on these intentions if I purchased toys on base, she took me instead to a small trailer outside of the hospital that contained a few boxes of donated toys. While there were no large white stuffed animals, I was able to secure a small white Beanie Baby cat, a gray Beanie Baby dog, a red-breasted robin, and a Wyle E. Coyote that looked like a consolation prize at a second-rate carnival.

I'll be honest; the kid didn't care much for Wyle E. Coyote. I guess if one is not aware of his *Roadrunner* shenanigans, he could look a little creepy. Through the translator, he worked out a trade—Wyle E. Coyote for the red-breasted robin.

Before I left the hospital, I gave the boy a wallet-sized photo of my younger children. I'm not quite sure why I did this. I think so that he might have something directly from me instead of through a colonel or chaplain.

Last night, as I lay down, hoping sleep would find me, I again thought of that poor child. I thought about the terrorist as well. I thought about our service members and the sacrifices they have made. I thought of the dangers they face every day and the holidays that would pass without their loved ones near. I still don't know what to think of our attempts at democracy in both Afghanistan and Iraq, but if democracy brings with it food, shelter, and kerosene heaters that don't set little kids on fire, then by all means, these attempts will be worth the price we've paid. But I don't know if that will happen. I do know that brave Americans like the ones I've met at Bagram Air Force Base have sacrificed their lives in pursuit of this bold goal. I also know that mere feet from where our service members breathe lie two Afghan citizens, separated only by a six-foot white tile aisle and an armed guard. I know that their feelings toward our country cannot be more opposed. One sees the United States as pure evil, while the other sees the United States as an answer to his dreams.

Can the United States truly be the answer to one's dreams? For millions, it has been, although I don't think this is true for Midikula. Maybe I was the answer to his dreams, and instead I gave him a carnival doll.

I've been thinking about an old Irish prayer that reads, "God grant me the strength to change the things I can, the serenity to accept the things I cannot, and the wisdom to know the difference."

It's doubting that I have that wisdom that will haunt me most of all.

Dear Hardcore Diaries,

I really wanted to write this yesterday, when the events in Lubbock, Texas, were at their freshest in my mind. Unfortunately, I was just too tired to do any writing on the plane, opting instead to watch *Glory Road* on the second leg of the trip, from Dallas to New York.

I'm glad in a way that I waited a day, because it gives me a little time to reflect on what went down in Lubbock, and it will also give me a chance to write down my feelings while I actually watch our promo on videotape.

I was nervous as hell, as well I should have been, before such an important moment, because this promo would determine whether there was indeed magic in our midst or if the ECW show would simply be a good build, with some decent interest based on whatever aura the company name still gave off in the minds and memories of fans.

Still, I was confident. Nervous, but confident. I had faith in myself, and despite Vince's misgivings, I had faith in the Funker. In my entire career, I have only seen two performers who seemed to exude a love for the business in their every in-ring step. Two guys who really felt "it," who seemed to be "on" every time they stepped into the ring. Ric Flair was one. Terry Funk the other. I felt like I had history on my side.

But maybe Terry Funk didn't have Father Time on his side. The guy had been through amazing wars, but unlike other saner men, never showed the common sense to slow down once the years and injuries had taken their toll. One of the greatest matches of my career took place in front of 150 people in a near-freezing gym on January 10, 1995, in Guma, Japan. Despite the scattered few in the building, it was a big match for me because of the attention it would garner in the Japanese magazines—a must for small promotions like our

Terry Funk.

IWA that didn't have the benefit of their own television shows. The things Terry and I did to each other in that match would have gotten us arrested in many places in the world. It was brutal. I was twenty-nine at the time, with two small kids and a mortgage. I needed that job with IWA. Terry was almost fifty. He managed to stay with me punch for punch, move for move, and chair for chair (including one that was on fire). Terry Funk simply cared too much to give anything but his best in front of any crowd, anywhere.

Eleven years had passed since the Guma "No rope, barbed wire" match. Terry's sixty now, and showing his age from time to time. I remember watching Terry do a promo in WCW about five years ago. I looked at Terry on that television and felt a little sad for him for the first time, because for the first time he looked old, confused, at a loss for words.

But a year ago, I refereed a Terry Funk versus Dusty Rhodes match, a blast of nostalgia from one of wrestling's greatest feuds, and witnessed Terry put the fear of the Funker into even the smartest of fans. He was out of his mind and on that one night, hands down, still the best heel in the business.

A big question loomed in my mind as I climbed the stairs and awaited my music cue behind the curtains at the top of the stage: Which Terry Funk would step forward tonight?

I watched with great interest as a Mick Foley teaser aired. It was just a pretaped walk backstage, filmed a few hours earlier, but not without considerable importance. How would fans react to seeing me for the first time since Anaheim? There I am. Boos. Yes! Sure, boos mixed in with cheers, but I detect genuine interest as J.R. says, "What is going on in the mind of Mick Foley? We're going to find out . . . next."

Many people felt disappointed in the reaction Edge and I had received in Anaheim. Actually, I think it would have been shocking if it had garnered a huge reaction. After all, it had been a blatant case of bait and switch. We used the premise of a *WrestleMania* rematch of Edge and Foley as bait and then switched them with a turn on a largely unknown Tommy Dreamer instead.

It was confusing. It didn't have any heat in the way a turn on a beloved WWE personally like, say, Shawn Michaels, would have. But that would be easy. I hadn't walked into Vince's office in Stamford to propose "easy." I wanted to create main-event interest from the ground up in less than five weeks. And in some ways, I felt like I'd had my best tools taken from me. The chunk out of Vince's ass was a huge tool that was no longer ours to work with. This was Lubbock. A few weeks ago I thought this city would play host to one of the all-time great *Raw* episodes. Now I wasn't so sure. Still, I felt like Edge and I had built a sturdy foundation the week before. But no one shows up at a homesite to marvel at a foundation. It was time to get to work. Time to start the real construction on the house.

Three minutes of commercials can seem to take a lifetime when anticipation is so high. You want to be relaxed, but at the same time, don't want to lose focus. My challenge is a simple one: take the promo that seemed so real inside my head, and bring the thing to life in front of all the fans.

A video of Terry airs, solely "for the house." We are fortunate to be in Lubbock, where Terry is a legend. But this video will reinforce his lofty status to those who know him, and give a crash course on the Funker, to those who aren't quite as steeped in professional wrestling lore.

Crash! The sound of breaking glass, followed by a distinctive three-chord guitar riff, sends me through the curtains. As was the case with my backstage walk, there are some boos, some cheers, but fans are mostly all standing. At least it's an enthusiastic mixed response. But I will act like all is well. I have made up my mind that I am still WWE's lovable muppet—a good guy, a babyface. As long as I believe my actions are justified, I'll be fine. I just have to make the fans believe that I believe. Fortunately, I've spent a lot of time in Promoland this past week. I really believe in everything I'll say.

"He's got to have a viable reason," J.R. tells the fans. I do, and I'm about to share it with you. But first, a little fun. And a small seed to plant for later on down the road—a day after *SummerSlam*, to be exact.

"Hold on, you're being a little judgmental. Let me explain myself," I say in response to the boos. It's been a good eight years since I've been booed by WWE fans, and it feels a little strange.

"I want to answer the question that's been on everybody's mind . . . what was I doing hanging out with Melina at Kane's movie premiere? Did you see the way she was looking at me?"

Yes, the planting of the seed. I didn't see fit to pass this comment by anyone. Someone may have overthought the moment and overruled it, and I didn't want to take a chance. It's just a simple comment and doesn't screw with the heart of the promo, but it does loosely place Melina and me together in the fans' minds. All in all, an important throwaway line. Plus, it makes the fans laugh a little, which is good. I want this promo to be an emotional roller-coaster ride. Nothing wrong with a little fun first.

"Now as far as that other thing, that unfortunate incident involving

Tommy Dreamer, well, I guess that's a little unbelievable—unbelievable in the literal sense, because I can't believe I took a barbed-wire bat and bludgeoned somebody who'd been a friend of mine for ten years. A guy with the heart of a lion, the innovator of violence, ECW's own Tommy Dreamer."

I want to build Tommy whenever I can. Hopefully, even a little mention of his heart will help in the long run. Or at less than four weeks to go at this point, the not-so-long run.

"Even more unbelievable, it seemed that I was in cahoots with Edge; arms up in the air with my sworn enemy, even going so far as to kiss Lita on the hand."

Lita's awesome and has worked hard to become WWE's sleaziest character. I fully intend to treat her like a lady, a princess, during the course of this run to *One Night Stand*.

"Now I could offer a lot of excuses, I could say it was the shots to the head that made me act a little goofy, but I'll tell you what, you people deserve better than excuses; you deserve an apology. So I'd like to say two big words to the big state of Texas . . . I'm sorry."

All right, quite a few cheers. This is going well. I think they'll really buy a ticket to this emotional place we hope to send them.

"Now, I wanted to say sorry personally to Tommy Dreamer, but unfortunately he couldn't be here. It seems as if he had an adverse reaction to a barbed-wire bat making contact with his genitals."

The crowd laughs as I hoped they would. "Who knew?" I say jokingly. "So I'm going to bring out another guy you might be familiar with, a guy who berated me on my telephone answering machine, saying I was a better man than I had shown on Monday night. Hell, he was hardcore before the word existed. He is a legend. He is my mentor. Ladies and gentlemen, Terry Funk."

The crowd greets the Funker in a way befitting his legendary status. Geography is on our side here. WWE only hits West Texas every couple of years. We are fortunate indeed to be in Lubbock for Terry's big return. Sometimes perception really is reality, and the perception to all those watching *Raw* is that Terry Funk is a very big star.

Terry greets the crowd with arms wide open, embracing the fans as J.R. and color commentator Jerry "The King" Lawler sing the Funker's praises. The TitanTron plays an image from *WrestleMania XIV*'s Dumpster match, where Terry and I won the World Tag Team titles. J.R. is great as always, summarizing my long, complex history with Terry in a few short sound bites. "Terry Funk has been a profound influence on Mick Foley's career," J.R. says. "Mentor may be putting it mildly."

Terry's now in the ring, and we're hopefully ready to make history. "Terry, it's great to see you out here," I say, extending my hand as if everything is just fine.

But Terry's not fine. "Not so fast, Cactus," he says, using the name he'd known me as for years. Terry refuses my hand, and circles the ring as a loud "Terry" chant begins. This is a good sign, a really good sign.

Terry holds up his hand, silencing the crowd. Many a man wouldn't have been able to resist the urge to bask in the adulation, which would have hurt the promo. By choosing dialogue over the "Terry" chants, he is showing the importance of the moment.

Terry looks me in the eye and says, "I know the reason why you humiliated Tommy Dreamer. I know the reason. You humiliated him, and I want to know . . . why, Mick, why did you humiliate him, why? Tell me."

Was I mistaken, or did Terry just say he knew the reason before asking me to tell him the reason? This is a bad sign, a very bad sign. Was it possible the wrong Terry Funk showed up on this night?

I figured I better take over the reins. "Well, I'm going to tell you why, Terry," I say. "Because at *WrestleMania*, Edge and I made history. We had the greatest hardcore match the world had ever seen."

"The greatest?" Terry asks skeptically.

"We tore the house down," I yell. "We stole the show!"

Terry starts to offer a little more resistance than I was expecting, continually questioning the validity of my statement. I want people to question it. Just not now. So I try to silence the Funker. "You listen to me," I say with emphasis. "Because I will be damned if a few short weeks after making history, I'm going to stand by as a bunch of second-rate ECW scumbags come into *our* house, play in *our* ring, and portray themselves as if they're what hardcore is all about. It's not going to happen." Some definite boos are building. "So maybe Edge and I made a little pact to defend what we created. Because Terry, I'll tell you this, there are three things in this life I will defend, with my *life* if necessary." I've got a finger in the air. "The honor of my wife." A second finger. "The honor of my children." A third finger. "And the honor of my legacy as the hardcore wrestling professional legend."

Damn, I screwed that last one up. Should have just been "legacy as the hardcore legend."

It's Terry's turn to talk. "You just don't get it, do you, Mick?" Terry says. "You just don't get it." His confidence is back, a good sign. "You *are* ECW! ECW is family! Your family is ECW. And I'm family. And I want to tell you something, Mick. I've been with you through the years. And I've fought you, and I've battled you. And I'll tell you that you've broken my nose, and I've broken your nose, and you've beat the hell out of me, and I've beat the hell out of you. And we've been in barbed wire, and we've been in fires, and everything else, but I always put my arm around you and said, 'Mick, dammit, you're a hell of a tough guy.' And I wanna go one step further. Mick, you're like a son to me." Terry's got one hand on my head, tousling my hair as if I were a rambunctious, misguided child. The audience is starting to stir, thinking they might be on the receiving end of a genuine feel-good moment. Boy, are they in for a surprise.

I put my hand on Terry's shoulder and close my eyes as Terry continues with the heartfelt pleas. "You're like a son to me, Mick," he repeats. "Like a son to me." I lean my forehead on the Funker's shoulder and take in a mild dose of warm applause. I really like where we are going.

"I'm like a son to you?" I ask, my voice muffled, almost inaudible.

"Yes, you're a son to me," Terry says decisively, and the applause is louder, prompting me to full-out hug my mentor.

"I'm like a son to you?" I ask again, this time louder, into the microphone.

"Like a son," Terry yells.

"Then let me . . . tell you . . . something . . . Dad!" The last word, "Dad," is sarcastic and cold, prompting a break in the embrace as I prepare to get to the heart of the promo.

"This is the first time you and I have stood together inside a WWE ring since 1998. It's a long time, isn't it?"

"That's right. It is," says Terry.

"But it wasn't supposed to be that way, was it? Do you remember 2003, Terry? In Madison Square Garden, on one of the greatest nights of my life, I was honored in a hardcore ceremony. Stone Cold Steve Austin handed me the hardcore belt." Applause for Austin's name. "I was surrounded in that ring by men I'd fought, men I respected, hardcore legends in their own right. But when I walked outside that ring, I had one question: Where was Terry Funk?

And you know where you were? You were at the Double Cross Ranch in Amarillo, Texas." Cheers for the ranch.

"That's right, that's right," Terry confirmed. "I was at the Double Cross."

"Why? I ask. Because what I was told was, 'We're sorry, Mick, Terry wanted too much money to be there.'"

Some boos, sympathetic boos. Fans seem to feel bad for me. Hell, they should. This is a true story, and it hurt my feelings. And I have done with those hurt feelings what every wrestler should. Saved them up, let them fester in the unlikely event that those feelings can be used to kick-start a wrestling angle. Thank goodness I hadn't reached a sense of closure.

"How do you think that made me feel?" I ask, going face-to-face with Terry. We're only inches apart as I head for the homestretch, my finger jabbing the air. I turn the volume and intensity up. "It broke my heart! And now you have the nerve to stand here and look me in the eye and say, 'You're like a son to me'?"

"Yes, you are like a son to me!" Terry yells. He starts to say more, but I cut him off, concerned that he might be diluting the message.

"You shut your damn mouth," I yell, stepping away from him. "This is *my* WWE ring. These are *my* WWE fans." The fans boo loudly. This unexpected moment of ad-libbing had led to a really good crowd reaction. At this point, these people really don't feel like my fans. Which is a good sign, a really good sign.

"You see, one day, I'm gonna get that phone call," I say. "It's inevitable." I make the universal thumb and pinky phone sign and hold it in my ear and mouth. "A year from now, two, maybe three or four, saying, 'We're sorry, Mick, the Funker's gone. Would you like to maybe come out to Amarillo and say a few words at his service?'"

All right, Mick, time to nail this thing. I go into full yell mode. I think yelling is overused in the world of the wrestling promo, but there will always be a time for it. This is the time.

"And I'll say, 'I'd like to, but it's going to cost you an awful lot of money to bring me out to a dump like West Texas.'" Big boos. It might be considered cheap heat if not for the fact that I'd worked so hard to get to this point of the promo.

The remark gets the Funker's Texas pride up. "You watch your mouth!" he yells. "Watch your mouth! You'd better watch it right now!"

I hadn't been expecting a warning. I thought I'd coast to the finish line, but his unexpected words add realism to the situation. I do, however, need to get back to my point. And I promise it will be a good one.

"It won't cost you a dime, Terry."

"Why?"

"I'll come for free. I'll use my frequent fliers if I have to. Because I'm going to show up at your funeral, just to earn the right to crawl over and spit on your grave, you greedy, selfish, miserable SON . . . OF A . . . BITCH!"

The Funker comes alive, neck veins bulging, eyes wide. "You've got your nerve, Foley. I'm gonna John Wayne your ass! I'm gonna beat the hell out of you, Foley." The crowd is with us. They want to see the promised John Wayne–ing of Mick Foley.

"Then take your best shot!" I say.

"You take *your* best shot," the Funker fires back. "Take it. I said take it." Terry proceeds to set some kind of indoor slap record, catching me in the face nine times. The crowd chants "Terry," and I struggle in vain to make my actions live up to the toughness of my words.

I know how frustrating it is to face a heel who refuses to show fear and vulnerability. I don't want to be that fearless, invulnerable guy. So I turn my back to the challenge, prompting Terry to hit me and the Lubbock fans with an insult he later admits was used on him in grade school.

"Hey, Foley, if I had a head like yours, I'd have it circumcised." The crowd erupts in a

Having a difference of opinion with Terry Funk in Lubbock.

chorus of oohs and cheers, prompting me to turn around. Terry had used this line against my wishes at the afternoon rehearsal. It wasn't that I didn't like it—I loved it. I just didn't want to risk having it rejected by the powers that be. When in doubt, do it live, then apologize. But Vince had loved it; it had even included a classic coffee-spit take from him.

"What did you say?" I asked. Although I had heard it perfectly well.

Terry knows he has the people. There's no need to yell. He savors the line before saying it, mulling it around like the bouquet of a fine vintage wine. "I said if I had a head like yours . . . I'd have it circumcised." The reaction is even better the second time around, prompting me to believe the sophomoric insult will be repeated in hallways and schoolyards across the country.

I know it's time to leave. I'm about to cut my losses and go home when Terry reaches for an insult never heard by WWE fans. "Hey, Foley, hey, Foley, your wife's a whore." Fortunately, my TiVo had a little "accident" that night and "forgot" to record *Raw*. I'm sure Colette would have loved it. Something tells me that Colette's copy of this book will arrive with one "missing" page.

J.R. admits that the comment might be a little too heavy, but Terry's about to go heavier. "Hey, Foley . . . hey, Foley! Your kids are bastards." A huge ooh of disbelief from the crowd. At the rehearsal, I had told one of our handheld cameramen to get a two-shot, with Funk right behind me, almost speaking in my ear. I told him it was the money shot. And it certainly was.

Terry Funk, however, is about to go too far. "Hey, Foley, heeeey, Foley . . . the WWE sucks!"

Bam! I wheeled around and nailed him. Like Popeye, I stands all I can stands and I can't stands no more. On one hand, the premise is funny—I won't defend my wife or kids' honor, but I will defend the WWE in a heartbeat. On the other hand, I don't think Colette will care a whole lot for it.

I proceed to hammer Terry with some forearms and punches, sending him into the ropes, doing his distinctive Funker sell. He's reeling, but firing himself up simultaneously. Finally he's on the comeback, catching me with three jabs and a big left hand. This was classic Funk, but I had been unsure of how the crowd would react. After all, no one throws jabs anymore. But they seem to like it just fine.

Edge slides into the ring with the barbed-wire bat, but is met by three jabs and a roundhouse left that send him down as well.

Terry fires up to the crowd's delight, eliciting the type of response that only WWE Superstars, even with years of TV exposure to their credit, will ever experience. He's still got it! I was right all along.

But here comes Lita from behind with an uppercut to Funker's nads, sending him down to the canvas, where Edge and I devour him, like a pack of hungry jackals. It wasn't our kill, but we'll enjoy its spoils, nonetheless.

It's Barbie time. Barbie was the nickname for my barbed-wire bat. I haven't used the name in a few years, but I need to start. Edge picks up the weapon. I recognize the fact that this can't look like *my* show out there. It has to be *our* show. For a few weeks, I'll do most of the talking, but then I want an allotment of equal mike time between us. After all, when this angle's done, Melina and *SummerSlam* included, I'm back out to pasture. Edge will continue to play a main event role with WWE, including an inevitable run with a babyface Triple H that, if correctly done, will be big box office. I look at our time together as one of those things that has to be correctly done. If Edge doesn't come out of this thing stronger than ever, then I will have failed to accomplish a major part of my goal.

Humiliation time for Terry. Mr. Socko time. It's shocking how quickly the fans have turned on poor Mr. Socko. I salivate at the mere thought of how he'll be received at the Hammerstein Ballroom on June 11 for *One Night Stand*. It should be classic.

I shove the dreaded sock into Terry's mouth. Edge readies himself for the spear and drills him with it, sending Funk to the canvas with a flying shoulder block to the gut.

I've worked hard for this moment, and I intend to bask in the aftermath. It's like a cigarette after great sex. Not that I would know anything about that. The cigarette, I mean. Yes, I realize I used the same stupid joke in *Foley Is Good*.

"Mick Foley and Edge on the same page," J.R. says disgustedly as Lita, Edge, and I raise our arms in triumph. "Who in the hell would have ever pictured that? And now destroying Foley's mentor, his father figure, Terry Funk. I don't like it a damn bit!"

Amen, J.R.—hopefully no one will.

Dear Hardcore Diary,

Thankfully, a kind woman at the Delta Business Lounge took pity on me and allowed me in as her guest. Otherwise, I'd be sitting in a packed airport with my notebook on my knee, trying to get into my writing "zone" amid the cacophony of running kids, CNN, the occasional autograph seeker, and those damn cell phone people who feel they absolutely, positively have to share the details of their personal and professional life with everyone within a half-mile radius.

Every one of those calls sounds the same to me. "Yeah, we shipped about a million, million five—should be a net of about twenty mil. Yeah, my cut's about half. All right, call you when I get there—I'm at the Ritz, penthouse—about two grand a night."

Why don't I ever hear a real phone conversation? Something like, "Yeah, she broke up with me. Said twenty-eight's too old to be working the checkout line at Burger King. Minimum wage wasn't good enough for her. She mentioned something about my penis being too small. All right, I'll call you when I get there. My parents said I could sleep on the couch for a few weeks."

It's been a hectic few days. I have a basic verbal outline for Monday night, and it seems good. There was a little concern that Edge might get lost in the shuffle if he stood on the sideline again, so a scenario was created to make him the emcee of sorts for a special hardcore tribute to yours truly. I think it will make for great TV, and is actually a better idea than my previous pitch, which would have been me in a similar emcee role on Edge's behalf. This will spotlight him more, but also better drive home the ridiculous premise that made me and Edge laugh so damn hard when we first came up with it. You see, tomorrow night in Las Vegas, live on

Raw, the Edgester and the Mickster (our names for each other) will become the first-ever coholders of a singles title. Not only that, but we will be coholding a single belt that doesn't even exist anymore—the Hardcore title.

Over the years, I've often visualized how J.R. would call a certain move or situation, while it was still in its creative infancy. Wait, can you actually visualize words? There's probably a more correct term for it, but as you've probably already guessed, my vocabularic range is not likely to send anyone sprinting for their dictionary. "Mom, help me. The wrestler's words are too difficult." Anyway, every time I think of Edge and I coholding a nonexistent singles title, I picture/hear J.R. saying, "My goodness King, Mick Foley and Edge are parading around the ring with a title that was last seen on Foley's mantel."

I've also come to treasure the anticipated ridiculousness of our ring announcer, Lilian Garcia, making the official announcement. "Ladies and Gentlemen, here are the coholders of the Hardcore Championship: Mick Foley and Edge!"

Writing about Lilian reminds me of my buddy, Chris Giordano, who is one of Lilian's biggest fans. Yeah, I know I last spoke of Chris when I was calling Trish Stratus from his house. But Chris, although he is versatile enough to like quite a few of the WWE Divas, is a Lilian Garcia guy. Most of our fans are like that—they appreciate many, but have a clear favorite.

I feel very fortunate to have such good relationships with so many of the Divas. Over the years, I've asked the girls to help me on so many occasions, and they have never failed to put huge smiles on the faces of kids I've known, many of whom had been through tough times where reasons to smile could be few and far between.

Stacy Keibler used to be great about taking my calls. I remember putting her on speakerphone in the older boys' cabin at Camp Adventure, a place on the east end of Long Island for kids who have or have had cancer, and their siblings. The boys, sixteen to eighteen years of age, surrounded me, their faces awestruck, as they hung on Stacy's every word. I tried not to jump to conclusions, but I did find it odd that at the conclusion of the call, three boys immediately headed for the showers—at four in the afternoon.

•　•　•

It's sometimes difficult for me to admit that I'm wrong. It shouldn't be. I've been married fifteen years, and have a lot of practice in the area of error admissions. But sometimes I become so locked in on an idea that any alternative opinion seems almost like sabotage (wow, could I have used a dictionary myself for that word. I'm sure it will be corrected in the editing process, but right now it's a little ugly). Which I guess is my way of admitting that Edge and I are better off without Vince dragging us down. Wait, let me rephrase that, keeping in mind that the guy I just wrote of is the guy signing my checks.

I've been thinking a lot about that promo with Terry, wondering if we might actually be better off without Vince's direct involvement. After all, the Funker and I made quite an impact in Lubbock. Sure, I could argue that biting a chunk out of Vince McMahon's ass might have been even more impactful. But last Monday's promo assuaged my deepest fear that Terry Funk would leave our *Raw* fans without the impression that he was a big star. We just have to keep the ball rolling.

The whole scene is more personal now. It's not about Vince. It's about me and Edge, two guys who will do whatever it takes to defend what is theirs. Almost as if our *WrestleMania* match was our very own child, and here comes ECW social services workers Dreamer and Funk doing their best to take it away.

Dear Hardcore Diary,

Okay, I lied. I wrote "aboard Delta Flight #1823" before finding out my flight is to be delayed another two hours. So I'm back in the airport lounge, where I have changed my writing spot, so as to better watch, or at least occasionally glance at, the final game of the Pistons/Cavaliers series. I know I am clearly sending a signal that this particular "hardcore entry" doesn't deserve my undivided attention, but this has been a roller-coaster series, and I do want to see who wins it.

I like to catch a few pro sports games every year just to regain some respect in the eyes of my oldest son. Most fathers will never have to face the day in which they come home to find that their son's room looks different, mainly due to the fact that all of the Dad posters are down, replaced by Sammy Sosa and Shaq. Even though Dewey has grown up watching people make a big deal out of me, it's only when he sees people who are a big deal to him making a big deal out of me that he seems impressed by it all.

So when he sees football great Tiki Barber (who I've known for five years through MDA) give me a hug, it's a big deal to me. When he sees Allen Iverson come up to me and say, "You're crazy, man," it's a big deal to me. And when he finds out Christy Canyon called, inviting me onto her radio show, it's a big deal to . . . oh, wait a second, he doesn't know about that one.

I think my favorite father/son bonding moment occurred three years ago at Yankee Stadium on opening day, in early April of 2003. This was during my WWE estrangement, and as a result, I'd been on television very little. I still did personal appearances and volunteer work, but in Dewey's eyes, out of televised sight, out of mind, which meant the hardcore legend had been reduced to ordinary dad. My daughter Noelle used to get on my case, wondering if I could become an anesthesiologist, like her friend's dad, so that we could live in a big house like they did.

Well, on this cold April day, with the evidence of a late-season snowfall piled up on busy Bronx streets, I waited in frustration for my buddy, Phil Castinetti, to meet me at the stadium's giant "bat" landmark with my tickets.

I'd been standing out there a while, attracting more attention than I wanted, when Phil reached me on my cell, complaining of traffic, warning me that it might be a while before he got there. He told me to explain my situation at the Yankee ticket office, in the hopes I could find refuge from the storm of fans around me.

I sat down on a bench next to a woman at the will-call desk and managed to get a look at the guest list, which included names such as: Whitey Ford, Rudy Giuliani, Billy Crystal, and former secretary of state Henry Kissinger. I

With Dewey and football great Tiki Barber.

also saw members of the Mantle and Maris family as they made their way to the stadium.

Then I heard Dewey's voice in a hushed, reverent tone. "Dad, it's George Steinbrenner." I turned to see the Yankee boss, no more than ten feet from me, his eyes focused on the elevator doors in front of him, so as not to greet the gawks of geeks like me.

"Should I say hello?" I asked

"If you want to," Dewey said.

"Mr. Steinbrenner."

Nothing.

"Excuse me, Mr. Steinbrenner."

Not a thing. Not a peep. Not even the slightest sign of interest. If there had been nineteen thousand more like him, it would have resembled a Garden crowd during a Test match.

I had a single ace up my sleeve. One last chance before admitting defeat, acknowledging to my son that I was just a normal dad, albeit one with his own action figure and a distinctive missing ear.

"George, it's me, Mick Foley."

With that, the Yankee boss, one of the most famous names in sports, wheeled around, his eyes sparkling, his mouth open in a joyous smile. Dewey's mouth was wide open as well, but I believe it was due to shock, not joy. How did his plain old ordinary dad know George Steinbrenner?

The answer was simple: I had previously had a top-secret meeting with Mr. Steinbrenner at the 2002 "Old Timers Day." I guess someone had pointed me out in the crowd, and as a longtime wrestling fan (he even wrote the foreword to Dusty Rhodes's autobiography), George had summoned me to the office. But Dewey didn't know that—as I mentioned, the meeting was top-secret.

All he knew was that the Yankee boss patted him on the back, chatted amiably, and signed a baseball before heading back to the business of berating, intimidating, and firing employees—just kidding. Actually, a friend of mine, Stanley Kay, a longtime Yankee front-office man, shared a story with me that showed Mr. Steinbrenner in a different light.

"I'll tell you," Stanley said. "When I was sick, Mr. Steinbrenner took care of everything. Everything. I can't say enough nice things about that man . . . so he yells a little."

• • •

Well, it looks bad for the Cavaliers in this one. Down by fourteen, three minutes left. Rasheed Wallace had guaranteed a Pistons sweep, and was on the verge of eating some serious wordage when the Cavs took three in a row. But now it looks like Rasheed's prediction is safe.

I met Rasheed in Portland, and procured a quick autograph as the Trailblazers star forward was making his way to ringside for a front-row viewing of *Raw*. While taking in the WWE action, Rasheed received a call on his cell, letting him know he'd been traded to Detroit. So, it is quite possible that I have in my possession the last official Rasheed Wallace Portland Trailblazers autograph.

I visited John Grill in the hospital a few days ago. John is the young man who was paralyzed during his first-ever pro wrestling match a short while ago. I was very apprehensive about the visit. Usually, when I visit someone, I can always count on a mutual love of wrestling to guide me through the experience. In this case, due to the circumstances surrounding John's injury, I feared that wrestling itself would have been seen as the culprit. So I showed up at the hospital, armed with a new *WrestleMania* DVD and very little confidence, for a visit that really should have taken place a month or so earlier.

To my relief, the visit was a pleasure. John's attitude was great, and he had far more use of his arms than I had previously believed. His mother didn't seem to blame either me or wrestling, although no one seemed thrilled by the referee's decision to push the seriously injured wrestler out of the ring instead of simply calling for the bell and stopping the match immediately.

But I do remember when I was much younger, and had the heartfelt belief that every match was of utmost importance. Poka, West Virginia, in front of twenty-six fans? It might as well have been *WrestleMania*. Every match was that way. John kept talking about his next match, challenging me and Raven to take on him and his partner. "Okay," I said. "But Raven's taking all the bumps." It's the least he can do for corrupting my poor mind.

As I was leaving, I spoke to a few nurses, who remembered my last visit to the hospital, about two years earlier. They remembered that I had not been alone that day; I had arrived with a special guest, whom I will speak about in a few minutes.

As I stepped out of the elevator, I was greeted by a face from my past—my first girlfriend, Katie McDevitt, who had sworn long ago that she was going to marry me. What's a guy supposed to do in this type of situation?

Should I ignore the past we shared, just pretend it didn't exist? Or did I take the right course by inviting her to sit and talk for a few minutes in the lobby, to reminisce about the good old days of innocent love?

And once I finished reminiscing with my first love, should I admit the conversation to my wife? Or should I keep it hidden, secret like my meeting with Mr. Steinbrenner? That was my first instinct, but the secret didn't last very long. Sometimes it feels as if I have Jiminy Cricket hanging around me 24/7, pooping on my party, forcing me to confess my simplest indiscretions.

Shortly before dinner, I approached Colette, ready to bare my soul. "Um, Collette, could I talk to you?"

"Sure," she said. "Is something wrong?"

"Well, I just wanted to let you know that I bumped into an old girlfriend today."

"Oh, was it serious?" she asked, slightly concerned, as is only normal when discussing the topic of past loves. She may also have been slightly confused, as "past Mick Foley girlfriends" are something of an endangered species. Not that they've been killed off or anything. There were just not that many out there to begin with.

"I guess it was pretty serious," I said.

"Oh yeah, how serious?" Now she was more than concerned. Slightly bothered.

"We used to talk about getting married."

"How old were you when you knew this girl, Mick?"

"Three."

"Three?" she asked.

"Yeah, it was the first conversation we'd had in thirty-seven years." (Okay, I'm on the plane now. It's ten minutes after seven.)

A few hours later, I made my way over to Albertson, a drive of slightly less than an hour, for the big "Sports Night" event that I wrote of earlier in *The Hardcore Diaries*—my annual opportunity to hang out with Olympic figure skaters and dress up like a woman for the sake of Abilities, which consists of the Henry Viscardi School, a top-notch educational center for kids with disabilities, and a job placement center for disabled adults.

Except earlier in the week, I'd received the bad news; no cross-dressing

"Sports Night"
cast, 2006.

this year. Instead, I had to learn lines for my role as Howie Mandelson, complete with the worst bald wig in America, in a takeoff of Mandel's role on the *Deal or No Deal* game show.

As always, the best part of the day was interacting with the great kids of the Viscardi School, not only in rehearsals of *Schpiel or No Schpiel,* but in backstage conversations where they actually propose possible future WWE storylines, some of which are pretty good.

I also get to get in more hangout time with my favorite skating sisters, the Hughes girls, and their mom, Amy, who gave me one of my all-time favorite compliments when she said, "I'm so glad you and Sarah are friends." Oksana Baiul was there as well, the beautiful Russian skater who won Olympic gold in 1992, the year of the infamous Nancy Kerrigan/Tonya Harding kneecap angle. I enjoy talking to her, but always sense an aura of sadness surrounding her; proof, I guess, that life goes on even after dreams come true. I had some difficulty dealing with the aftermath of fame, the complicated residue of childhood dreams realized, back in 2000, when I retired from full-time wrestling. But at least I was thirty-four; Oksana Bauil was only sixteen. And I'm not sure she's figured out what to do with her life just yet.

She did, however, look great in her *I Dream of Jeannie* outfit, and I got a kick out of hearing her explanation of her tendency to sprinkle her sentences with frequent obscenites. "This is how I learned English," she said. "The first words I learned were 'Blow me.'"

Which reminds me of Lada, a lovely young Russian woman who was an invaluable help to our family, back when Mickey was just a baby. One day, Lada made a discovery and summoned Colette to survey the situation. "Colette, Colette," she said, in her thick Russian accent. "Meekey has a scratch on his right ball."

Damn, Johnny Cash's "Hurt" just came on my headphones—about the heaviest, most emotional piece of music I've ever heard. I know I touched on the song in an earlier *Hardcore Diaries* entry, but as is the case in almost everything in life, I think a parallel with the world of wrestling can be formed.

How is it that Cash, his health ailing, his voice failing, could make such an indelible footprint on the fabric of society with a mournful Nine Inch Nails song? I think it comes down to emotion, conviction in one's own message, and an audience's ability to see through the hype and identify the real deal once in a while. Could you imagine Cash singing "Hurt" on *American Idol*? He'd have been laughed off the stage. But can you imagine Clay Aiken singing "Hurt"? It would be a crime.

Sometimes it seems to be the same in wrestling—at least, I hope it is, for my sake. Hopefully on June 11 enough fans can overlook the obvious lack of athleticism and glamour in that ring, and focus instead on the emotion and conviction on display. Hopefully that will be enough. Emotion. Conviction. Oh, and maybe a baseball bat wrapped in barbed wire. And thumbtacks. And garbage cans. And especially the return of the ten-pound weight taped to my foot that I intend to kick a field goal with—assuming, of course, Terry Funk's nuts play the part of the football in this match. Hey, Lada, there's going to be more than just a scratch on the Funker's right ball.

As I mentioned in my earlier diary entry, "Sports Night" attracts some of the biggest stars in athletic history. While very few of these stars have the time or willingness to make fools of themselves in the play, they nonetheless give up their time for a great cause, often traveling considerable distances to do it.

The first hour of the official event is a cocktail hour, where all of the stars are available for conversation and autographs. Because most guests have already paid pretty substantial money to attend the event, there is no extra charge for these autographs. As you can probably imagine, not all stars are equal in the guests' eyes, and therefore, the line for Jim Brown (perhaps the greatest football player of all time) is considerably longer than the line for Mike Masco (the Olympic bobsledder whose name I forgot in the earlier entry).

I'm somewhere in the middle—lots of kids, some adults. But by the forty-minute mark, I was on the verge of being lonely when I was approached by two nice young ladies, in their mid- to late thirties, I guessed.

One of them, a blonde, seemed genuinely happy to meet me, saying, "Out of everyone here, my son is going to be the most excited to hear I met you."

The three of us proceeded to chat amiably for a few minutes before the blonde said, "Well, I don't want to bore you, so I'll leave you alone."

"Listen," I said, confiding in them both. "Anyone who wanted to meet me has already met me. You can feel free to stay and talk as long as you want."

So they did. They hung out while I expressed my concern about the "Lunch with Mick Foley" that was up for bid as part of the silent auction.

"Well, at least it's up to $450," I said. "At least that's respectable, right?"

"Oh, definitely," one of them said.

"Yeah, they asked me if I'd mind doing it, and I said 'Sure,' just as long as its not part of the live auction. Because I'd really be terrified that no one would bid on it, which would be humiliating, you know."

They nodded in agreement. That would be humiliating. I then regaled them with a story from my glory days, where two people paid $32,000 each for the "Dinner with Mick Foley" package.

"Yeah, for a while, I put a dinner up at every event I went to, but that price slid down pretty rapidly, to the point where it barely covered the cost of dinner. But hey, $450 is respectable, right?"

"Definitely," the blond woman reconfirmed. Then she said, "Mick?"

"Yes?"

"Would you mind if I introduced you to my dad?"

"Oh, of course not," I said, thinking it was actually quite sweet that she would bring her dad out to meet all his favorite sports stars.

"Mick, this is my father," she said.

I looked up to see Jack Nicklaus.

"No," I said in disbelief. It couldn't be.

She laughed and said, "Take a close look at me."

She looked exactly like him. Like looking at a photo of him on the cover of my dad's 1970 *Sports Illustrated*. I'm not a golfer, or a particularly big golfing fan, but even I understood how important Jack Nicklaus was. I was stunned.

After talking with Jack and his wife for a minute, and thanking them for supporting Abilities, I turned to the blond woman, Jack's daughter. "Can I have your permission to tell this story everywhere I go?" I asked.

"Of course," she said.

The main item on the live auction list was a round of golf with Jack Nicklaus, with an opening bid of $50,000—a number that was the main course of conversation over dinner. Following the cocktail hour, each athlete (or sports entertainer in my case) sits at a designated table with guests, for dinner and the grand Jo Jo Starbuck production. Of course, those foolish enough to perform leave the table immediately after dinner.

"How much do you think it will go for?" I was asked.

"Right around a hundred," I said. "How about you?"

"One-fifty."

"One-fifty," I said in bemusement. "No way."

Good thing I'm not a gambler. A round of golf with Jack Nicklaus went for $300,000—twice. A grand total of $600,000 for the honor of putting and driving with golf's greatest legend.

The show, as usual, was a blast, even if someone forgot to tell Irish tenor Ronan Tynan that the adults are supposed to embarrass themselves with bad acting, humiliating costumes, and Ashley Simpson–esque lip-synching. So instead, Tynon went out there and had to ruin it with "God Bless America" and some Rogers and Hammerstein tune that wowed the crowd. How the hell was I going to follow that with a bald wig and some overacting worthy of Vince McMahon?

Uncle
Dee

Brian Hopkins has been a friend of mine since somewhere around the end of 2000, about the time I moved back to Long Island. Somewhere around that time, I called up my local Make-A-Wish, asking if they knew of any wrestling fans, who might want to hang out, kind of like a bonus wish for a kid who loved wrestling, but might wisely choose a Disney vacation or trip to Hawaii over a chance to meet a guy in tights who pretends to fight.

Yes, I was told, they had two "wish" kids who had listed WWE as their second choice. Hey, I don't mind being second—I'm just flattered to be in the top hundred. I was given the numbers of both kids, and was told that as long as I initiated the contact, any meeting I set up would not be considered a "wish."

One child was facing serious back surgery. Despite what some people may think about "wish children," not all of them are terminally ill. I think by definition they are kids under eighteen facing life-threatening illnesses or procedures.

The other one, Brian, suffered from cerebral palsy, and was brought into the world under the most trying of circumstances. He was one of twin boys. His brother, Jerry, was born without any physical complications. Their mom, unfortunately, died during childbirth, leaving a grief-stricken husband and two newborns without a mother.

Following our initial meeting in late 2000, I became a sporadic guest at the Hopkins house for random *Raw* or *SmackDown!* viewings. Watching the shows seemed like a fun way to spend time with a great kid who'd endured more than his fair share of hardships along the way. I would bring my older kids, eat for free, exaggerate tales of my wrestling past, and never have to worry about leaving my comfort zone. As long as a WWE show was on, I could show up, have some fun, make a little bit of a difference, and never have to worry about addressing difficult issues.

But I feared that eventually some kid would pose a question that didn't deal with Hell in a Cell or teaming with The Rock; a query that might actually involve some insight or knowledge on a subject I was not completely comfortable with. It's one thing for me to say "I don't know" to my kids—they hear it all the time from me. It's another for a kid who has faced serious challenges to hear the same thing. Granted, twenty years in the world of sports entertainment, traveling the globe, experiencing the highs and lows of human nature on a regular basis, has been an invaluable education in its own right. But it hasn't necessarily prepared me for questions of life and death, or qualified me as a provider of comfort or dispenser of wisdom.

I wanted to change that. So in the winter of 2002, I took a seven-hour workshop entitled Good Grief, offered by the American Cancer Society, that dealt with the emotional consequences involved in death and life-threatening illnesses and conditions. I found the course to be invaluable, especially in emphasizing what I took to be the workshop's main theme—people want to talk about what's troubling them.

Wow! This was the complete antithesis of the Mick Foley *SmackDown!* visit. No, no, no, my job was to show up, eat, watch TV, tell an amusing anecdote or two, and then leave without ever even acknowledging a kid's physical limitations. Wheelchair? What wheelchair? Those types of things were simply out of my area of expertise. So I ignored them.

But shortly after the Good Grief workshop, I received a phone call from Brian, in which he asked if I would like to go to an Islander game with him before he underwent serious spinal surgery. Brian's cerebral palsy, it seemed, was causing him to lean to the side of his chair, twisting his spine and causing a domino effect of subsequent health problems, all of which combined to cause him a great deal of pain.

So I drove my Chevy Impala over to Brian's house in Lindenhurst (hometown of Pat Benatar) and had his dad take us the rest of the way to the Nassau Coliseum in their wheelchair-accessible van. He dropped us off like we were on a big date, and after making our way to the special handicapped section, I realized that I felt woefully out of place.

The skates, the ice, the Zamboni—it was all foreign, like a huge audience reaction in a Test match. So, after watching warm-ups in a state of near silence, I fumbled for words that might make me sound like a little less of a loser than I was actually feeling like.

My choice in cool words? "Hey, Brian, how does it feel to be a member of my posse?" Oh yeah, great, Mick, that was really cool, you're a real modern-day Fonz. A member of my posse? What was I thinking?

Brian mumbled an unenthusiastic response, and I went back to watching the warm-ups. Maybe there'd be a fight or two so I could make a smooth transition from real fights to my fights; a way to bring it all back around to my comfort zone.

But Brian had a question. "Mick?" he asked shyly.

"Yeah, Brian?"

"Am I really a member of your posse?"

Holy crap, he thought it was a cool question. Which meant, yes, that I was cool for saying it.

I looked Brian in the eye, my confidence suddenly returning. "You better believe you are, Brian," I said. "You better believe you are."

Now, what I didn't tell Brian is that I didn't actually have a posse; that by process of elimination he was the sole member of the Mick Foley posse. With thoughts of Good Grief in mind, I decided to use this opportunity to actually venture outside my comfort zone; to ask an important question that didn't involve the WWE.

I said, "Brian, how do you feel about this operation you've got coming up this week?"

Brian paused for just a moment, then proceeded to confide in me, telling me all about his fears, hopes, and dreams. Finally, he said, "It's just too bad I've already had my wish, or else maybe some Islanders could visit me in the hospital."

I thought I had an answer. "You know, Brian, I work with this one group [the Marty Lyons Foundation] that sometimes grants second wishes."

Don't get me wrong, a wish granted through Make-A-Wish or other groups can be invaluable in lifting the spirits of children and their parents. I've known many children who cherish the memories of these granted wishes, and always consider the chance to look through family photos of these trips as a special honor. It's amazing how often the memories involve Give Kids the World, a special village unto itself in Kissimee, Florida, that serves as a home base for "wish" families as they visit the great destinations (Disney, Sea World, Universal) the Orlando area has to offer.

But for a family facing a serious long-term health condition, a wish granted at age four can seem like an eternity ago as that same child reaches his teens. For those families, a "second wish" can seem like a godsend.

It certainly seemed like one for Brian, as he looked up toward the nose-bleed seats in Nassau, seemingly staring off into space. "I'd like to meet Metallica," he said, almost in a whisper.

"Really," I said. "Is that the type of music you like?" I had no idea. Although I'd been to the house on many occasions, I didn't have a clue as to what his interests were, outside of WWE. By the way, Brian likes what I did to Tommy Dreamer and Terry Funk. He thinks I make a better bad guy.

"Yeah," Brian said.

"You like heavy metal?"

"Yeah."

"Do you like Twisted Sister?"

"Do you know Dee Snider?" Brian yelled. I don't really know what prompted that sudden question. I guess Brian knew that Dee, lead singer of the classic 1980s band that belted out such rock radio staples as "We're Not Gonna Take it" and "I Wanna Rock," was another Long Island guy, and that it was not outside the realm of possibility that I might know him.

Now, during the course of my career in wrestling, I have had occasion to meet many famous people. And in truth, if I talk to any of them for longer than ten seconds, I consider them my friend. Like Katie Couric. I've been on the show, she held my baby. She's a friend. But I've got a shocking confession to make—she's not my friend. Not really. Which doesn't mean that we couldn't be friends sometime. If we, you know, spent some time together, maybe talked a little more, maybe a phone call, or . . . Oh sorry, where the hell was I?

Oh, yeah, real friends. The truth is, I only have three famous real friends. Sarah Hughes is one. Kevin James, "the King of Queens," is another. Kevin went to both high school and college with me—we were even on the high school wrestling team together—and we still talk every few years. He even called me up onstage last year and gave me a big public hug, then ridiculed me about my fashion sense once I sat down.

My other real friend? You got it—Dee Snider, one of the great bad boys of rock and roll. But in addition to being a bad boy, he's a great guy, and over the last five years he's become a good friend.

So I told Brian that, yes, I knew Dee Snider, and I'd ask Dee if he could possibly give him a quick phone call while Brian was laid up in the hospital recovering from surgery.

My high school wrestling team photo. That's Kevin James to my right.

With the hockey game over, our big date finished, we waited for Brian's dad to show up with the van. Once inside, Brian shared the new information with his father, saying, "Dad, Mick knows Dee Snider."

"You know Dee Snider?" his father yelled, displaying a type of enthusiasm rare for grown men who aren't either at a football game or institutionalized. Brian's dad was neither. He was simply a huge fan who had come of age while following the band around the prefame seventies club dates of their Long Island stronghold. Things were different then, before the drinking age hit twenty-one and teens were entirely shut out of the club world. It used to be a rock-and-roll band could cut their teeth in the clubs and show up on the big stage of national exposure as a polished, finished product.

These days, big pop stars like Jennifer Lopez have TV specials touting their first-ever concert. But I guess, like all things in life, there is yet another parallel to be drawn from the world of pro wrestling. In the old days, guys who worked the old regional territories could hone their craft for years, and when given the opportunity could show up on the national stages of NWA (later WCW) or WWE as polished workers. Hell, I'd been in the business for eleven years before I finally got the call from J.R.

In today's WWE, talent is often brought up before they've really had the chance to mature as performers. I don't begrudge any of them for anything they're given, but I'm glad it took me a long time. I was given a chance in WWE, and I was able to make the most of it, largely due to the poise and experience I'd developed along the way.

Any good athlete can be taught the moves. But you can't teach poise. You can't teach experience. And you can't teach passion.

Back to Dee. Sure, a phone call would have been good, but as far as I was concerned, for Brian Hopkins, good wasn't good enough. I gave Dee a phone call. Because as it turned out, Dee owed me a favor. And it wasn't a "Could you pick up a dozen eggs at the Dairy Barn?" type of favor. It was, "Could you drive eight hours round-trip and do my radio show for four hours for free while I play myself in a VH-1 movie about the Senate obscenity hearings of 1985?" type of favor. I decided to call it in.

We made quite an impression upon entering the hospital. Dee had his long blond hair tied back in a ponytail. He wore a knee-length black leather duster, snakeskin boots that went up to his knees, and a pair of black leather pants that I wouldn't be caught dead in. Even if you didn't know who he was, you knew he was somebody. I, on the other hand, could have easily been mistaken for the plumber. Red and black flannel, sweats, sneakers.

As we neared Brian's room, I told Dee to hang outside in the hallway for a minute. I figured I was kind of like the hors d'oeuvre, Dee was the main course. I didn't want to ruin the meal by serving up both dishes at once.

Brian was happy to see me, despite the considerable pain he seemed to be in. But let's face it—I was old news. I guess the first time he met me, he was thrilled and then the excitement started to wane. I was no longer a really big deal. I was just a friend who happened to have his own action figure.

Brian couldn't hide his disappointment when he said, "I was kind of hoping Dee would call."

"Well," I said, "you know Dee's been really busy. They're getting the band back together for a USO tour in Korea."

"I guess," Brian said.

Hell, I couldn't make the poor kid wait any longer. It would be tantamount to torture. So I excused myself, saying something about having forgotten something in the hallway.

"Oh . . . my . . . God!" Brian said when I returned, upon seeing just what it was I'd forgotten. "It's Dee Snider."

Over the last twenty years, I've been involved in some pretty good entrance reactions. But this was among the finest for me, because even though Dee was the recipient of the adulation, I felt responsible for its existence.

Dee sat down at Brian's bedside and proceeded to talk for an hour, maybe more, about the glory days of Twisted Sister; the music, the videos, the lawsuits, the verbal smackdown of Tipper Gore.

He wasn't just going through the motions, showing up because it was in his contract, like that guy in the ESPN series *Playmakers,* who swiped kids' pain medication while he was in their room. I heard a rumor that Rush Limbaugh used to pull the same sleight of hand when he visited hospitals to brighten the spirits of young bedridden conservatives. Just kidding—I doubt Rush Limbaugh visits kids in the hospital.

Dee and I headed home, stopping first at his favorite bakery so he could arrive with warm fresh muffins for the hungry Snider clan. I pulled up the drive and stopped the car, and Dee playfully punched me on the shoulder, saying, "Thanks a lot, man," before getting out. But as I backed out of the drive, I saw Dee stop and put his arm out, signaling me not to leave just quite yet. I rolled down the window as he slowly approached. Actually, I just pushed a button and the window went down, but I think you get the point. Once at the door's side, looking into the window, Dee seemed somehow different. A man who usually exuded self-confidence seemed to be uncomfortable, almost shy, as he struggled for words.

"I just want to thank you," he finally said. "For helping to make me a better man."

As I drove home, reliving the day's events in my mind, I realized the significance of Dee's words. After all, I was no longer just a three-time WWE Champion. I was no longer just a two-time *New York Times* best-selling author. No longer was I just a guy who'd been interviewed—twice—by Katie Couric. Now, in addition to those previous accolades, I will forever proudly consider myself to be the guy who made Dee Snider a better man.

Dear Hardcore Diary,

I pulled into an Extended Stay America about half an hour ago, and after discovering that the air-conditioning wasn't working in the first room, and finding out my key didn't open the door of my second room, I finally settled into a semi-comfortable room that may or may not be my home for the next three nights. I say "may" because basically the chair at the tiny desk makes my orange Worcester Centrum folding chair seem like a king's throne, and I just don't know if putting my 315-pound body on it for extended periods of writing seems like the wisest idea.

The next two days are designated writing days. I'd like to put in a minimum of ten hours a day into the writing, pausing only to eat, sleep, and work out. I'm determined to have *Hardcore Diaries* finished by a day or two after the *One Night Stand* show, but I have to continue to work out, so as not to have a cardiovascular debacle to write about. I worry that everything will fall into place except my conditioning, causing the *Diaries* to fall victim to a flat ending.

Because, let's face it—we need a hell of a match to really make the book. Otherwise, it's like Ralphie not getting the Red Ryder BB gun on Christmas morning, or Rocky losing the big fight to Creed. Wait a second, he did lose that fight. But at least he didn't gas out and stink the place up. At least he still had the energy to call out for his pet-shop girlfriend, even while the judge's scorecards were determining his fate.

But honestly, even if my conditioning is not what it should be, we'll probably have enough bells, whistles, and extracurricular activity to put on a good show at *One Night Stand*. Plus, the atmosphere should be unbelievable. But I've just been asked (yesterday) about my feelings on wrestling Ric Flair at *Vengeance* only two weeks later.

I'm not against it on principle, as I was two years ago following the publication of his book, which wasn't exactly a glowing testimonial to the hardcore legend. But I am worried about how my body will react to the rigors of the ECW show, and how quickly I'll be able to bounce back for the fast-moving, intense matchup that the Flair match really needs to be.

I've found that it's really tough to simulate an in-ring pace with any piece of cardio equipment; it's just a completely different feeling. I pretty much told Gewirtz and Michael Hayes that I'd probably be limited to tag teams or hardcore-type matches, which are easier for me to set the pace on. But this proposed Flair match does make sense, especially if he decides to get involved in our match at *One Night Stand*.

Vengeance is in Charlotte, Flair's hometown, where he's like the unofficial mayor. So it should be another great atmosphere, provided, of course, that I don't use up all the oxygen in the building. And provided that my knee holds out. Right now, it feels like it's hanging on by a thread. I'm pretty sure it's the left posterior cruciate ligament. I had the right one replaced with a cadaver (dead person) tendon back in '92, but it tore again in 2004 following the *Backlash* match with Randy Orton. Injuries to the posterior ligament are rare, so I could be something of a medical marvel should I be without both of them.

I've got an MRI scheduled in a couple of days in L.A., which should help me figure out which plan of action to take for conditioning and match preparation. The pain has been getting gradually worse, to the point just getting into and out of the car is a considerable struggle.

It looks like Melina will be coming over to *Raw*, following her *SmackDown!* "firing" by general manager Theodore Long at last night's *Judgment Day* Pay-Per-View. I wish I knew more. Hopefully she'll be coming with Nitro & Mercury, her tag team, as one of them (Nitro) is her boyfriend. Should she arrive solo, I'd feel greatly responsible for the breakup of the team, as I can't help but feel it was my proposed scenario that led to the *Judgment Day* results. I don't want to break up a team or put strain on a relationship, no matter how good an idea I have.

Relationships within wrestling are rough—the success ratio is not encouraging. I had a failed one of my own back in 1988, with a wrestler twelve years my senior. She'd wrestled all over the world, and was far more accomplished than I was—a fact that dipped into my already shallow supply of self-confidence. As a result, I was pretty miserable for most of our two months together, although I must confess to reacting quite favorably to my initiation into the world of dirty talking—a dish she served up quite nicely with her sexy Australian accent and imaginative choice of words.

Dear Hardcore Diary,

Well, I called several of the hotels in the area, and they are all sold out, so I may end up checking out and moving out of Pasadena, somewhere closer to Glendale, where the upcoming Christy Canyon interview will take place. As you could probably guess, Colette is not exactly thrilled with the prospect of that one.

Last night's *Raw* went very well, although it didn't feature the definitive Paul E./Mick Foley verbal toe-to-toe I had been anticipating. Which is probably good, because last night's segment did an excellent job of setting up the actual match, and left the Vegas crowd awash in an enthusiastic chorus of ECW chants.

Much to my surprise, I'm actually a bad guy now. I had assumed that some people would boo me, but figured my ultra loyalty to WWE would keep people on my side for a while. Sure, some of the fans were cheering, and there was a subdued but noticeable "Foley" chant when I came out, but I guess I need to accept that I am now a wrestling heel—at least for a while. The truth is, I could probably take my six months off after *SummerSlam* and return to a babyface reaction, as if nothing had ever happened. After all, guys like Undertaker have been heavy heels, and come back after extended breaks to huge babyface reactions. But for the sake of successful storytelling, I want to have a sense of cohesion and logic to my departure and eventual return. And hey, if the return can generate interest in this book, then so be it.

Extended Stay America was nice enough to bring me a padded office chair, so it looks like I'll be staying a while. The poor chair—it's about to become better acquainted with my ass than anything, living or material, really deserves to. Maybe it's not the rustic log cabin where so many writers seem to do their best work, but then again, it's not an airplane or the front seat of a broken-down car, where I wrote part of the Uncle Dee chapter.

Unlike last week, I don't have a videotape handy to offer word-for-word promo analysis. Besides, this was a very good but not historic or particularly emotional promo, and I don't want to get so in-depth all the time that you guys are actually skipping over these "promo" entries in order to get to more Diva stories. Still, it was a very good segment, and an integral piece of the bigger puzzle, so utilizing the powers of recall that hundreds of chair shots haven't yet stolen, here's what went down last night, right there in Las Vegas.

Oddly, I didn't show up at the Thomas and Mack Center raring to go. This West Coast *Raw* still throws me off. It just doesn't seem right to go live in the middle of daylight. It had been a few days since I'd spent any substantial time in Promoland, and I'd already let the image of the "hardway promo" drift from my mind, accepting, I guess, that it just wasn't going to happen this time around. Besides, trying to tie the eye injury into *SummerSlam,* as I hope to do, is a bit of a stretch. Three months is an awful long amount of lead time for what I have planned. Maybe a hardway at *One Night Stand* would work better, as it could be seen in all its gory glory the following night on *Raw,* allowing it to become part of the Flair match buildup, before continuing on to *SummerSlam.*

It continues to cross my mind that writing a book is not the best way to fire oneself up for such an emotional match as ECW's promises to be. Maybe there's just not enough hours in a day to write, hit the gym, be a father to four children, and make daily sojourns to Promoland as well. I don't want to burn myself out too soon emotionally, as I may have done at *WrestleMania XX.* But it is a distinct possibility.

Whore and *balls* are a major concern. Can we say them (repeatedly, in *whore*'s case) at the nine o'clock (ET) hour? Just to be safe, we decide that Paul E. will go with *prostitute* and *nuts.* Paul's central theme will involve labeling me as a prostitute. Hey, I give him credit—he can't be charged with making claims in private that he's not willing to make in front of millions around the world.

I've always gotten along with Paul E., and had until recently considered him a good friend, but as I've come to realize and accept, there are very few real friends in wrestling. Lots of business relationships, lots of friendly acquaintances, but very few friends. But whatever disappointment or hurt I felt at discovering his opinion of me, it can't tarnish Paul's legacy as one of the most creative, incredibly gifted minds I've encountered in our business. We can definitely do business together, even if business will often involve what Terry Funk calls "borderlining," coming very close to what you really feel and mean about an individual.

Paul made it very clear that nothing is off the table as far as his life is concerned. I can say anything I want to. But Brian Gewirtz has assured me that we will get to that previously mentioned definitive Foley/Heyman promo. Oh, yeah, for those of you who don't know, Paul E. and Paul Heyman are the same guy, and the two names will be used interchangeably. But my feeling is that now is not the time to address Paul's changes. We'll let them stew in the minds of fans, let them try to figure it out, before I give my side of the story.

Basically, I plan to paint ECW as a fanatic cult, a latter-day Jonestown, if you will. Paul is the charismatic cult leader, the Jim Jones of ECW, lording over his naive, trusting flock of hardcore wrestlers. Why shouldn't they have been loyal? After all, most of them were guys who'd bounced around the independents for years, seemingly going nowhere, when Paul breathed new life into their careers. The guys worked their butts off, don't get me wrong, but Paul E. was the maestro, conducting an eclectic blend of bloodshed, humor, emotion, and good old-fashioned ingenuity into a symphony of hardcore entertainment. During its heyday, it blew away what WCW and WWE had to offer.

It was fresh, it was exciting, and it did wonders for the careers of many, especially those for whom it served as a conduit, a way to get noticed by the big boys—guys like Eddie Guerrero, Chris Benoit, and Dean Malenko, who were something of anomalies in ECW. They were actually *wrestlers*, having *wrestling* matches, which stood out amid the potpourri of weapons, blood, and bad language that was the staple of the ECW diet.

The company also served as a creative springboard for so many, myself included. Paul E. didn't script interviews, he nurtured them. He was like a father figure in that way; bringing out the best in his children simply by believing in them, by giving them the room to grow. I grew immensely under Paul E.'s guidance. Stone Cold Steve Austin did as well, as did many others who were fortunate to have called ECW their home, if only for a little while.

But I never drank the Kool-Aid, although I did come mighty close. WWE, at that time, was not even a possibility for me. Jim Ross had been pulling for me for years. Nothing. I called the WWE offices once a year on principal. Nothing. I had even thought about calling WCW and offering my services, as a strictly TV performer. By combining my ECW, Japan, and prospective WCW bookings, I could have made a pretty good living for my family.

My bread and butter was Japan, where by engaging in incredibly physical matches with Terry Funk, I was becoming something of a minor cult hero. WCW might have been some gravy for the bread, although in all likelihood I would have been used up, beaten, and discarded quickly by the group. But my heart belonged to ECW. Until I saw it for what it really was—a dead end.

I had the glass of Kool-Aid right up to my lips. I saw Paul E. smiling contentedly, another soul for him to keep, another career gone for good. You guys do realize I'm speaking metaphorically here, right? There really wasn't any Kool-Aid there, unless of course the Sandman had poured a quart of vodka into it.

The "Cane Dewey" sign is usually seen as the defining moment in my ECW career. Before the sign, everything was good. After the sign, I saw things a little clearer. "Cane Dewey" was a sign held up by a fan that seemed to encourage the "caning," or beating with a kendo stick, of my then-three-year-old son, Dewey. I knew it was meant as a joke, and had even told the "sign guy" who made it that it was okay to show it. But the sign made my wife physically sick to her stomach, and served as the catalyst for my ECW heel turn, which is still spoken of reverently in wrestling lore.

But it was actually an incident involving longtime Philadelphia-based indy wrestler J. T. Smith that affected me more. I'd known J.T. for years and thought he was a heck of a guy, although he seemed intent on wrestling a style that his body just wasn't made to handle. He liked the wild stuff, the big, high-impact bumps, which always seemed to leave him in incredible pain. But man, he would have done anything to please the fans, including risking his life. Eventually, he found love in ECW in a comedy role as wrestling's first full-blooded Italian black man. His biggest impact on my life, however, was the time he slipped off the top rope at the ECW arena (Viking Hall) and crashed headfirst to the concrete floor below.

His head swelled up immediately, dangerously so, maybe even life-threateningly so. But that didn't stop the ECW faithful from reveling in his pain. "You f'd up, you f'd up," they chanted, over and over. But as you can probably guess, they didn't just say the first initial. I was really pretty

Back in my ECW days.

stunned. Sickened. Because in that one moment, I realized that ECW was a dead end—that to stay any longer than necessary would be the death of my career.

For me, it all comes back to just where my life would be if I'd listened to ECW fans who chanted, "You sold out," upon learning of my imminent defection to WWE. If I'd listened to good friends who said WWE would be the death of my career. Or even Paul E., who warned me that my program with Undertaker would be "a dead deal." Where exactly would I be? Broken down, bitter, probably divorced, possibly penniless, and looking at WWE's proposed new ECW brand as a life-saving measure.

All right, maybe that's melodramatic. I probably could have done wild matches in Japan for years and lived a fairly decent life. Or perhaps gotten out of wrestling completely, and had the intestinal fortitude to actually make my way in the real world. And I've often considered my final ECW match, with its completely unexpected hero's farewell, to be a highlight of my career. I really did love so much about ECW. So it was a love/hate relationship that for Pay-Per-View purposes I will only be dwelling on the hate side of.

But I'll go out on a limb and say that most of what I have has been made possible through my experiences with WWE. And no, this is not a blind tribute to the philanthropic nature of Vince McMahon. I was given an opportunity, and I made the most of it. I paid a price, and I was paid a price for doing so.

But there would be no *Hardcore Diaries* without WWE. No *Have a Nice Day,* no *Foley Is Good,* no children's books, no novels. I've had my share of battles with Vince McMahon, and I'm sure I'll have more in the future. Maybe Vince only gave me the ball and I did the running, but at least I was running somewhere with it—not on a path to nowhere, like so many of ECW's finest ball carriers.

Good stuff, done really well, makes for great TV. Good stuff, done decently, makes for forgettable TV. I thought the stuff we had was really good, and I knew we had the potential to do it really well, so I wasn't all that worried about the finer comparisons of *whore* and *prostitute* and *balls* and *nuts.* It was going to be good. So what if I didn't know my lines? I could make it up while I was out there. We'd be fine.

And we were. I came out to a far more mixed reaction than a week ago. Very cool. Once inside the ring, which I had considerable trouble actually getting into (I know my knee is bad when I have to push off the ropes to stand up), I informed the fans that there had been a misunderstanding, that I was actually a good guy, letting parents know it was okay to give their kids permission to cheer me.

"After all," I said, "I'm the cuddly guy, the human Muppet, the guy who puts his thumb up in the air and says, 'It's great to be in Vegas!'" A big, cheap pop. Sure not everyone is buying into it, but enough are to make the next line work.

"Except it's not really that great to be here in Las Vegas."

I then explained the problem I had with millions of people attempting to change their lives with a lucky hand at cards or roll of the dice, instead of working hard for their accomplishments, like I had. After all, I hadn't won three WWE championships by rolling sevens on the craps tables, or written two *New York Times* number-one best-selling books by putting a quarter in a slot machine. I'd earned them.

I then introduced a man who had earned everything in his life as well, Edge. Edge then came out to participate in a major-league schmoozefest, during which I presented him with the old hardcore title, in recognition of him truly embodying the spirit of hardcore. Edge declined the title, claiming that I was the more deserving of it, for having toiled in obscurity for so long in ECW, and for tolerating the words of a so-called legend like Ric Flair, who had referred to me as a "glorified stuntman" in his aforementioned book. So the first seed of the Flair match had been planted.

I began my rebuttal of Edge's rebuttal, noting the irony of a man who called me a glorified stuntman earning his *WrestleMania* paycheck by basically not getting killed in a ladder match. "That's fine," I said. "What's not fine is, it seems like we've got a little problem here. I think you deserve the hardcore championship, and you think I deserve the hardcore championship. So as far as I can see, there's only one way to resolve the issue—you and I beat the holy hell out of each other, right here tonight!"

The crowd went wild. They bought it. They actually bought it. Fortunately, for the sake of my knee, no such match was going to take place. Because Edge had another option. He whispered into ring announcer Lilian Garcia's ear, and Lilian, after a moment of befuddlement, made the announcement I had been picturing in my mind for weeks, even months, when Edge and I were first hatching this plan prior to *WrestleMania*.

Paul Heyman, aka Paul E., one of the most brilliant guys in the business.

"Ladies and gentlemen, the new coholders of the Hardcore title, Mick Foley and Edge."

Yes, we had done it! We had a vision, and we saw it through. One of the cheesiest moments in WWE history; two men willingly sharing a single title. How much more unhardcore could holding the hardcore title possibly get? Proudly, the three of us, me, Edge, and Lita, held the title belt aloft, floating in the rising tide of boos that were so richly deserved.

Then Paul E. had to ruin it. Like a turd in the punch bowl of life (not the same punch bowl he served the ECW Kool-Aid from), he had to arrive on the scene to the accompaniment of the ECW music, and a surprisingly loud ovation.

"Look at this," he said, obviously relishing his return to the spotlight. "In the only state where it's still legal, a blatant display of prostitution right in that very ring."

Everyone cheers as Edge and I console Lita, who, the fans of course believe, is the object of Paul E.'s derision.

"Oh, and there's Lita, too," Paul says, temporarily confusing the audience. "because the prostitute I'm talking about is you, Mick Foley." I act stunned, like the thought has never entered my mind. Actually, it hadn't, until a few weeks ago when I first heard a rumor of his claim.

Paul then went on to cut a masterful promo, accusing me of prostituting my name, my likeness, my legacy, the fans' faith in me, even the term *hardcore*. But he does far more than just make charges. He builds me up first, so that our fans realize the significance of the charges. "Build him up before you tear him down." It's old-time wrestling psychology but it still works. I'm not just a piece of crap—I'm a guy who has chosen to become a piece of crap. There's a big difference.

He concluded his diatribe by asking how it felt to look in the mirror and see a shell of my former self. Paul had previously asked me backstage about mentioning my wife and kids in the promo, and I hadn't been in favor of it. Sure, they'd been referred to, respectively, as a "whore" and "bastards" just a week earlier, but I felt once was enough. I don't want my older kids under any more pressure than they already are. Adolescence is tough enough without a WWE storyline hanging over their heads.

"Do you know what I see when I look in the mirror?" I say. "I see the coholder of the WWE hardcore title. I see a WWE Superstar. I see a real-life action figure. I see a man who has written seven books and who's working on another that will be available in bookstores everywhere next spring." By this point I'm yelling, my emotion is high, even when getting in a blatant plug for *The Hardcore Diaries.*

I continue, saying, "I see a man of immense power, unlike you, Paul, who has none. You're not general manager of *SmackDown!* anymore, you don't own your own company, you're nothing."

Paul agrees that his power is limited, but he does have the power to make a suggestion, or to issue a challenge. Here it comes, the official challenge for the coholders of the Hardcore Championship to face any ECW scumbags of his choosing.

I've slummed long enough, I tell Paul E., so listen to the authoritative voice of a WWE Superstar as he tells you, "No way."

But Paul E. is laughing, throwing me off my game, causing me to demand an explanation for the inappropriate anger. Actually, I think I just said, "What's so funny?"

Paul E. continues to laugh, then says, "It's just that I'm looking at Lita, Edge, and Mick Foley in the ring, and the only one with any NUTS is Lita."

Sure, balls would have been better, but it's the nine o'clock hour, so out of respect for the children watching *Raw,* Paul puts forth the less offensive of the testicular references. Actually, I thought he might seize the moment and the advantage of live television to let "balls" fall out of his mouth—wait, I'm not sure that sounded right—but he does the responsible thing. Otherwise, the only seizing done would be by Vince, when he seized Paul E. after the segment.

The insinuation of female ball possession is enough to send Edge over the edge (a deliberate play on words by the best-selling author), and against my wishes, he accepts the challenge, and offers to show Paul E. a little sample of what's to come on June 11.

Paul E. then reveals our opponents, Funk and Dreamer, who proceed to administer the obligatory butt-kicking, sending the coholders of the hardcore title fleeing for safer grounds, through the crowd and out the exit.

Sure, Paul E. got chewed out for the segment going three minutes over, but in this case, rushing things would have been detrimental to the angle. We all realize that our angle is second in significance to the reformation of DX, but nonetheless, we all believe in the importance of what we're doing and we don't want to undermine it by skimping on important details, like not maximizing audience reactions. Besides, I've seen some stinkers that seemed to go on forever, and there didn't seem to be any ramifications for the over-run, or any loss in future mike time for the people who overran. We'll have to closely consider the time next week, however, as I don't want to risk the potential last two weeks of promo time for having been slapped with an "overrunner" label.

Dear Hardcore Diary,

I'm sitting in the spare bed at my manager Barry Bloom's house, resting my notebook on a large green stuffed alligator as I write. I would have been happy to spend most of yesterday as a designated *Diaries* day, but a quickly scheduled MRI appointment threw a wrench into my literary works.

At least I'll know what I'm dealing with from a health standpoint. I'm pretty sure something is wrong into the back of my knee—the posterior cruciate ligament is still my best guess—but the MRI should help me be better prepared to deal with it. Maybe I'll need a special brace, or can be given a specific training routine. For now, I'm doing a lot of work on recumbent bikes and a variety of elliptical trainers. But I'm staying away from weights with my legs—not that I'm bombarding my upper body with weight work either—and as always, staying far, far away from tanning beds of any type.

In the old days, I had my own tanning bed—a Chrysler LeBaron convertible. By 1991, I'd become adept at the act of the cover-up wrestling attire, which displayed only my bare arms. So a few days a week, I'd simply go sleeveless in the LeBaron and, presto, instant farmer's tan.

I do continue to wonder if I've bitten off more than I can chew these next few months. Gearing up physically and emotionally for *One Night Stand* would be trying enough, even if I weren't attempting to pen a towering best seller at the same time. Plus, I've got the Flair match looming on the post-ECW horizon, meaning I'll have little time to relax and enjoy what we've all worked so hard to create at *One Night Stand*.

That was always one of the biggest demands of life with

WWE—continually having to climb to emotional highs without a decent downtime to enjoy them. At least I was able to sleep in late after *WrestleMania,* and take an early-afternoon flight home. Edge, who was hurt worse than I was, had to actually wrestle the next night on *Raw.*

I'm sure I'll be hurting after our June 11 show, possibly even injured. But there will be no rest for the weary, as I'll have to crank up the emotion that very next night to start creating interest for the June 28 match with Ric Flair. There will be some people out there expecting an awful lot out of the match, myself included, but unlike most of those people, I don't have a whole lot of confidence in Mick Foley's chances of really tearing down the house.

Of course being in Charlotte will help a great deal. Unlike most cities, where I'll probably be cheered by a decent portion of people no matter what I do, I'll be hated in Charlotte. Which is cool.

It's been a very productive trip from a *Diaries* standpoint. Over a three-day period, from Sunday afternoon to yesterday (Wednesday) afternoon, I'd written 20,000 words by hand, including almost 9,000 on Tuesday alone. Hopefully as you read, you'll be able to get a sense of how much I've enjoying writing it. I know some chapters may seem like emotional downers, and there may be some extended periods where I don't talk about wrestling at all, but nonetheless, I hope you don't regret your decision to pick this thing up.

I saw Chris Jericho last night, who is writing a book of his own—about his formative years in wrestling, leading up to WWE. Chris and his family came over to Barry's for dinner, and we all laughed and told exaggerated stories until almost midnight. I always liked Chris, and considered him to be a great wrestler, a tremendous promo guy, and a class act. And his wife Jessica, for some reason, has always thought I was cool.

Chris remarked on how odd it seemed that so few people stayed in touch after he left WWE about nine months ago. It just seems to be the nature of the business. You can work intensely with somebody, draw money together, trust that person with your life, share that obligatory post–Pay-Per-View honeymoon period watching your previous night's match on the lunchroom TV monitor, and then, poof, that person is more or less out of your life. You're both on to new partners, and what you both worked so hard to create just fades into history. Unless of course you write a book about it, and then it lives on in perpetuity.

Hey, I plead guilty. As much as I like Chris, I haven't stayed in touch, even though I've been very happy for his successes outside the ring. He's got quite a lot going on, singing, acting, writing, so I'm not sure if wrestling even fits into his future. But should he ever choose to return, WWE fans would love to welcome him back.

I told Chris that I'd actually had something of a George Bailey moment a few nights earlier. George Bailey was the Jimmy Stewart character in *It's a Wonderful Life*, the guy who becomes convinced that his life has been meaningless until an angel shows him just how full of meaning his life really has been. Okay, maybe I wasn't in need of an angel, and I certainly don't think my life's been without meaning, but I was lying awake, following a late-night *Diaries* session, trying to figure out just how many real friends I'd made during the course of a twenty-year career.

The answer? Not many. Not many at all. I get along with almost everybody. I like almost everybody. I'm genuinely thrilled to see most of the guys (and girls) in our WWE family during the course of my sporadic returns. But when it comes to "real" friends—wow, there's not an awful lot there.

The actual low point of my career, a defining moment of sorts, came in Calgary in 1999, on a hospital visit to see Davey Boy Smith, who had been laid up for several days with a bad staph infection that had gone into his spine. At his peak, Davey, as one-half of the British Bulldogs tag team, was one of the top wrestlers in the world, and as a singles competitor had engaged in many great battles, including a couple of classics with his brother-in-law, Bret "Hit Man" Hart.

He was well liked by all of the guys, and had several close friends that he traveled and trained with. He had an infectious laugh and a great sense of humor, often pulling elaborate pranks that eased the monotony of the road, but really hurt no one.

I remember talking to Owen Hart, getting directions to the Calgary hospital, which was just minutes away from both the airport hotels and the arena. "Davey's really excited to see everybody," Owen said. "I think it's going to really help lift his spirits."

Except "everybody" wasn't there. In fact, nobody was. Except me and Biff Wellington, a longtime Calgary wrestler. And I wasn't even a good friend of Davey's. Not like some of the guys were. Yet nobody showed. I guess there were tanning beds that were lonely, or weights that needed lifting, or any number of reasons not to complete a ten-minute drive. But the message it sent me was chilling and simple—this isn't family. And on that day, I promised myself that I would make as much money as possible and retire on my terms, without kidding myself that I owed the wrestling business a thing.

Dear Hardcore Diary,

If I am ever to mount a congressional run, this will probably be the day that will come back to haunt me. What was I thinking? Christy Canyon? Ginger Lynn? An interview? Man, am I in trouble. I asked the show's producer just what I could expect, and she said, "Oh, the girls will probably just play around with you a little bit."

Now some of you longtime Foley fans might recognize Ms. Canyon's name from 2001's *Foley Is Good* as being something of an inspiration in the conception of little Mick—or at least in one of the many attempts over the course of a grueling three days.

Christy knows about it, too. How? I was kind enough to send her a copy, along with a letter, telling her how much I'd enjoyed her autobiography *Lights, Camera, Sex*. I told her there was an underlying sweetness to the book, and that it read like a very good action adventure/coming-of-age tale that just happened to center on the world of adult films.

So Christy had written me back, with a very nice letter of her own, telling me about her radio show, and inviting me on when I came to town. So, I guess I actually have two famous pen pals. John Irving and Christy.

Along with the copy of *Foley Is Good* I had sent a signed copy of *Tales from Wrescal Lane*. Because I remember way back in the eighties, sometime around '85, when a friend who I won't name here showed me a film of a young, twenty-or-so Christy. I vividly remember seeing the spirited, naturally busty young lady in action and having one distinct thought: "Someday I'd like to sign a children's book for her."

That was over twenty years ago. But I'll never forget how she stepped into my solitary young sex life, filling a void that English veteran Kay Parker's retirement had left. Kind of like Mantle replacing DiMaggio in centerfield for the Yankees, or Hogan stepping down for a fiery Sid Vicious.

Back in the dog days of the summer of '89, following my return home from the World Class territory in Dallas (know as USWA by the time I left), I was in the process of transferring a Christy video onto a blank VHS tape when I heard a knock on my parents' door. Outside stood a young lady who should best remain nameless, who I had known for years and had always carried a small torch for. Which, at the risk of falling victim to outmoded phrases, meant I had a longtime crush on. Obviously, I turned the Christy video off. Fortunately, I hadn't been in the process of going a few rounds with my baldheaded champion, if you know what I mean. Unfortunately, I looked kind of ridiculous, which was a pretty constant fashion statement for me back then. Really long hair, red flannel shirt, an old pair of shorts, cheap snakeskin boots, and a burgundy cast, just short of my elbow—a hard-earned trophy from a Fort Worth Scaffold match landing that didn't work out quite as I'd hoped.

The girl sat on the couch, and I began consoling her. She'd been through a rough few days, and felt comfortable allowing me into her confidence. I just thought she was beautiful. The more she talked, the more beautiful she became, until it reached a point where I had never been more attracted to a girl in my life. Well, at least until Colette came along about a year later and set a whole new standard for me.

Keep in mind, I was shy. I still am, in a way. And the attraction I felt wasn't of the Christy Canyon video variety. It was more innocent. Like a first-love type of thing. A mutual thing. Perhaps I should have leaned forward, just gone for the kiss, instead of asking permission—which is what I ended up doing. Asking permission, that is.

"Can I kiss you?" I asked, feeling almost sure the request would be granted.

Maybe I should bring in Marv Albert to make the call. "Foley drives the lane, takes the shot. It's no good! Rejected!"

The girl swatted my attempt away as if she was Dikembe Mutombo in his shot-blocking prime.

What had gone wrong? Well, I took a wild guess. There was only one person to blame—Christy Canyon. It was karma. To this day I believe that had I not been taping the porno, the kissing attempt would have been successful. Well, I don't want to be too hard on Christy, because after reading her book, I know that she's sensitive. Come to think of it, it may have been the shorts-and-boots combo that cost me the kiss. Not a real fashion winner in any era, even an era that featured the mullet.

May 26, 2006
12:10 A.M.—Toluca Lake, CA

Dear Hardcore Diary,

I'm now at the home of Barry Blaustein, who I met ten years ago when he began work on *Beyond the Mat,* a wrestling documentary that was well liked and acclaimed by just about everybody who saw it, except Vince McMahon. Years ago, back in 1999, the release of the movie caused some friction between me and Vince, but to this day, I stand by it, and will always be proud I was a major part of it.

It seems funny now, but at the time of our first meeting, Barry thought my career was fascinating, but was thinking of covering me as the guy who'd had a few years of stardom before heading back to the minor leagues. Luckily all that changed.

Barry went on to direct *The Ringer,* a real funny film with Johnny Knoxville as a guy who pretends to be mentally challenged so he can win the Special Olympics for big money. Despite its coldhearted premise, the film has a nice heart, was warmly received by many critics, and is currently the number-one video across the United States. Hanging out at Barry's house has always been a pleasure, and just as importantly, it saves me big bucks on L.A. hotels. Okay, maybe it's not quite as important, but it does help. I learned a long time ago that its not how much you make in wrestling, but how much you save, and though I may no longer be the tightest man in the business, the guy who pinches pennies so hard he makes Abe Lincoln scream, I am always aware of how easy it is to live life too large while on the road.

As for that once planned congressional run—you can forget about it. Following last night's appearance on *Night Calls* with Christy Canyon and Ginger Lynn, I would be a ridiculously easy target for any attack ad. I could just hear the voice: Mick Foley claims to be for family values, but is he really? Cue specific sound bites from any number of the show's shenanigans, and I'd be lucky to get a job cleaning toilets at a top-secret CIA wiretapping meeting.

Which isn't to say I didn't have fun. I did. The girls were both great, and I think I did a reasonably good job of being a good sport while the deviant duo assaulted whatever is still left of my innocence with a barrage of innuendos, straight-up sex talk, half-nude wrestling, mutual boob groping, and a litany of lavicious one-liners that had me shaking my head in sheer disbelief. Christy even whispered sweet nothings into what was left of my right ear, prompting a telltale tingling in my trousers that hasn't completely subsided.

Colette called during a break in the show, and I was dumb enough to answer, freely admitting to my locale and the company I was keeping. For some odd reason, she wasn't thrilled. Sure, I felt like I was promoting the ECW Pay-Per-View while engaging in some harmless fun, but I guess I need to see some things from her point of view.

We are about to leave Pornoland—no relation to Promoland—but not without one last stop, which took place at the nation's largest video convention, back in 1999.

I was representing WWE at the convention, signing videotapes (DVDs weren't yet big) in front of a respectable line—a couple hundred strong. Occasionally, I would notice a scantily clad woman cutting the line with permission, getting an autograph, before heading back behind a massive curtain. This strange occurrence happened several time before I asked our sales rep, 1980s WWE Superstar Hillbilly Jim, about the mysterious destination of the nearly naked girls.

Hillbilly laughed. He's a gregarious guy, and a heck of a salesman, from what I have heard. "Son, they're from the adult annex," he said, slapping me on the back for emphasis.

"Adult annex?" I asked.

"Son, they've got their own little world right behind that curtain."

"Really."

"Sure," Jim said. "How would you like to go there after you're done with your signing?"

Wow, what a question. Would I like to go? I thought it over momentarily.

Colette was 2,000 miles away. How would she find out? Unless, of course, I was going to be dumb enough to write about it in a book or something. Besides, I would be just walking around. I wouldn't really be doing anything wrong. After my signing, I took that walk.

Behind that curtain lay a whole new world. I posed for pictures that, if discovered, would have cost me a shot at any type of political career long before the *Night Calls* naughtiness. I saw old stars I remembered from my much younger days, and new stars with whom I wasn't even vaguely familiar. Then I saw a glimpse of one of the world's beautiful women, Janine, a goddess in the adult film industry.

I don't really know how she ended up in adult films—she should have been on the cover of *Cosmo*, with her radiant looks. She commanded a lot of attention from what seemed to be a legion of fans: a long line that snaked out into the vast reaches of the annex.

Hillbilly smiled. "Do you want to meet her?"

"Sure."

But just as Hillbilly Jim was ushering me to the front of the line, a big-time wrestling fan jumped between me and Janine.

"Do you know who this guy is?" the fan said. "This is Mick Foley. Cactus Jack. Mankind. He's done the most unbelievable things that you've ever seen. He's been thrown off the cell, he's been blown up, he's been in barbed wire."

This was pretty cool—almost like a dream come true. A daydream come true, at least. I mean, I used to literally daydream about someone singing my praises in front of a beautiful girl. Even back when I didn't have praises to sing about. This daydream goes back quite a while, like back to eleven or twelve, when I daydreamed about looking real good in front of the girls in Mr. Perkins's sixth-grade class. The realization of this dream in front of Janine was almost enough to make up for all the heartbreak and ridicule I'd suffered at the hands of unrequited loves during my formative years. Almost enough to make up for the incredible rejection I'd suffered on the couch in my parents' living room after dubbing the early Canyon video offering onto a blank VHS. Almost.

"Wow, who was that guy?" I said to Janine, after the fan had finally finished up his fond Foley affirmations.

"Oh, he owns the video company," Janine said. Before asking, "Which group do you wrestle for?" with genuine interest.

"WWE," I said, proud of the company, proud of myself. But I saw Janine's nose and eyes crinkle in a look of great disappointment. "What's wrong?" I asked.

"Well, no offense, but I don't let my son watch you, because of the 'Suck it.'"

"Well, that's quite a coincidence," I said.

"What is?" said Janine.

"Well, I don't let my son watch you either."

The train is now leaving Pornoland. Please leave all your bad thoughts behind.

Plan B

I may indeed have made Dee Snider a better man, but to the best of my knowledge, I didn't inspire the Twisted Sister reunion. Dee and the boys had done a couple of USO shows in Korea for the troops, and had decided to hit the road in the summer of 2003 for a full-fledged comeback tour. As a tune-up, the band, under the clever subterfuge of "Bent Brother," kicked off the tour with a couple of club dates, including one at Long Island's "Downtown," which as a pal of Dee's I received a VIP ticket to.

Quite frankly, I was a little worried for Dee. He'd had such massive success in the 1980s and was a veritable cultural icon. Why ruin it almost twenty years later? I thought I'd seen the last of old guys in tights with the fall of WCW.

My preshow concern for my friend triggered one of the dumbest comments of my life, during a conversation with Dee's teenage son, Shane.

"Is your dad excited about the tour?" I said.

"Yeah, he's been working out and doing a lot of yoga."

"Yoga?" I said, with joking sarcasm. "I bet he doesn't want anyone knowing about that." Yeah, I know it's great exercise and that my good buddy Diamond Dallas Page wrote a book called *Yoga for Real Guys*, but you can't deny that it still has a certain stigma surrounding it.

Apparently that stigma didn't mean that much to Shane, who said, "Mick, my dad dressed up in women's clothing for ten years, I don't think he cares if people knows he does yoga."

So having been put firmly in my place by a teenager, I went out toward the stage, fearing that I was about to watch a good friend embarrass himself. Hey, I knew how this felt. I'd been embarrassed by the last several months of my active wrestling career, before an early 2000 angle with Triple H allowed me to retire with my dignity, courtesy of a couple of classic matches. From time to time, I'd even considered a comeback. Every once in a while, I'd see a great match, and I'd get the itch, and every month when I got my financial statements, I'd be reminded that my Clinton-era plan of living off the interest from my investments was just not going to happen.

Sure, I'd saved a lot of money. And unlike a lot of investors, I hadn't bailed out at a loss when the market got rough in the wake of 9/11. Within a couple of years, the markets had largely stabilized, but I also knew I could never count on them again. As soon as the Dow Jones got close to 11,000, I shifted most of what I had into fixed-income investments, meaning I would never fall victim to the volatility of the stock market again. But neither could I sit back, do nothing, and reap the late 1990s harvest of yearly double-digit gains. *Tietam Brown* had done okay, but not as well as I'd hoped. I had another novel, *Scooter*, largely written, but I wasn't foolish enough to expect any type of sales miracles from it. Writing novels, I realized, was not going to provide a whole lot of extra security for my family—which, with the additions of Mickey and Hughie, was obviously of slightly more concern. My refereeing experience at Hell in a Cell had shown me that there was still a market for Mick Foley, the wrestler. I would be a fool not to consider it. After all, I felt better than I had in years. But I really feared returning, to find that Father Time had played a rib on me. I had been proud of the legacy I'd left

behind. I didn't want to mess that up. Let Dee Snider mess up his own legacy.
I was going to leave mine alone.

Dee took the stage. And I stood mesmerized, awestruck as a near-fifty-
year-old rocker blew away all my preconceptions. He wasn't just the Dee
Snider of old—he was better. Full of emotion, full of passion; full of all the
things you can't teach in a studio, or fake in front of fans. He still had it. And
I vividly remember thinking that I would not return to WWE unless I could
be as good at wrestling as Dee was on that stage.

Meanwhile, I had been watching Randy Orton. Watching him progress
and mature into a rising young star. Perhaps I could play off my Madison
Square Garden mishap after all.

Scooter was now approaching the final editing stage, although it would
not be published for another year and a half, in the late summer of 2005. One
of *Scooter*'s central themes involved incidents of inaction or cowardice at

inopportune times in the main character's lives, leaving the reader to wonder whether a life should be looked at and judged in its entire context, or whether it should be judged based on one regrettable moment.

How, I wondered, would our fans judge me if I were to fall victim to such a moment? I sat on the idea for months, letting it grow, visualizing it, waiting until it kept me awake for many nights. Then, in late fall of 2003, I gave Vince a call.

I am a firm believer in backup plans, especially when trying to stay afloat in the tumultuous ocean that is WWE. The *Scooter* scenario was actually my backup plan. Plan B. Here, let me show you plan A.

"Vince, I was thinking about showing up as a surprise entry at the *Royal Rumble*. I would win the *Rumble* and then, because I wasn't technically a *Raw* or a *SmackDown!* wrestler, would challenge both champions to a three-way match at *WrestleMania*, which I would win, making me the undisputed WWE champion."

"No," Vince said. "I have no interest in doing that."

"Okay, I've got a different idea involving Randy Orton."

I told Vince that I wanted to be the first pro wrestler to ever chicken out of a match—accept a match and just walk away from it. Vince nodded his head, intrigued.

"Then, after I walk out, Randy will launch a political attack ad campaign on me."

"Attack ads?" Vince asked.

"Yeah, you know those things. Everyone hates them. Imagine that deep voice we always hear, saying, 'Mick Foley *claims* to be the hardcore legend . . . but is he really?'"

Vince laughed and began writing feverishly.

He liked the idea. On December 15, in Tampa, Florida, I was going to make history.

But it didn't happen without a fight. A couple of nights before the Tampa show, I received a call from Stephanie McMahon, telling me that a variety of well-respected wrestling minds had voiced opposition to my idea, feeling that quite simply, any character who walked out on a match would never be forgiven by our fans. Instead, Steph told me, I was going to walk out for the match, and be jumped by Orton's brothers in Evolution—Triple H, Ric Flair, and Batista.

So it seems that our fans can indeed accept gullible, naive, stupid wrestlers—just not courageously uncertain ones. Man, I was confused and upset. I will always love certain aspects of WWE, but the unwillingness to take chances with characters is akin to creative suffocation. And no, by taking chances, I'm not talking about doing angles involving necrophilia or terrorism. I'm talking about allowing characters to show faults and vulnerabilities that our fans can empathize with and talk about.

We can't get away with just being shocking or cutting-edge anymore. So many of the elements that made WWE so big in the late 1990s have been borrowed, stolen, or hijacked by various elements of the entertainment spectrum that the onus is on us to give our fans scenarios that they can become emotionally caught up in. From Bill Clinton's arrival at the 2000 Democratic Convention being captured with the *Raw* low-angle shot, to rappers wrestling on video games, to the everyday shock and awe of reality shows, the new pop culture seems to have a never-ending hunger for crumbs from the WWE pie. We have to constantly adapt. And in my opinion, that means broadening our characters' range of emotions, and giving our fans enough credit to broaden their expectations of what WWE can be.

I stated my case as best I could to Steph, and then left a long, rambling message on Vince's machine. I knew that a nonmatch with Orton might displease some viewers, but argued that those types of fans weren't likely to order Pay-Per-Views anyway.

I remember one specific line from my return call from Vince. "Did you ever see the movie *Shane?*" I asked, in reference to the classic 1953 Western in which a reformed gunfighter is forced to confront his past demons to defend his honor.

"Yes," said Vince. "I have."

"Well, go back and watch that movie some time," I said. "And tell me how good it would be if Shane accepts the heel's challenge the first time."

"Okay, I get your point," Vince said. "But, Mick, you're the only person who could make this thing work."

We did make it work. I walked out, and Randy hocked a major-league loogie right in my face. He ran several weeks of major attack ads, building from the somewhat subtle to the outright shocking.

They worked, too. I watched with pride as Randy Orton's confidence and star seemed to grow with each passing week. As general manager, my old buddy Steve Austin played a valuable role as well, more or less promising WWE fans that I would be returning for vengeance at the *Royal Rumble*.

And return I did. Where I learned two valuable lessons. One—three months of hard training and strict dieting didn't mean anything when I got into the ring, where I gassed out in less than a minute. And two—the very real punches that Randy and I threw at each other during the *Rumble* didn't look any different than the punches WWE fans see every week on *Raw*. Actually they might have looked worse. As a matter of fact, as of this writing not one person has ever commented on those punches, leading me to believe that the very thought of them was a waste of time, pain, and swelling. Sadly, the lesson of the real punches was not one I would fully absorb, in 2004 or 2006.

January 26, 2004, was my day—for explanation and for retribution. It was one of those promos I'd done so many times in my head that it seemed to beg for a chance to escape and have a life of its own on millions of televisions across the world. Rarely have I been so fired up as I was on that night. And rarely has a promo lived up to my expectations of it as it did that night in Hershey, Pennsylvania.

> **MICK FOLEY:** Thank you . . . it's very nice. But I think that following the events of December 15, 2003, maybe a little explanation is in order; every day since that day, I've heard one comment over and over: "Why, Mick, why?" I think I have finally come to a place where I can answer that question as best as I can, but I think to understand "why" you need to understand where I've been, or maybe, more accurately, what it is that got me there. When I think about my career—when fans refer to my career— they come up with a lot of really nice accolades. They talk about my heart, my guts, my courage, my love for the business. The truth is, yes, some of that came into play, but the main benefit I had was hatred—the ability to take something in my life, to hate it very much, and then channel it in a very useful way. To go into a deep dark part in my heart and produce things inside this ring that were thought to be humanly impossible. That's really good, as long as I was an active wrestler, but then I thought of a guy like Pete Rose—the most competitive player of his era— who when I was a kid played the game as if he was angry at the

world. To see Pete Rose dive into third base headfirst was pretty cool. To see Pete Rose knock over Ray Fosse at the '70 All Star game or take a swipe at Bud Harrelson in the '73 playoffs was really cool. But to see that same guy, ultracompetitive, still angry at the world at age sixty-one, lying about betting on baseball, is pretty sad. I don't want to be the sad guy. I don't want to be the bitter guy. So when I retired from wrestling, although it was very difficult, I had to let go of all that anger. And I heard throughout my career, "Mick Foley is a hell of a guy." I was a hell of a guy as long as I had that avenue to channel all the hatred toward. When I retired, I needed to let go, and after a long time I did, and got to a place where I was truly for the first time happy with myself. So I'll admit to making a big, big mistake on December 15, 2003, in Tampa, Florida. The mistake was not walking out on the match. The mistake I made was accepting the match to begin with, because as I walked down that ramp to face Randy Orton, who is the Intercontinental Champion and is a hell of a wrestler, I realized I wasn't willing and maybe not able to go inside that place in my heart to do what was necessary to get the job done. Now, Randy kind of seized that opportunity, and I think he took advantage of it a little bit, and he's chosen to make my life a little bit difficult over the last seven weeks. So even though I know he is probably very angry at me for costing him his shot at the main event at *WrestleMania,* I still think Randy Orton, all things considered, owes me a little favor. So what I'd like to do is call Randy Orton down to the ring without Evolution. One on one, right now. Randy, I will wait here all night if I have to.

Randy Orton comes to the ring.

RANDY ORTON: You want a favor from me, Mick? I dare ask, after blowing my chances at a main event at *WrestleMania!* I dare ask, what do you want from me?

MICK: Wait, wait . . . hold on! Don't be so angry. This may seem out there . . . this may seem downright kooky, but what I would like you to do is, I'd like you to spit in my face again.

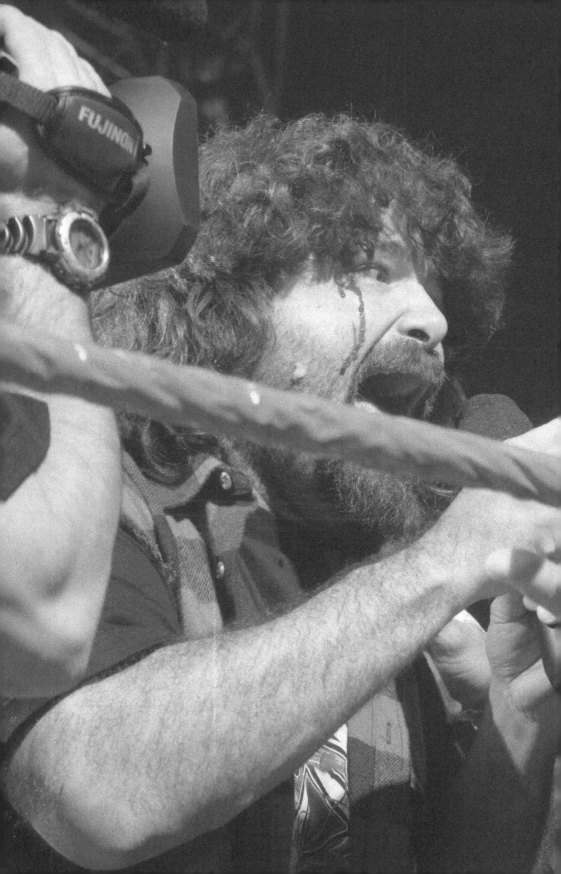

RANDY: You want me to do what?

MICK: I told you it was kooky, and look, I know you can do it, because I felt the warmth of your spit that night in Tampa. I've seen the replays seventeen times, I've seen it in slow motion, hell, I've even seen it in rewind, but I'm just wondering if maybe that was a fluke and if you have the guts to spit in my face again right here in Hershey, Pennsylvania.

RANDY: Mick, listen, man, listen. [Mick snatches his mike and throws it.]

MICK: Listen here, you little bastard! I was spilling blood on six continents while you were still latched onto your mother's breast! I've been hearing you run your damn mouth for seven weeks! Now I've got the microphone and I'm talking, and you do as you're told! I am telling you, no, I am ordering you, to spit in my damn face! Do it! Do it! Do it! [Mick smacks Randy in the face a few times.]

Randy spits. A yellowish green wad of phlegm can be seen on Mick's cheek.

MICK: What! What! Why, I ought to . . . why—I am not going to hit you, Randy, I am not going to hit you. Not only am I not going to hit you, I'm going to take the advice of a very good book I read a little while ago that said "Turn the other cheek," and I am going to turn that other cheek. What I'm going to do is ask you to spit on that one as well, but I couldn't help but notice that this was one lackluster loogie, Randy. My goodness, it's cold and flu season, the harshest winter in fifty years, and I'm willing to bet that you can exhume something real green from way down deep. Dig it up and plant me right here! But hold on, hold on, maybe Randy needs a little inspiration, so if you join me, maybe we can get a chant going, "Loogie, loogie, loogie." Deeper, deeper . . . there you go!

Randy spits.

Yeah! Wooahhh! Take a good shot of that! Realize that you can look at it close, and it is still only spit. Still just spit, and, Randy, you have to realize, I've got four children. During the course of twelve years of raising those kids . . . I've been peed on, I've been pooped on, I've been thrown up on, I've been sneezed on, and yeah, I've even been spit on. So being spit on by you one more time is not really a big deal. When it came to you calling me names, I had it on good authority that "sticks and stones may break my bones but names, that's right, they'll never hurt me." I am willing to bet that whoever came up with that helpful adage was never referred to as Randy Orton's "bitch" on national television. You see, Randy, it was about at that point that something sank into my brain. Something that never occurred to me before—that is, people were starting to believe you. Understanding the definition of the big lie, which says, "If you tell a lie that's big enough and you tell that lie long enough, the public will accept it as fact no matter how big a pile of crap what you're saying actually is." Randy, the idea of you as a hard-core legend is one big pile of crap! Take a look, because this is not just spit anymore. Because I have come to realize that when you spit on my face, you spit on my name, you spit on my legacy, you spit on the very business that I love and I cannot . . . cannot [Mick punches his own face] accept that, you under-stand. I worked too hard and I suffered too long to have my reputation torn up by you. You little bastard! I've seen my ear thrown away in Munich, Germany! I've seen my skin hanging off the barbed wires in Japan! And I've been bludgeoned in Nigeria! [Blood starts streaming from Mick's eyebrow.] Now I no longer have to wonder whether I have a place in my heart where darkness dwells, because I'm already there! I'm already there, and I don't have to deny the hatred anymore, and that's why I accepted the hatred that exists in my heart. I will welcome it home as a long-lost friend, saying, "Welcome home, where you been?" because there is a time and a place for hatred, Randy Orton. The place is Hershey, Pennsylvania . . . and the time is now!

I later learned that several top WWE stars had not liked the promo, thinking that it made Randy Orton look weak. Yeah, I know that in the era of the ultra-cool heel who no one actually boos, doing something as heelish as showing fear might seem like the death knell to a career. But come on, guys! Give me a little break here. Sure, maybe it wasn't a promo that was going to sell T-shirts, but I sure as hell do believe that it sold tickets and *WrestleMania* Pay-Per-Views.

And as far as making Randy Orton look weak? I'm not always right on everything, but I think I know a little bit about the human mind, and its capacity for evil and revenge. Randy Orton, once taken out of the comfortable cocoon of self-assured cockiness he had created for himself, would feel an irresistible drive to overcompensate for his perceived shortcomings, causing a violent, uncontrollable reaction toward the revealer of those shortcomings. Thus, what some very good wrestlers saw as weakness, I saw as potential for character growth. Of course, you'd have to ask Randy Orton himself whether or not being involved with me was a good idea.

Marcos

Following the promo in Hershey, I was awash in compliments, from both fans and fellow wrestlers. Indeed, there has never been a time when I was part of so much emotion following a show. Yet I knew very little, if any, of the response had to do with my promo with Randy Orton. For something far more special had taken place inside that arena.

A few weeks earlier, I was contacted by the Marty Lyons Foundation concerning a boy, Marcos Diaz, whose time on earth appeared to be drawing to a close, and whose wish, it seemed, had been to be a part of WWE. I have a photo of Marcos on a bookshelf, revealing him to be a handsome, well-muscled teenager. At one time, he dreamed of being a WWE wrestler. But cancer, and the countless operations that accompanied it, had stolen those dreams, and now, with only a short time to live, Marcos's dreams had unfortunately been altered. He wanted, more than anything, just to be a part of WWE. In some way. In any way.

I rode with Marcos to the show in Hershey, where he was treated like a king by all who crossed his path, from Ric Flair to Stone Cold to RVD to Vince McMahon. I wheeled him down the entrance ramp to ringside, and Marcos just stared, eyes wide open, at the WWE ring; the very space he had yearned to enter for so long. But Marcos was so frail, so devastated by the long battle with his disease, that his goal would never be realized.

It was Richie Posner, the "magic man," the man responsible for everything from painting Mankind's old referee shirts to formulating Mae Young's prosthetic sagging boobs, who suggested bringing Marcos into the ring. Without hesitation, Dave Batista picked the young man up in his massive arms and handed him to Randy Orton, who was waiting to help Marcos into the ring. A little earlier, Bruce Prichard, a longtime WWE fixture best known from his days as Brother Love, had given Marcos an official WWE replica belt as a gift from the company. Marcos took a couple of labored steps inside that ring and then held the belt aloft, closing his eyes, savoring the sound of cheers he must have known he'd never live to hear.

Except he did live to hear those cheers. I made sure of it. So did Chris Benoit. So did Bill Goldberg. So did Stone Cold Steve Austin. For after *Raw* ended, with traces of Orton's loogie and a tiny trail of my own blood still on my face, I announced to the Hershey crowd that I had a special friend in the audience, who unfortunately didn't know what it was like to hear thousands of people chant his name. But with our help, he would. With Benoit's help. With Goldberg's help. With Austin's help. With the help of the thousands of fans in Hershey that night, we accomplished something special. We made one of Marcos Diaz's last nights on earth one of his best.

A few days later, I asked Vince if I could address the entire *Raw* roster— the first time I'd ever done so. Vince, for all his faults (which I've been kind enough to discuss in detail), has always had a heartfelt belief that what we do on our TV shows actually matters in the most important of ways; we entertain people, we take their minds off their problems. He has often said that short of curing diseases, the most important role in life is to make people happy through the gift of entertainment. Until that day, I'm not sure I ever really agreed with that.

"Mick Foley has asked for the opportunity to speak to you," Vince said. "You know, so many times we travel from town to town, doing what we do, that we forget about the difference we sometimes make while we're there. I think Mick would like to remind you of one of those times."

I just started shaking. I'd addressed so many crowds, so many times, often without hesitation or concern, but this situation was so different. I was addressing my peers. About a kid I'd grown to care so much about in such a short time. A kid I'd eulogized at a funeral service just hours earlier. A kid I'd seen laid to rest, buried in the clothes we'd given him. A Stone Cold shirt, a Socko cap, the championship belt.

I know that during the course of this book, I have sometimes seemed like an outspoken critic of things I see wrong with WWE. But on this particular afternoon, at Penn State University, I just wanted to thank all of the guys for all their acts of kindness. Every single person in that room had gone out of their way to make that kid's day a special one. Every single person. And I appreciated it. And every one of them had made me so damn proud to be part of the business.

I concluded by telling the whole group that I hoped they would feel like they could come up to me at any time and ask me about ways they could help out. Unfortunately, I didn't actually know of any ways to help out.

I don't know Dave Batista that well. To this day, I'm not sure I've had a conversation with him that's lasted more than five minutes. But I'll never forget that he was the first person to come up to me, his eyes filled with tears, and say, "How can I help?" No, I don't know Dave that well. But I will always respect him, and I will always be grateful to him for fulfilling the last wish of a dying young man.

Comeback

 How would I feel about The Rock being part of the *WrestleMania* · match? About making it a Tag Team match?

To tell the truth, I was a little confused. "I'm fine with it," I told Brian Gewirtz, the placer of the phone call. "But I read that Rock only wanted to come back if it was a really big deal."

"He thinks this *is* a big deal," Gewirtz said.

"Really?" I liked The Rock, had done great business with him in '98 and '99, and had long gotten over whatever problems we may have had during our working relationship. But I honestly wouldn't have guessed that The Rock considered anything involving me to be a big deal. I was flattered.

"Yeah," Gewirtz said. "We wanted to make it a handicap tag. You and

Rock against Evolution—Orton, Batista, and Flair. Do you have any problems working with Ric?"

"No," I said. "I'd be glad to have him in the match." Hey, until Ric's book was published, I actually liked the guy, and considered it an honor to have him involved in our deal.

So, for the next few weeks, we set about creating an urgent need for The Rock's return. And what better way to necessitate his return than to beat the living crap out of the hardcore legend on multiple occasions, including a battering in Bakersfield, California, on February 16, 2004, that has to go down as one of the most brutal in sports entertainment history?

The WWE seems to be constantly going through phases, be it the "serious" phase, the "real people don't play kazoos" phase, the "hot lesbian action" phase, or the "necrophilia equals ratings" phase. On February 16, we were in a short-lived "wrestling" phase, where no damage could be caused by or attributed to an outside object, such as a sledgehammer, barbed-wire bat, or even a set of ringside stairs. Blood was also not an option. So I wondered how, exactly, to make a three-on-one beatdown seem brutal enough to inspire a Hollywood movie star to play the role of my knight in shining armor, riding in for an "Emotional Rescue," which for you trivia buffs is the name of a dreadful Rolling Stones song—probably the worst one they ever recorded.

I called Randy Orton over right before we went out.

"You know, Randy, sometimes in this business we make our own breaks." Randy looked at me, eyes wide open. Despite the grumblings of those stars who thought I'd made him look weak in Hershey, Randy trusted me implicitly. "I want you to catch me with a couple of punches right here," I said, pointing to the outer part of my left eyebrow. "Try to split it open. If you get any heat from the office, just tell them that I called it in the ring, okay?"

"Okay, Mick."

And with that I was off. Off to catch eight punches in the left temple. Off to feel consciousness leave my body like a Garden crowd streaming toward the popcorn stand during a Test match. Off to drive to LAX with the left side of my skull swollen like the Elephant Man, making only a brief pit stop to puke all over the interstate. Despite the throbbing in my skull, my biggest pain of the night came from realizing that Randy Orton had never bothered to check on me following the Bakersfield beatdown. I have always gotten along very well with him, and I always appreciate how willingly he gives me credit for the success he's enjoyed, but unfortunately, the first vision I have when I think of Randy is the vision of no Randy at all backstage at Bakersfield.

I was supposed to be off for a couple of weeks following Bakersfield, at which point I would reappear with the other half of the "Rock 'n' Sock Connection," hell-bent for vengeance, and a potentially huge 'Mania payoff. This angle had really been connecting with fans, and it figured to be a major part of what we all felt would be an extremely successful WrestleMania.

Four days after Bakersfield, however, I gave Vince a phone call. "Listen, Vince, I know we talked about keeping me off for a few weeks, but I think you really need to get me on camera. My eye is a mess."

Indeed, it was. Despite the fact that the botched hardway attempt had not yielded a single drop of external blood, the internal bleeding had been severe, leaving my face a work of abstract art: splashes of purple, greens, and black, with a dash of red thrown in the eyeball for good measure. Kind of like a Jackson Pollock rendition of Rocky Balboa.

I drove the ninety minutes to Stanford, cut a short in-studio interview with Coach—Jonathan Coachman—and drove on home, not completely thrilled with the interview, but relieved that we had captured the eye in all its swollen beauty.

Vince, however, was a good deal less than completely thrilled with the interview. In fact, he wasn't thrilled at all. Deeming it "the worst work of his career"—meaning mine, not Coachman's (which would really be saying something)—Vince demanded an immediate reshoot, this time with J.R. manning the microphone. Dutifully, I climbed back into the road-worn Impala and put a slightly better threat down on video, warning Orton and his Evolution cohorts that I wasn't coming into Atlanta alone.

The Return of The Rock was one of my finest moments. Sure, it was *his* pop, technically speaking, but I savored it as if it was my own, for I had worked so very hard to set the table from which he dined. And what a meal it was: know-your-own rolls, a pint of shut-up juice, and a special helping of The Rock's favorite pie for dessert.

Speaking of "pie," that most thinly veiled of sexual euphemisms in the WWE repertoire, the following week in Bridgeport, Connecticut, on March 8, the word *pie* was responsible for one of the great unintentionally hilarious moments in WWE history.

As you know, I'm not a big fan of rehearsing segments for television. I'm

very much a believer in improvisation and the resulting magic it sometimes provides. In Bridgeport, however, The Rock was hosting a "This Is Your Life, Mick Foley" segment—an ode to a similar segment I had hosted for him in 1999, which has gone down in lore as an all-time great wrestling moment. That segment was slotted for twelve minutes—it went twenty-six. The 2004 version was set to end the show. It had to go home exactly on time. Plus the segment included a cast of thousands (actually eight), with specific time cues for each, so in this case, I grudgingly accepted the need for rehearsal.

The Rock's first guest for me was Mrs. Snyder (no relation to Dee), the kindly old neighbor who used to willingly serve her pie to all the neighborhood kids. Cue The Rock's abject look of horror and the requisite double entendres that made Jack Tripper's old *Three's Company* look almost Shakespearean by comparison. Take this gem from Mrs. Snyder, in regard to The Rock inquiring as to whether she still served pie to the neighborhood kids. "Well, I don't leave my front window open for pie, but I do leave my back door open for strudel."

Jimmy Snuka was next to emerge. "The Superfly" was one of my idols when I was growing up, and it's doubtful I would have dared enter the wild world of pro wrestling had I not journeyed to Madison Square Garden in the fall of '83 to see Snuka sail majestically off a steel cage onto the prone body of Don Muraco, seventy-five feet below. Or was it fifteen? Or was it eight? Who can tell when nostalgia and myth mix with facts and videotape so many years down the road?

The Superfly was supposed to acknowledge the fact that he occasionally enjoyed a piece of pie, yielding yet another horrific Rock reaction shot, pondering the image of "The Superfly" and Mrs. Snyder entwined in the timeless embrace of carnal desire.

The Superfly, however, must have gotten his bakery preferences confused, a result, I guess, of too many chair shots, too many high-altitude landings, or the rumors of a prolific past of partying—legendary even by wrestling standards. For when Snuka entered the ring, grabbed the mike, and began his declaration of culinary affection, this is what came out. I understand that many of you out there in literary wonderland (to borrow a phrase from Snuka, who used to refer to the viewing audience as "TV wonderland") are familiar with Jimmy's unique vocal stylings. For those of you who are not, the best I can do is combine a young Marlon Brando with Brenda Vaccaro on a particularly bad voice day.

"Let me tell you something, Brother Rock, Brother Mick. The Superfly LOVES . . . cake."

I actually had my own request for "This Is Your Life." I pitched this to Vince and thought it was a sure winner, only to see it rejected like one of my feeble high school/college/mid-twenties romantic overtures.

Here's the pitch. Ready yourself for tenses that shift from past to present for no apparent reason. The Rock says, "Our next guest, Mick, is a former Tag Team partner of yours. A man you went on to have legendary matches with."

"I think he's talking about the great Terry Funk," J.R. interjects.

But before any further announcement can be made, piano music of the mid-fifties Jerry Lee Lewis type drifts forth from the sound system, heralding the arrival of "Cowboy" Bob Orton Jr., Randy's father. Throughout his career, Bob was known as a consummate technician, a great heel, and the source of a subtle in-ring sense of humor that was often lost on the masses. There he is, a good six months before his actual return; same greasy leather hat, same greasy leather vest, same cast from an injury that never seemed to heal. Sometimes I think "Cowboy" Bob and Iron Mike Sharpe are in a contest to see who can work their injury the longest. No one, however, can compare to Mike Sharpe when it comes to length of showers taken (several hours), number of plastic Baggies within a plastic Baggie protecting a bottle of baby oil (up to twenty), or any other number of curious phenomena that have made Mike Sharpe stories a locker-room staple for over two decades.

Anyway, Bob's arrival would amuse me, but confuse me as well, prompting me to ask just what he was doing in the ring on my big night.

Once again, I'm sure many of you reading this are keenly aware of the unique (far different from those of Snuka, but unique in their own way) vocal stylings of "Cowboy" Bob Orton Jr. For the uninitiated, think Bob Dylan dueting with Tom Waits on a Kris Kristofferson song, while hung over and gargling with razor blades. Bob's voice, you see, is a little gravelly.

"Hold on a second there, Cactus," Bob would say, paying tribute to my old Cactus Jack days. "Is that any way to greet your greatest tag team partner?"

"Greatest partner?" I would say, laughing. "Sure, Bob, we tagged up a bunch of times, but as a team, we really weren't all that good."

"But, Cactus," Bob would plead. "What about Aruba? Don't you remember Aruba? You conceived your first child on the deck of the Holiday Inn in the room right next to mine. Did you know that I brought Randy on that trip, back when he was thirteen years old? That's right. As a matter of fact, Randy's first sexual experience was pleasuring himself at the Holiday Inn to the sounds of your old lady."

Obviously, I would take great offense to that, and would confront Bob immediately, intent on defending my wife's honor. Even if we really did conceive our first child on the deck of that Holiday Inn in Aruba.

"Hold on. Hold on," Bob would say. "Before you get all upset, let me take you on a little stroll down memory lane."

The WWE fans in Bridgeport would then have been treated to the worst video production values in the history of sports entertainment. Tacky, wimpy music. And one old snapshot of me and Bob, doing a variety of early eighties home video moves: the swirl, the twist, the starburst. Just when you thought it couldn't have gotten any worse—you got it—it would. Because gravelly-voiced Bob Orton would start singing "Memories"—the Barbra Streisand song. It wouldn't even matter if he knew the words. Let him butcher them. The worse, the better. As in, "Memories, of a misty moonlight run. Memories of all our groovy teaming fun."

It would have been hideous. It would have been great. It would have caused both me and Rock to laugh, letting our defenses down, allowing Evolution to sneak in and do the damage they were supposed to do anyway. Better yet, it would have given a perfect reason for Snuka to be in our corner, and for "Cowboy" Bob to be in theirs, bookending the original *WrestleMania*, when Snuka was in the corner of Hulk Hogan and Mr. T and Orton was in the corner of Roddy Piper and Paul Orndorff.

Alas, it was not to be, for reasons that were never made quite clear to me.

Back to *WrestleMania*, and my match that had held so much promise. Promise that, unfortunately didn't quite materialize. We didn't exactly stink out the place, but we didn't tear it down, either. We had a good match. But a good match was not what I was hoping for. Not after four years away. Not after so much buildup, so much thought, so many hours spent visualizing the great things to come.

What was most disappointing to me was realizing that I'd settled for "good enough." I heard the Evolution music and specifically remembered hoping I didn't suck when I got out there. That was it. Not exactly reaching for the stars, huh? It would be like Michael Jordan taking the last shot in game seven, hoping just to hit the rim. Like Albert Pujols stepping to the plate, bases full of Cardinals, his team down by three, hoping just to foul a couple off. Like doing a scene with Christy Canyon, in her spirited late eighties heyday, hoping for a peck on the cheek. I'd been guilty of setting my sights too low. I'd pitched this idea with adrenaline in my veins and stars in my eyes, then fell victim to my own nerves and the blinding glow of the Garden's bright lights.

I had five weeks to atone for this sin of complacency. *Backlash*. One-on-one with Randy Orton. Hardcore rules. A second chance to make a lasting impression.

It was a conference call with Vince and Gewirtz, while sitting in a car at Dewey's Little League practice, that got my mind working for Houston. My gut was churning, the result of one of those protein drinks I'd been subsisting on since *Mania*. I'd weighed in at just under 290 for *Mania*, the lightest I'd been since 1996, and a good 40 pounds lighter than I'd been for the past few years. But I wanted more. I trained harder. I dieted stricter. I'd been 280 for most of 1995 and 1996, a time when I had done much of my best work, in ECW, Japan, and WWE. I'd been 280 when I worked with Shawn Michaels in Philadelphia in September of '96, which still stands out as my best personal performance, if not match, largely because I was in shape and could keep pace with a lighter, better athlete for close to thirty minutes.

Vince wanted to talk about the April 5 *Raw* in Houston. I had requested promo time in front of the live crowd, but Vince had other ideas.

"I want to have you in a rocking chair, Mick," he said. "Rocking back and forth. In a room by yourself. No fans. Holding a box that we think will be flowers, but which will turn out to be your barbed-wire bat. I don't want to know what you're going to say. I want you to surprise us. Just say it from your heart."

So I did. I sat there alone (except for the camera, lighting, and sound crews) in that room, rocking back and forth, holding a box, speaking from my heart, letting loose on one of my favorite personal interviews.

Foley is backstage, sitting in a rocking chair, holding a tulip and a flower box with a ribbon on it.

MICK FOLEY: It's been said many times that you never . . . never forget your first. Call me sentimental, but I . . . but I think that's true. Because, in my life there have been many . . . dozens. Maybe hundreds. But I've never quite forgotten my very first one. There were times on the road where I'd pick up a couple a week. Use them for a couple of days and then . . . hand them off to a lucky fan. But I've never forgotten my first. My first flannel shirt. Given to me the Christmas of 1977. Three sizes too large. And not worn, in the last ten years, until just a few days ago I went to a box of my favorite things and gleefully withdrew it, intending to wear it in my match at *Backlash,* in Edmonton. It may sound funny, for a guy whose name is synonymous with hardcore wrestling to become so fond of, even in love with, an inanimate object. But I've always found the word *hardcore* really had nothing to do with chairs. It had nothing, to do really, with tables, garbage cans, cookie sheets. The term *hardcore* signified that I had an attitude that meant I was going to go above and beyond what it took to give the fans the greatest show possible. It was a word that said I loved the business, and I loved the fans enough to put my body through unimaginable pain. And even when I had the chance to go to Japan and take part in some barbaric matches, I did it with love on my mind. After all, in 1994, I had a one-year-old baby girl. I had a three-year-old boy. I had a mortgage to pay, and I did what I had to do to pay the bills. So even though some of the matches I took part in may have been described as inhumane, deep down in my heart I rested with the comfort and knowledge that I was doing it for love. And I swore I'd never go back. I swore I'd never watch those matches again. Never watch what I put those poor Japanese people through. But, in trying to recapture the fire and the passion that I thought I lacked at *WrestleMania,* I went back and I looked at the tapes. And I did barbaric things. I did inhumane things, but it wasn't the moves. It wasn't the barbed wire. It wasn't the tacks that caught my eye. It was my eyes! Over and over I'd watch the tapes. Rewind, play, rewind, play. And it was there. It was a look in my eyes that said deep down, maybe there was a little part of me that didn't mind inflicting that type of damage. Deep down, maybe there was a little part of me that even liked it. Deep down, I heard the screams. The suffering! The agony! Maybe, maybe deep down . . . I even loved it. Randy Orton, these were honorable men. Nice men. They never spit in my face. They never conducted a calculated campaign calling me a coward. They never took cheap-shot, triple-team efforts to send me to the hospital. But the fact is, when I had the chance, I wrapped my arm in barbed wire and I tore them apart! So, if I were you, I'd be asking myself a simple question, and that question would be, "What the hell is this man going to do to me at *Backlash*, knowing full well he hates my guts?" The answer, Randy Orton, is simple. I AM GOING TO KICK YOUR ASS ALL OVER ED . . . No. No, I'm not going to kick your ass all over Edmonton. Because I hear that all the time, it's become a cliché. *[Sarcastically.]* "I'm going to kick your ass, man! I'm going to kick your ass!" I'm not going to kick your ass in Edmonton, Randy. I'm going to be a little more descriptive than that. In order to be descriptive, well, I'm going to have to introduce you to another old friend of mine. Another friend that I saw in my box of favorite things, Randy Orton. *[Pulls barbed-wire bat out of box.]* Say hello to my friend . . . Barbie. And Barbie's not going to kick your ass. Barbie is going to get sunk into your skull, AND I AM GOING TO CARVE CAVERNS OF GORE INTO YOUR VIRGIN FLESH! I am going to . . . I'm going to bring on the type of bleeding usually reserved for special effects teams in Mel Gibson biblical efforts. Randy Orton, I am going to tear you apart. I am going to take Barbie, and I'm going to . . . TEE OFF! *[Hits table on floor.]* I am going to take Barbie and . . . *[Hits lighting fixture.]* I am going to take Barbie and I'm going to teach you what it means to be hardcore! *[Hits rocking chair.]* I am going to rip! I am going to tear . . . I am going to gorge! I am going to possibly dis-embowel! And I am going to . . . love it.

Backlash against Randy Orton—
this may have been my favorite
all-time match.

Unfortunately, little Mickey got sick a few days later, a victim of the rotavirus, which he suffered, we're pretty sure, after a run-in with some unknown child's fecal matter at a fast-food ball pit. The virus worked its way through part of the family, putting Mickey in the hospital for two days before catching on in my system for a couple of bedridden days—including an absolutely miserable Easter on the day before the April 12 *Raw* in Chicago—before doing its worst damage on poor Hughie, only a year old at the time.

Little Mick had just been hospitalized when I headed out to Edmonton for *Backlash*, a confused study in emotional contrasts. I wanted so badly to right my *WrestleMania* wrongdoing, but I felt so damn guilty about even caring about the match.

But I really did care about the match. And I think it showed. For Randy Orton and I had a classic hardcore battle that night. Wild, intense, bloody, and very well interpreted by both parties. Randy still claims it was the best match of his career, which is a tremendous compliment, considering some of the great ones he's been involved in over the last few years. It may have been my best match as well. But as is usually the case with these type of things, there was a hell of a price to pay for *Backlash*.

I had over seventy-five cuts on my body, mostly the arms and fingers, courtesy of a board laced with generous amounts of barbed wire. Hey, at least there weren't explosives in there, like in my old IWA King of the Deathmatch days in Japan. My knee gave out a couple of days later, resulting in a July surgery. And as I pulled into a Tim Horton's doughnut shop, intent on celebrating my hard-fought match with a glorious jelly-filled delicacy, I was immediately reminded of the consequences of human skull meeting steel. Yeah, I puked in the parking lot. But I still got that doughnut, then headed off to the airport, for the red-eye to Toronto—where a delay in international baggage handling screwed up my connection, tacking an extra three hours onto my travel time—before finally arriving landing in New York, where I immediately drove to the hospital, giving Colette some relief from her tour of duty as hospital mom.

Oddly, sadly, or ironically—depending on how you look at it—I have written this entire "Comeback" chapter while sitting at Hughie's hospital bedside, where he has once again contracted an intestinal virus. The poor little guy. He'll be okay, but it's a terrible feeling for a parent: watching someone you love lying helpless, monitors clicking, tubes hissing, the sounds of children laughing, crying, or silently dying just down the hall.

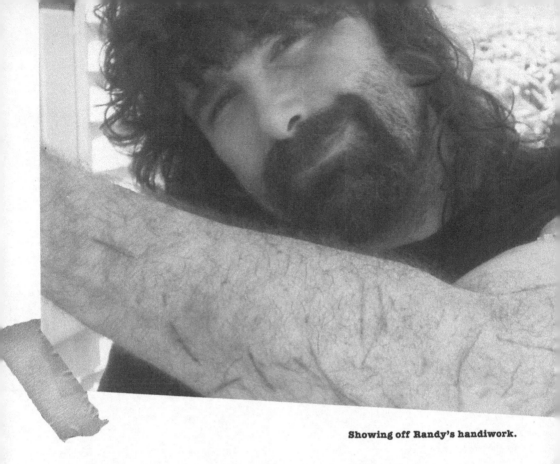

Showing off Randy's handiwork.

I never really got to enjoy *Backlash*. Between the hospitalized children, the postconcussion vomiting, the red-eye flight, and the postmatch knee problems, I just didn't have time to reflect on how special it had been.

Rumor had it that the match wasn't particularly popular with a few big stars in the WWE locker room—pretty much the same guys who didn't care for the Hershey promo. Funny, I don't seem to remember them having too many problems with the way I did things back when it was benefiting them.

Dear Hardcore Diary,

A fire was officially lit today. A fire under my ass, that is. Today, during a midafternoon phone call with head *Raw* writer Brian Gewirtz, I was informed that the Tag Team match at *One Night Stand* was being turned into an eight-man match. Why? Apparently because Terry Funk had some trouble getting down to the ring on Monday night, including a near fall on the ramp, leading to speculation that he might not be physically up to a big main event. So, instead of taking a chance that one of the greatest performers of all time would be able to defy Father Time and Mother Nature for a night, a decision was reached to sabotage all the hard work, emotion, and planning that had gone into making the angle, in exchange for four more bodies.

At first, I was tentative with my response, saying something along the lines of, "I don't really think it makes sense." Fortunately, I must have hit a dead cell-phone spot and the call was lost, allowing me to throw the new idea quickly at my manager Barry Bloom. Barry's been around the wrestling business a long time. I first met him in 1992, when he was Jesse Ventura's manager in WCW. Jesse was the first pro wrestler with official representation, a fact that was looked upon with scorn by wrestling's old-school establishment, which saw the idea of official representation as unwanted and unnecessary. In other words, everything would be better if the talent was not aware of their options or real worth to a company. Even WWE was slow to embrace the idea. Hell, I remember when we were told it was a good life experience to negotiate our own contract, prompting a classic retort from former WWE performer Don Callis—who was more or less shunned in WWE dressing rooms for having the audacity to be introverted—when he said, "I guess it would be a good life experience to perform brain surgery on ourselves, too."

Eventually, sports entertainment climbed out of the contractual dark ages, even yielding guaranteed WWE contracts for the first time in 1996. Sure, I came in about a week before those contracts started being offered, but by the summer of 1997, I too had a new guaranteed contract, even if I negotiated it myself. I guess I ended up doing pretty well for myself, but having Bloom's expertise helped immensely, since I hooked up with him on nonwrestling projects in 1999 and have continued to do so with my new contractual wrestling issues since returning to the ring on a sporadic basis in 2004.

Barry didn't care for the new eight-man idea. As I alluded to earlier, there is a time to concede certain points in order to protect what is really important—a time to lose a battle in order to win the big war. In this case, losing this battle would mean losing the war. I needed to win this battle, and I decided to start on the offensive with a few precise, direct words as my initial assault.

"I think the idea is awful," I said. "I think it ruins the whole angle." I decided to go back to the initial pitch meeting for emphasis. "If I had pitched my idea in Stamford, and you guys suggested an eight-man instead, I would have said 'No, thanks.' And walked away."

"I know," Brian said. Hey, I know in this case Gewirtz was just the messenger, but the message was so freaking lousy that in this case, he deserved to be shot.

"Brian, at this point, the angle doesn't even resemble what I suggested. Tell Vince his idea sucks."

"It's just that—" Brian said.

"It's just what?"

"Well, Vince is concerned that Terry—"

"That Terry what? Won't be able to work a good match? Why, because he nearly tripped?"

"Well, kind of."

It was time for me to go into full Funker defense mode. It wasn't enough that we'd proved the naysayers wrong in Lubbock, with one of the most compelling promos of the year. Now, I was going to have to make a case for the greatest wrestler I'd ever seen. Sure, he's sixty and broken down. So is Vince McMahon. But that didn't stop Vince from putting on a hell of a show in one of this past *'Mania*'s main events. He did it by playing to his strengths and avoiding his weaknesses. Just like Terry will. Just like I will. Just like Dreamer will. Fortunately, one guy in our match, Edge, doesn't have any weaknesses.

"Look, I know Terry's knees are bad," I conceded. "They've been bad for twenty years. They were bad when we used to tear down the house in Japan, eleven years ago. His back is bad, too. It was bad in '89 when he was working with Flair, and had a cracked sacrum. He'd have to get out of his seat after takeoff and get on his knees, leaning over his seat, for the entire flight. And then he'd go out and tear down the house, every night."

"This is good," Brian said. "I can take this to Vince."

"Hell, take this to Vince," I said. "Tell him I saw Terry wrestle less than a year ago at *Hardcore Homecoming*, and he tore the house down there, too. There's going to be a hell of a lot of emotion in that building on June 11. We'll all feed off it. We'll put together a hell of a match."

I'd be lying if I told you I knew how we got to the subject of Ric Flair, but I know I brought him up, possibly as a partial concession to the possibility that having three broken-down wrestlers in a main event might indeed be slightly risky. I know I told Brian of my concern for my left knee, and told him there was a decent possibility I wouldn't be able to walk after *One Night Stand*, let alone have a good singles match with Ric Flair in his hometown of Charlotte, only two weeks later. I did bring up the possibility of making *Vengeance* a six-man Tag Team match.

So though I'm uncertain of how Flair's name came up in regard to *One Night Stand*, I know I did try to mount a decent campaign for why he'd make a hell of an addition. "He's the one non-ECW guy those fans will accept as part of that team. They'll love it. And they'll love the idea that they're getting the first crack at seeing Foley and Flair. And it won't really hurt a potential singles match a couple weeks later—it might even help build it."

"Okay," Brian said. "I'll take it to Vince. I've got a meeting with him in an hour. I'll call you when it's over."

By the time he called back, I was on the road from L.A. to 'Frisco, fifty miles or so into a near-four-hundred-mile trip.

The eight-man, per my request, was history. Flair, however, was not going to be a part of *One Night Stand*. We would apparently start our program from scratch the following day and shoot for a singles match, ligament tear or no ligament tear.

I'm a little worried about this, as despite my history with Ric, I want to be able to do my part to have a good match in his hometown of Charlotte.

I asked Brian if in retrospect they'd have had Ric lose in two minutes in the last *Raw* Pay-Per-View, if they knew they'd be counting on him to have a big match at *Vengeance*.

"Probably not," Brian said.

Listen, I know booking *Raw* and *SmackDown!*—four hours of prime-time programming a week—is no easy task. And I don't meant to be hard on Brian Gewirtz, because I think he does a tremendous job in a very high-pressure, often thankless job. And I understand that Umaga, the wrestler who defeated Ric at that last Pay-Per-View, needed a big win. But not to realize that Ric Flair, one of the greatest wrestlers of all time, might be playing a big role on a big show in Charlotte, where he's practically royalty, is a stunning lack of foresight.

As a footnote of some interest, *I* was the guy originally slated to be Umaga's first victim, on his debut, the night after 'Mania. I resisted the idea, on the grounds it would greatly minimize Edge's big hardcore victory at *WrestleMania*. Above and beyond helping draw a buy rate for 'Mania, and having an extremely large check (I hope) sent to my house a couple months later, the match with Edge was supposed to help keep him at main-event status. I thought my being crushed the next night by an unknown entity would greatly minimize Edge's accomplishment.

"Well, I disagree," I was told by "Freebird" Michael Hayes, one of the business's best minds, but who in this case was someone I couldn't agree with.

"Listen, Michael, after my match with Randy Orton, he bragged for over a year about beating me."

"That's true," Hayes said.

"After Triple H beat me, he bragged about it for four years. I mean, he was still talking about retiring me even after I was no longer retired."

"True, again," Hayes said.

"Both of those guys got a lot of mileage out of those wins, which is great—that's what those wins are for, to get mileage out of. Now, tell me how much mileage they would have gotten if the night after either of the matches, a new guy squashed me in thirty seconds?"

"I see your point," Michael admitted.

"Besides," I said. "I may have an idea for the ECW show."

. . .

So Ric got squashed instead of me. And now we have to figure out how to unsquash him in two weeks, so he can wrestle a guy with one leg. Still, it can be done, and it might even be done well, provided someone decides to let Ric Flair talk. It seems Ric has gotten hit with the label of giving "eighties 'rasslin' promos," which despite having drawn money all over the world, simply won't do in the era of the homogenized, scripted interview, circa 2005. Wooooo!

Back to *One Night Stand*. No eight-man, no Flair, but Vince does want a change. He wants Lita on our team, and Tommy Dreamer's wife Beulah (thankfully, not her real name) on theirs, to make it a mixed-gender six-person match. I think it will work. Even if I concede this point to Vince, I consider the battle a victory. But Brian has one more point for me to ponder as I make my way to 'Frisco.

"Vince says it looks like the match is going to be the shits."

I hate to use the *S* word there, but not only is it a direct quote from Gewirtz, who was directly quoting Vince, but the term "the shits" is a popular, almost universal term for describing a match that is thought to be no good. But I didn't actually hear the Gewirtz quote. I thought it was part one of a two-part quote. I thought he said, "*If* it looks like it's going to be the shits." As if Vince was suggesting a mid-match remedy, if indeed the match was in danger of suffering.

So, I said, "Okay, *if* it looks like it's going to be the shits, what? What does he want me to do?"

It took Brian a second to figure out what I meant. Once he did, he was quick to correct me. "No, Vince says, it looks like it *is* going to be the shits."

Pretty straightforward. No real room for interpretations. Vince's cards were on the table.

"Well, tell Vince I disagree," I said. "And I intend to prove it."

Dear Hardcore Diary,

Maybe I won't be proving Vince wrong after all. I barely slept, after finishing up last night's entry around 2:00 A.M., and making the decision to use the hotel health club's elliptical trainer for half an hour before going to bed. It seems it's hard to sleep when your leg is throbbing, and as a result, I woke up somewhere around seven, tired, aching, and barely able to walk.

I was in a situation like this two years ago, when, two days after my *Backlash* match with Randy Orton, I found myself unable to walk, after getting out of a chair in which I had been watching Mickey and Hughie play. Injuries seem to occur that way quite often for guys with a lot of previous wear and tear on their bodies. It's not always a major mistake or tremendous collision that leads to injury, but a minor action at the tail end of a long line of abuse. It was as if my knee was pulling a Popeye, saying, "I stands all I can stands, and I can't stands no more." I know this is the second time that I've quoted the grammatically incorrect sailor man, but it's such a profound, powerful statement that it deserves to be read twice. Besides, this is actually the first time my knee has quoted Popeye. By the way, Raven, the master of psychosexual warfare, does a tremendous Popeye imitation.

11:39 A.M. Sorry. I just ran to the hotel dryer to put my now clean clothes into the dryer. The move may take me out of my writing zone, but my "guys" will be deeply appreciative of the clean undies.

Just yesterday, I was so sure I could pull this thing off. Now I'm not so sure. After all, other than being carried to a really good 'Mania match by Edge, one of the top guys in the

business, I really don't have much in my plus column since the *Backlash* match with Orton.

11:59 A.M. Sorry, I just got off the phone with Brian Gewirtz, and it seems that Paul E. and I are going to go toe-to-toe verbally in two days at *Raw*. The key challenge for me on Monday is to resist the temptations to rip into ECW just for the sake of ripping into it. I'm sure Paul E. and I would both fare very well in a true battle of verbal one-upsmanship, but my feeling is that I should actually lose this battle in a very close contest in order to enhance the interest in the match. It would be easy for me to get a cheap laugh by pointing out that Funk and Dreamer, the two ECW loyalists who never sold out, did in fact wrestle in WWE, and were last seen wearing panty hose (Funk) and drinking water out of a urinal (Dreamer).

But why go there? I want to draw money, not laughs—at least, in this case. So on Monday, I will portray Funk as the greatest and toughest wrestler I ever saw (true), and Dreamer as a guy with as much heart, desire, and talent as any of the WWE legends I battled over the years (a little less true).

I'll make my best points, but I'll make sure Paul E. has better ones lined up.

12:10 P.M. Back to the knee. At least for thirty minutes, when I'll leave for my personal appearance at Lee & Woo's—an optometry office in downtown San Francisco. I know it seems like an odd place for an autograph signing, but they've had WWE appearances there for years, and seem to do just fine with them.

I had X-rays and an MRI done on my left knee in 2004, which revealed a torn meniscus and severe arthritis, but nothing that could explain the intense pain behind the knee or inability to walk.

A few days later, I received a call from Barry Bloom. "How's the knee?" he asked.

"Not too good, Barry."

Terry Funk (right) and Tommy Dreamer.

"Can you walk?"

"Not very well."

"Can you wrestle a match in five days in Japan?"

I thought it was the most ridiculous question I'd ever heard, until Barry gave me a dollar figure for the match. It seemed that Bill Goldberg, for whom Barry had negotiated an incredible per-match deal for the new Hustle promotion in Japan, had injured his hand in training and would be unable to wrestle. The promotion was desperate, and he was willing to give me Bill's money for the match. I stood to make more for that match than for my fourteen previous Japan trips combined.

I said, "I'm not sure I'll be able to walk, but for that type of money, I'll be in the ring in five days."

The match didn't suck, although it won't go down on anyone's list of the all-time mat classics, unless seeing Japanese star Toshiaki Kawada kick the crap out of me for ten minutes is anyone's idea of a good time. Sure, I spent the hours after the match puking in the toilet following a really hard kick to the back of the head, and needed a wheelchair to get through the airport, but I did these two things as a somewhat wealthier man.

I'll admit, I took the match solely for the money, which may make me a whore, but at least for that one night, I was an extremely high-dollar one.

I finally had the operation on July 5, and was able to view the procedure on a television screen as it was happening. Once inside with the scope, the doctor quickly found the source of my suffering—the cadaver tendon that had been used to replace my torn PCL (posterior cruciate ligament) back in 1993 had completely given way. The doctor cleaned the mess up, but said another repair was inadvisable. So, I'm just going without one. This left knee is giving me exactly the same type of pain, which makes me think the left PCL is history, too.

I just wish I knew. My MRI result is in limbo, at least until Monday. Maybe I can get some type of special brace for just such an injury, and get by until after *SummerSlam*. I hate to think I might have to start taking pills, but the pain is so bad that I might not have a choice.

Dear Hardcore Diary,

Tomorrow is *Raw*—the big showdown with Paul E.—and my adrenaline should be flying. But for some reason it's not, as I have been conspicuously absent from Promoland, with the exception of several hours of the L.A. to San Francisco drive, where my attention was actually absorbed by my post-*SummerSlam* promo. Granted, the *SummerSlam* deal should be intense, and I even had tears in my eyes as I went through it in my mind, but I fear the prospect of peaking on it too early and wish my mind would allow me to cut these promos in correct chronological order.

Perhaps I'm hung up on the post-*SummerSlam* promo because my recent knee problems have caused me to question the likelihood of the match taking place. And while it was the incredible creative rush of the ECW show that brought me to the table in Stamford, I'm not blind to the idea that a big *SummerSlam* match with Cena as champion could mean far more to me financially. Besides, no match with Cena means no postmatch angle with Melina, which means I would be forced to live with the guilt of building up hopes and then letting them die.

Melina will be heading to *Raw* soon, along with Johnny Nitro—so no matter what happens, I'm not responsible for any kind of professional breakup, which is always a strain on a real-life couple. I can't get a straight answer on whether the move is any of my doing, but have been told that my random Melina comments will not be so random anymore. I'm pretty sure I'm being left in the cold on this one, so I won't share what I know with Melina, who is apparently on a need-to-know basis in regards to her future.

Though I'm no fortune-teller, I do see big things for her in the future, with or without my *SummerSlam* deal, but it would sure make me feel good to be part of her push.

History was not made last night at the Giants game, where Barry Bonds was looking to hit home run 715, which would have put him at second on the all-time list, ahead of the legendary Babe Ruth—although Bonds did hit a screaming line drive into McCovey Cove, just wide of the foul pole. It was a nice way to relax, though, as I always enjoy catching a game in a different major-league city. I hope to hit the road a few times this summer, just to catch a few games with my two older kids. Mickey has been to a couple of Mets games this year, but as far as he's concerned the Long Island Ducks are the real deal in his life, and the little guy has set some kind of minor-league record for most games attended without actually paying attention to a single thing on the field.

Maybe I can bring Hughie along to a few Ducks games this year, provided his allergy to peanuts doesn't keep him away. Obviously, he can't eat the nuts, but as of a year ago, a stray shell fragment or husk could cause a real problem.

Okay, back to Bonds. I actually met Barry last year while on my *Scooter* book tour, when I stopped by the Giants clubhouse to say hello to second baseman Ray Durham, a big wrestling fan. As it turned out, when I showed up, there were more fans than just Ray, which is usually the case with any sports team. You can usually count on five or six guys who will admit to watching our show, and a couple of others who swear that they don't but just happen to know the Cell match with Undertaker.

I had a good time hanging out with the guys, while being aware of Barry's larger-than-life presence and his own personal space, which seemed to take up a good third of the clubhouse. It was as if he was Adam West, and the rest of the team was Burt Ward. Sure, when "Play ball" was called, they'd do battle together, as if the Mets, Phillies, and Braves were Penguin, Riddler, and Joker, but when that last out was over, there was not a whole lot of camaraderie between Barry as Batman and the entire roster as Robin.

On my way out, I was stopped for a moment by a man who I thought was a coach, but was actually Barry's personal trainer. He liked my Negro League jersey, which I had purchased a couple years earlier at the Negro League Hall of Fame in Kansas City. He asked me a couple of questions, then said, "Hey, show that to Barry. I think that he'll like it."

Except that he didn't tell Barry I was coming to see him. So as I reached the end of my lengthy journey from regular Giants clubhouse into Barry's domain, feeling very much like a frightened young Dorothy about to encounter the great and powerful Wizard of Oz, I saw Barry's right eyeball glaring at me. He hadn't actually turned his head, indeed my lowly status as a hardcore legend didn't merit a movement of Bond's neck. So, I did the best that I could to address his eyeball's concerns.

"Um, your coach said you might like to see my jersey."

Then I turned my back to Barry, while maintaining eye contact, so he could see the embroidered patches of so many teams of Negro League history. Barry's face broke out in a big smile. "I like that," he said. "I've got one from my visit, almost like it, except my jersey's white."

It was time for me to drop a name. "Yeah, I'm doing a book signing at the Hall in a couple of weeks. I thought I invented the idea of doing a signing there, but it turns out Tony La Russa did one there for his book, *Three Nights in August*." La Russa, as respected a name as there is in the game, seemed like a good name to drop. Plus, now Barry knew of my interest in the Negro Leagues, the long-forgotten contribution they made to our game's national pastime.

"Good luck with the book," Barry said, sending forth a subtle message that my allotted time had come to an end, no matter how good a friend of the black man I was. But as I left the clubhouse, I heard Barry's voice. "Hey, Mick," he yelled. I turned to face Bonds, who had his left thumb in the air. "Hell in a Cell!" he said. "Hell in a Cell."

Okay, so I made that last part up.

Dear Hardcore Diary,

I'm sitting in the fourth row ringside, attempting to write a few preliminary thoughts, before a rehearsal for my big showdown with Paul E. I'm more nervous than usual for one of these things, as I don't know whether to go full-tilt during the run-through, as I did with Terry Funk two weeks ago, or just go through the motions, as is usually the case on these things. If I had things my way, there would be no rehearsal at all, as Paul and I will probably be at our best when the situation seems most real. And, no doubt about it, when Paul gets going, speaking from the heart about the promotion he loves so much, it's going to seem very real indeed.

I talked with Paul very briefly when I arrived at the Tacoma Dome. Both of us take Vince's prediction/proclamation of the imminent shitty nature of the match as both a slap in the face and an incredible opportunity to make him eat his words. And man, do I look forward to seeing Vince McMahon with a big mouthful of shit.

I told Paul that I intend to be like a Hall of Fame–caliber pitcher out there, unloading my best fastballs on him. But they'll all be fastballs, no curveballs or other junk, and I have every confidence that Paul E. will handle my best stuff and knock it clean out of the park.

It's a little tough to write with guys working out in the ring, so close to me. The Predator/Sylvester Turkay has just finished making quick work of an aspiring young wrestler, under the watchful eyes of WWE producer Arn Anderson. Turkay is a former All-American collegiate wrestler, having finished second in the NCAA final in 1992, to WWE's own Kurt Angle, before claiming the title a year later. He's bounced around Ohio Valley Wrestling and Japan, and been involved with shoot fighting for the past few years, so it will be interesting to see what the future holds for him in WWE.

9:09 P.M.—Sea-Tac Airport. I don't know quite what to make of today. I'll have to check the replay video to see if I was throwing my best heat, as it seemed to be just a step off. It felt as if I didn't have my best stuff, and Paul simply didn't seem as fired up as he's been in the past. The chemistry may have been tampered with a bit, as instead of feeling like borderline adversaries, we felt like comrades of sorts, each of us tired of our grand visions being tampered with.

I just feel beaten down by the constant tweaking, manipulation, time-limit reminders, and doubts about the ability of my *One Night Stand* opponents, Tommy Dreamer and Terry Funk. Despite his home-run performance in Lubbock, Terry Funk has been put on the end of Vince's bench, and it's doubtful his number will be called until June 11, when he will be expected to fail. Tommy Dreamer might just as well be faceless, for all the attention he's received.

Going back to the Anaheim heel turn, Edge and I had a foolproof method for alerting fans around the world that Tommy was a legitimate force to be reckoned with. Well, not quite foolproof, as our idea was overruled at every opportunity, and as a result, Tommy Dreamer came off as weak, inept, nondescript, and hopelessly naive. For all the confidence the WWE has shown in them, Edge and I might just as well be taking on a couple of first-year trainees. To the casual observer, it seems like we're gearing up to do battle with an old guy with a bum knee and a dumb guy with love handles.

I keep coming back to wondering if, all things considered, I would have still proposed this ECW angle. And the answer I keep coming up with is no. It should have been simple, it should have been fun, but instead, it's been neither. Nonetheless, I'm not writing us off yet; taking a page out of one of my characters in *Scooter,* I may strike out, but I am going to go down swinging.

Speaking of bum knees, I received my MRI results from Doc Rios, our WWE medical expert. I guess the good news is, there's no PCL tear, which shows how knowledgeable my medical opinion is. The bad news is just about everything else is in rough shape. The anterior cruciate ligament (ACL) is partially torn, as is my meniscus. There are some bone spurs growing on some part of my knee, and a large cyst that seems to be the primary suspect involved in the distribution of the intense pain I feel when any type of past-ninety-degree flexion of the knee is involved.

As a result of the pain, I have just taken my first pain pill in many months, a step I had hoped would not be necessary. But the prospect of being jammed into coach on a midnight flight was too much for me to chance, especially in my psychologically sensitive state, so I shoved my pride to the side and had a Vicodin and a beer with dinner. So if the subject matter begins to veer from postpromo depressions to heartfelt desire to save the world, you'll have some inclination that the medication was effective.

It has been said that alcohol or medication brings out a person's real personality. To which comedian Bill Cosby had a succinct and unusually blunt retort: "What if you're an asshole?" With that in mind, it gives me some small sense of pride to know that alcohol or medication rarely makes me dwell on questionable thoughts like sex, violence, or money. Instead, I think of all God's children, and the rough hand so many of them have been dealt—and how I might do my part to make the score between the haves and the have-nots a little closer. Oddly enough, I'm also thinking of calling Christy Canyon, just to let her know how much I enjoyed talking to her on her radio show.

Something must be severely wrong with me. I meet Christy Canyon and think of world peace. I watch Melina's entrance and think of Christmas mornings of my youth. To make matters worse, I'm even thinking of telling Colette to go out shopping, paying no heed to the balance on our credit card. Just how many times have I been hit with chairs over the years?

Melina and Johnny Nitro made their debut on *Raw* tonight. Obviously, I was glad to see her, and continue to be relieved that my idea didn't cause her any pain. I have to question the idea of beating Nitro in such a quick, convincing fashion on his first night on *Raw*. Sure, a good angle can always jump-start a guy with talent, but why dig the guy a hole so quickly?

I hate to look at excelling in WWE as an art of psychological warfare, but I can't help but think that somewhere in the McMahon house there's an old copy of Sun Tzu's *The Art of War* tucked into a bookshelf, along with the complete Mick Foley literary catalog.

. . .

As I get ready to board the flight that will carry me through the night to New York, where I'll arrive jet-lagged, tired, frustrated, and quite probably in a great deal of pain, it is really crossing my mind to just throw in the towel on the whole thing. Realize that I did indeed throw away eight years of goodwill with our fans for a heel turn on a second-rate Pay-Per-View that seems to be dying on the vine, and just flat-out stop caring about the whole thing. Sure, I'll show up at TV and do my part as well as I can, but as far as I'm concerned, they took an idea that was a no-brainer, a sure winner, and derailed it, possibly on purpose.

I really don't give a crap right now about *One Night Stand*, about *Vengeance*, about *SummerSlam*. I'll do them if I'm told to, provided I can walk after *One Night Stand*, a concern I voiced, but which I received absolutely no feedback on. I really tried to make a difference. From now on I'll just sit back and deposit the checks, thinking of how great this whole thing should have been.

Ladies and gentlemen. Promoland is now closed for the season. Due to changes in the business beyond my control, there is no longer any need for it in wrestling. Please check your passion and imagination at the door.

Dear Hardcore Diary,

I can't believe six days have gone by without a diary entry. But I'm aware that my last entry was a downer, and it's not as if I've had an incredible breakthrough to write about. I have come to wonder if this book will even be published, and if so, in what form? I'm not sure if WWE really wants a book on their label that constantly questions their judgment and criticizes their ideas. I'm guessing that quite a few people will voice their concern to Vince, and offer their opinions on where, how, and why certain parts should be cut. Then, ultimately, it will be up to Vince. Hopefully, he'll be in a "freedom of speech" mood that day.

In retrospect, I may have bitten off more than I could chew. Suffice to say, the next time I make a wrestling comeback, I won't simultaneously be writing a book about it and have a major overhaul on my house done. Sure, the floors looked old and dull, but refinishing the floor required removing all our furniture and actually moving the family into a hotel forty minutes away. Which meant an incredible amount of driving—kids to school, feeding pets, checking on house, working out, little kids to preschool, big kids to softball and baseball—and the aggravation that accompanied it.

Maybe it was a blessing, in that it took my mind off my *One Night Stand* troubles. I did receive a phone call from Brian Gewirtz, telling me of the basic plan for Monday, which seemed fine, although I expressed my concern that not nearly enough was being done to make Funk and Dreamer look like stars, threats, or even credible opponents. Without a late buildup, Edge and I face the very real prospect of headlining the lowest-grossing Pay-Per-View in recent WWE history, not to mention the possibility that, in accordance with Vince's prediction, the match will suck.

Even when pitching this idea in Stamford back in April, I left the last two weeks of buildup in WWE's hands, telling the creative team that the promotion for the match should be a snap, considering the very real, very dramatic past I share with both Funk and Dreamer. A past that is right at Vince's fingertips, given the treasure trove of goodies hidden in the ECW video library, which WWE owns. Granted, someone has to dig for that treasure, but incredible video production has always been a WWE hallmark, and I really doubt that the slight inconvenience of time should be allowed to sink an idea that once held so much promise. Hey, maybe I'll volunteer to go up there and help out on the search. I won't go down without a fight, but unless someone steps up to the plate and decides to put the WWE machine behind Funk and Dreamer, this whole thing will sink to the bottom of the WWE crapper faster then Buff vs. Booker in Tacoma, back in 2001.

I told Brian to take a look at the *Rise and Fall of ECW* DVD that shocked the video world by selling an astounding number of copies, almost single-handedly putting ECW back on the map as both a Pay-Per-View entity and possibly a returning full-time promotion.

"Maybe some people question Tommy's ability," I said. "But look at the DVD again. It's basically Paul E., Tazz, and Tommy. Hey, they interviewed me, but I'm barely in it. Tommy's in it because someone made the determination that he was interesting enough to feature in the story. Put a video package together with him. He's got the heart and pride, and our fans will see how much this match means to him. Plus, over the years, in ECW, he was a part of some incredible video moments. Please don't write him off just because a few people decided he doesn't have it."

So it's basically out of my hands. I'll make a last-minute plea to Vince, but it's possible he has his mind made up on this one. After all, he is "the decider." And the sad truth is, "the persuader" just doesn't care as much anymore.

I have actually started questioning my judgment for even suggesting this idea. What was I thinking? That by sheer force of will, I could sculpt a masterpiece in five weeks? While a bunch of other sculptors simultaneously chip away at it, rendering it almost unrecognizable?

I keep thinking that I should have gone with a dream match. A money match. A sure thing. Maybe I'm not quite on the level of a Rock, Austin, or

Hogan, and perhaps there is no singular "dream" match for me, but I'm pretty sure a properly done heel turn could have drawn big money with any number of guys. After all, I hadn't been a bad guy since 1998, an eternity by WWE standards, where the number of turns by top guys gets into double digits on many occasions.

I remember sitting next to Chris Jericho on an airplane a few years ago and passing the time by trying to list all the McMahon and Big Show turns. Kurt Angle must have turned four times in the past year alone. Good guy, bad guy, All-American patriot, troop-hating heel, etc.

Speaking of Kurt, I'm extremely bothered and confused by what exactly he may have been told to do to me last Monday night. I was told he was going to take me down, and let me up, leading to an Angle Slam, which would cause me to roll outside the ring in disgrace, leaving Kurt to stand as the triumphant new face of ECW, which I'm pretty sure constitutes yet another turn.

Except that's not quite what happened. Yes, Kurt took me down. But once I was down, he hammered me with some pretty damn real punches to the head, with a couple of legitimate headbutts thrown in for good measure. Hey, I'm a believer in realism, but come on; as one of the few remaining guys with long hair in the business, it's pretty easy to deliver a decent-looking headbutt without leaving lumps all over my head,

But the stiff stuff didn't bother me too much. After all, I've worked with some of the stiffest, most believable guys in the business, including Vader at his monster heel best, and Austin, when absorbing his comeback punches was no day at the beach. What bothered me more was learning of the possibility that Kurt may have told to take me down continually, without my knowledge—to embarrass me and to show off his wrestling expertise.

I had some serious words with Vince over this matter, which, if true, would have been unprofessional and dangerous, not to mention another nail in the *One Night Stand* coffin.

I said, "Vince, why would you tell Kurt to take me down without telling me, knowing that my knee is hanging on by a thread?"

Vince, however, didn't know my knee was hanging on by a thread. He also didn't know anything about telling Kurt to take me down continually. Signals, it seemed, had been crossed. Vince had apparently, after the fact, told Kurt that he *should* have taken me down continually, to show his wrestling superiority. According to Vince, Kurt was never told ahead of time to do so without my knowledge.

Is anyone out there skeptical besides me? I'm taking Vince at his word, but nonetheless, I'm going to be a little bit more cautious from this point forward, with Kurt, with Flair, with Vince. It's bad enough that my *ideas* have been screwed with.

From a business standpoint, *One Night Stand* could be the worst decision I have ever made. By throwing away my most valuable commodity—the trust of the fans—I have probably cost myself the huge payoff that a well-promoted dream match could mean. My *One Night Stand* payoff will probably be less than a tenth of that possible payoff, making me quite possibly the world's most naive whore.

I rented a car at LaGuardia and drove on to Baltimore, about 220 miles, in preparation for tomorrow's Walter Reid Army Medical Center visit in Washington, D.C.—the twenty-fifth time I've made such a visit in the last two and a half years. As I noted earlier, Promoland has closed its doors for the season—possibly until my post-ECW angle with Flair—so I went promo-free during the road trip. I did devote some quality time to thinking about the ECW match itself.

While my earlier visions of attaining "wrestling immortality" with this angle have turned out to be preposterous, I am hoping we can put on a hell of a match to prove Vince wrong, to heal my wounded pride, and to give a happy ending to this very frustrating story.

The more I think about a Lita/Beulah finish, the cheaper it seems. I'm all for having the girls mix it up during the course of the match, but making it a mixed tag reeks of desperation and may ultimately leave the fans unsatisfied. Hey, I understand the need for an ECW victory. Beat me! Please. That's what I'm good at. I've won exactly one match this decade, and I don't see any reason to change that.

I just hope that we'll be given the opportunity to improvise in this match. Sure, not knowing what Terry Funk will do is a little dangerous. So what? It also has the potential to be magical. And that potential is really all we have left.

•   •   •   •

I spent most of my time thinking about little Mick. Earlier in the day, the little guy and I had eaten breakfast together. It was actually my first time in that hotel restaurant since my August 2005 meeting with Jeff Jarrett, concerning the possibility of jumping the massive WWE ship and boarding the relatively tiny TNA boat—a jump I came very close to making.

The waitress looked at little Mick, who was making quick work of his French toast. A day earlier, at Adventureland, a misleadingly nice amusement park tucked into a shopping district on a busy thoroughfare on Long Island, I had told Mickey that he was eating his pizza way too quick.

"Mickey, please take only one bite at a time," I had told him. Instead, he was taking four quick bites, which he chewed and swallowed with great speed, eager to dig in for more.

The waitress was kind of marveling at him, as many people do. I know he's my son, but man, he's a handsome little guy. "Where did you get those big blue eyes?" she said. "Did Daddy give them to you?"

"No," I said. "My eyes are hazel."

"How about Mommy?" the waitress asked. "Did she give them to you?"

"No, his mommy has green eyes," I said.

The waitress said something about the miracle of recessive genes, but Mickey wasn't buying that theory. Why? Because he already knew the answer.

"I think God gave me blue eyes," he said. "That's what God does."

On our way out, Mickey grabbed a red apple—a "poison apple," as he called it—and we headed back to the room, where Colette and the kids were finishing off room service. Six people in a room can get a little claustrophobic, so we try to break the group up now and then. I gave the "poison apple" a good washing, then handed it to Mickey, before leaving the bathroom to forage for uneaten pancake scraps.

It was Colette who sensed the trouble. "Where's Mickey?" she said. Without waiting for an answer, she rushed to the bathroom. "Oh, my God," she yelled, her voice stricken with panic. "He's choking."

Mickey's face was red, bordering on purple, when I got to him. Colette was reaching into his mouth with her finger, trying unsuccessfully to fish for the blockage. "Mick, please help me," she said.

I grabbed my son from behind, interlocking my fingers, pushing in firmly and quickly underneath his rib cage. Once, twice, nothing. His eyes were bulging; his beautiful little face was a mask of fear and confusion. I tried to think. What more could I do? I remembered a story, thirty years ago, about my cousin Terry picking a boy upside down and whacking him on the back to dislodge a gum ball. That was to be my next move.

I pushed in one more time—the same Heimlich maneuver we'd practiced in high school health class and in advanced lifesaving at the Ward Melville pool. A piece of apple flew from his mouth and landed atop the blue hotel rug—one of the most beautiful sights I'd ever witnessed.

He coughed, a beautiful sound. He turned to me, his face still red, still scared, still confused. He whaled at me with both tiny fists and, crying, said, "You hurt me. You hurt me!" I dread thinking of his tiny mind, in his most vulnerable moment, wondering why the person he most trusted was trying to do such a thing to him.

A little while later, an hour or so, I guess, he put his little arms around me and kissed me. The little guy is big on hugs and kisses. While Hughie slips into preschool with a simple "Bye, bye," it's not unusual for little Mick to dish out multiple hugs and kisses before letting me depart.

"Daddy?" he said.

"Yes, buddy?"

"I know you were helping me."

"So you're not mad at me for hurting you?"

"No," he said, "I love you."

"I love you too, Mickey."

"But I love Mommy more than you. I love you a little, but I love Mommy a lot."

I kept thinking about those two morning faces—the big blue eyes from God, and the panicked face of fear. I have known so many parents who have lost children, and have always thought I couldn't imagine the pain those lost lives must cause. During those 220 miles, I tried many times to imagine that pain, and my brain would simply stop me from fully exercising my imagination.

Life is just so delicate. And at this moment, I am ashamed to think about how much of it I've wasted recently worrying about something as insignificant as WWE, ECW, and attempts at wrestling immortality.

Good-bye, Vince

"Hello, this is Mick Foley calling. Can I speak to Vince, please?"

This was a phone call I had dreaded making, but one I knew I'd have to make. I simply couldn't leave without saying good-bye.

Vince, I was told, was in a meeting. He would be busy most of the day.

I said, "Could you please tell him that I'm going to TNA?"

TNA stood for Total Nonstop Action, a promotion that had existed solely on Pay-Per-View since 2002, until a national television deal and an influx of new money gave it a considerably higher profile, and a legitimate shot at success. I had been contacted by them sporadically over the years, but had not really been interested, until some recent conversations with company cofounder Jeff Jarett about the new direction of the group sparked an interest.

I went outside to play for a while, an hour or so, with Mickey and Hugh—my two tiny safety valves, guarding me against the pressures of life. When I returned to the house, I was greeted by the flashing red light of the answering machine. Four messages. Two from Vince, two from John Lauranitas, head of talent relations. There were two more messages on my cell phone, both from Vince. He wasn't mad, just concerned, and made it very clear that he considered me a valuable part of WWE. What could be done, he wanted to know, to make things right?

But as far as I was concerned, there was nothing that could be done to make it right. I had made up my mind.

It wasn't about the money. If it *had* been, my decision would have been simple. I would have never even *thought* about leaving. I had met with Vince in June of 2005 and proposed a three-year deal that called for only two matches a year. Obviously, it would have been a good deal for me; a guaranteed weekly check for three full years in return for a very minimal investment in time. But I thought it was a good deal for Vince too, as it would allow him the luxury of either building to a big match with a guy who was a proven commodity, or calling me off his bench as a stopgap measure in the event of some kind of wrestling emergency, such as an injury to a major star at an inopportune time. From the standpoint of a publicly traded company, the deal would also allow WWE to freely promote me as one of their guys for three full years, a situation I was sure they would be more than happy to capitalize on.

The whole meeting lasted less than twenty minutes. It seemed like a no-brainer. But the WWE legal gears can grind awfully slow, and while they did, I did some serious thinking about who I was in the wrestling business, and what my ultimate legacy in it would be.

I had worked on some independent shows, over the past few years, serving in the capacity of the world's most dangerous referee. Sure, it was the same gig over and over—bad guy gets out of line, bad guy gets his just desserts, courtesy of Mr. Socko—but it was fun, paid well, and gave me a chance to meet some of the top new wrestlers in the game. I had also done a number of shows for ROH (Ring of Honor), working under the creative direction of Gabe Sapolsky, who I had known since he was a teenager, when he was helping out in any capacity he could for ECW in the mid-1990s.

I really liked the group, and thought highly of many of its stars, some of whom figured to be a major part of the new TNA. I recommended a few of them, such as Samoa Joe and C. M. Punk, to Vince personally, with varying degrees of success. Punk was picked up on a WWE developmental contract, and may eventually become a big star, if he's able to successfully dodge the minefield of political b.s. that dots the WWE landscape. Joe, despite being the most convincing badass I'd seen in years, wasn't thought to have a WWE look—a knock I'm somewhat familiar with, and one that continues to reek of backward thinking. After all, six-six and ripped only goes so far.

My old buddy Raven had affected my thinking as well, getting inside my head, convincing me that a jump to TNA would be in wrestling's best interest.

"Bro, I'm telling you," he said. "If you made the move and helped this thing work, it would literally dwarf anything else you've accomplished in the business."

So I talked a few times with Jeff Jarrett, and agreed to meet for a double-secret breakfast at the Long Island Hilton in August 2005. I'd known Jeff since 1988, when I got my first full-time break, in his father's company, and despite the fact that I didn't really enjoy my time in the Memphis territory, I had always liked Jeff and considered him to be a quality guy.

It was amazing to see how closely Jeff's vision of my future role in TNA compared to mine: an initial match with Abyss, a talented big man who has taken a page or two out of the old Mick Foley playbook. A couple big matches with Joe, including an angle that would have served as a new textbook example of how to get a guy over. And then a title shot with Jarrett.

I received an offer a few days later. Twice the work and far more pressure for half of the WWE offer—guaranteed for only one year. So essentially I was set to leave Vince McMahon, the man who'd played such a big role in so many of the positive things in my life, for one-sixth of the WWE's guaranteed offer. Wow. How many concussions *have* I had anyway? What was I thinking? Well, actually, I know what I was thinking. I was going to save TNA, and give aspiring wrestlers who don't happen to be six-six and ripped a viable shot at a career. Which begs the repeat of my previous question. Just how many concussions *have* I had?

Sure, it seems ridiculous now, but at the time, I was so focused on my new role in wrestling that I must have seemed like some Jonestown Kool-Aid survivor when I finally did have my talk with Vince.

I'm sure Vince must have been slightly bewildered to learn that my decision wasn't based on money, because in business, it's almost *always* about the money. But I simply had so many things that I wanted to do outside of WWE, including nonwrestling ventures that Vince would almost certainly not grant me the latitude. Vince is a great guy in many ways, but he is not particularly willing to let his wrestlers branch out into other areas of interest while under his business umbrella. I'd learned that lesson the hard way when fighting for my right to party . . . oops, I mean my right to publish my own novel.

Which reminds me of the Beastie Boys CD that Dewey had received for Christmas. I knew the Boys had been on the cutting edge of hip-hop for a long time, but nonetheless, not being a real hip-hop aficionado, I knew exactly one of their tunes—the song about fighting for the right to party. So I decided to impress the kids by singing all the words to the sophomoric tune while on the way to one of Dewey's basketball games. It turns out the only kid I impressed was little Mick, who at the age of five, proceeded to walk around the house for the next few weeks singing, "Living at home is such a drag. And your mom threw away your best porno mag."

Word had apparently gotten around the WWE offices that I'd been looking for a new contract because all of my outside ventures had failed. Which really bothered me, because it wasn't 100 percent true. More like 80 percent true. Sure, my novels had not sold all that well, and I may have been guilty of greatly overestimating my WWE fans' willingness to follow me into non-wrestling-related projects. But I had other deals, such as a syndicated radio show and a television reality show, that fell through simply because my heart wasn't in them. Yeah, I know everyone and his brother has a potential reality show in the works, but this was a legitimate deal, brought to me by Buena Vista Productions, a reputable part of the Walt Disney Company, created by Walt Disney himself as the distribution arm of the motion picture part of his vast business empire. In the end, I just wouldn't have felt right about putting my kids on weekly television before they were at an age to really appreciate the consequences of such a deal.

Reality TV has been great for a guy like Hulk Hogan, but his kids are at an age where they can make mature decisions about being in the public eye. I definitely could see the potential upside to being part of a successful franchise, but in my opinion, the price to pay would simply have been too steep.

Fortunately, my daughter Noelle thinks I'm really cool, because I regularly get to turn down offers from *The Surreal Life, Celebrity Fit Club,* and other offbeat offerings from the world of reality television.

Still, being labeled a failure by forces within WWE really bothered me, and I felt that signing with Vince would be tantamount to an admission of failure on my part.

Besides, there were some other things that had been bothering me for a while, so I took what I thought was my final opportunity to get them off my chest. One of them dealt with John Layfield's overly aggressive treatment of the Blue Meanie on the last ECW show, June 12, 2005.

"Vince, how could you allow something like that to happen on your Pay-Per-View?"

"Well, Mick, according to John, the Meanie went after him, and—"

"Come on, Vince," I said disgustedly. "The Blue Meanie wouldn't break an eggshell. That episode ruined my entire night, and by not condemning it, you're condoning it."

"Mick, I'm sorry you feel that way, but I assure you, we did not condone that."

"Vince?" Here it was, the question I'd been dying to ask.

"Yes?"

"In the months before Ric's book was published, didn't anyone in the company think it might be a good idea to give me a heads-up, about how negative the book was going to be toward me?"

I think Vince said something about it being an oversight, and taking responsibility for it, but it smelled like curiously strong bullshit from a guy who's usually a straight shooter. Okay, just a few more things to get out, and then I was done.

"Vince, do you know, it just about broke my heart to read that Triple H agreed with Ric. After all the great matches we'd had, after all the money we'd drawn?"

To be fair to Triple H, he did say something about having a lot of respect for me and thinking I was great at what I did, but that I wasn't a great hold-for-hold wrestler. Which is true. Except Ric didn't make the case that I wasn't a great hold-for-hold wrestler. Instead, he made the case that I was pretty much a talentless piece of garbage who had only drawn money due to the creative genius of Vince McMahon, who in the role of modern-day P. T. Barnum waved a magic wand, and presto, created Mankind, a future WWE champion.

"Vince," I continued, "every time I turn around, I'm getting bad-mouthed by one of our guys. I don't get treated like that by the TNA guys. They treat me with respect, like I'm somebody special."

I think Vince correctly interpreted that I wasn't thrilled with WWE, probably figuring that if someone was willing to openly criticize Triple H, they really must never want to work for the company again.

"So, I guess that's it," Vince said.

"I guess so," I said, before thanking Vince for all he had done for me, and reasserting my long-held belief that Vince McMahon should be considered on a level equal to that of United States presidents. Hell, I'll even put him way ahead of our current one.

The door was really closing on that part of my life. I'll admit that I was the guy who made the conscious effort to nudge the door open just a little.

"Vince, it's just that I know you wouldn't be willing to do what it would take to make me stay."

"What would it take?"

So I told him what it would take. A lot of freedom. Freedom to pursue pretty much any outside venture I wanted, without the need for approval from WWE. I had told Jeff Jarrett all along that there was always the chance that Vince would make me an offer I couldn't refuse. In which case I'd have to take it.

I used to travel down life's highway with an old cassette tape of Bob Seger's "Beautiful Loser," and always felt a deep connection to the title song. I'd always felt a deep regret at the song's refrain, which warned, "You just can't have it all."

With the help of Vince McMahon, I was able to prove Bob Seger wrong. I really could have it all. Vince McMahon made me an offer I couldn't refuse, and I simply had to take it.

So did I make the right choice? Yeah, I think so. In a way, I guess I feel the same way about TNA as President Bush feels about Osama bin Laden— I just don't spend that much time thinking about it.

I will always firmly believe that the wrestling business would be better off with two healthy national promotions, for the wrestlers' sake as well as Vince McMahon's. Hey, I remember the glory days of the Monday Night Wars, when everyone was reaping the benefits of healthy competition—the wrestlers, WWE, WCW, the fans. Okay, maybe Eric Bischoff's desire to put WWE out of business went outside the boundaries of healthy competition, but I think you get the point. Besides, there are so many talented wrestlers

How Vince may have looked when I told him I was leaving.

out there who don't seem to have what WWE is looking for. It would be nice if they could make a decent living, too.

I don't feel any guilt for the decision I made, because I was simply not the answer to all of TNA's concerns. I may indeed have been a nice shot in the arm for the company, but long-term success will ultimately depend on many factors that I would not have played a role in. Besides, the jury is still out on whether or not I can put together a string of quality matches. Chances are, I can't. And then, where would I be? Out of luck after a year, wondering why I turned on a guy like Vince McMahon for one-sixth the money—less than 17 cents on the dollar. Wow! Just how many concussions *have* I had?

Yeah, I think I made the right decision. And with TNA's help, I was able to secure concessions from Vince that would have previously been unthinkable. I have my home and security, and get to live like a sailor at sea. But it hasn't come without a price. For I believe it has cost me the friendship of Vince McMahon. I think he still respects me. He probably still likes me. But for all intents and purposes, I'm pretty sure all vestiges of genuine friendship disappeared the day I told Vince I was leaving.

Dear Hardcore Diary,

Sometimes I wonder whatever happened to the old Mick Foley. The thrifty guy. The guy who slept on the cot at the Red Roof when he was WWE Champion. The guy who, in 1990, achieved legendary status by managing a record-low dinner bill of $7.49 at Sabbatino's, one of the finer restaurants in Baltimore. Does that old Mick Foley bear even a passing resemblance to the guy writing this book—the guy who just plunked down $112 for a Hampton Inn?

The old Mick Foley would have made a point to stop by every front desk in town, trying to secure the best deal possible, trying to perform a financial limbo dance under the $80 top figure he'd set up in 1990. Well, maybe adjusted for inflation, $112 isn't all that high, especially considering the relative luxury of a Hampton, as compared to some of the rat holes I have laid me down to sleep in.

I think a turning point of sorts came in 1999, back when I was WWE Champion, in the middle of a week-long title reign. By that point, I was being compensated very handsomely by Uncle Vince, even if Uncle Sam seemed to show up with his hand out every three months, looking to take a major portion of my hard-earned cash.

Despite my handsome compensation package (did I just use "handsome" and "package" in the same sentence?), I just couldn't break my frugal ways, at least until a telling episode outside Indianapolis.

During the course of my travels, I had run into a couple of the area's independent wrestlers on a couple of occasions. So when one of them offered to put me up for the night, I accepted, partially to spare the wrestlers' feelings, and partially to save a little extra money. Actually, I think it was mostly a money thing, I doubt I really gave a crap about his feelings.

Nevertheless, I liked the guy, and his girlfriend was cool, so their rented house in a not-so-great part of town became a biannual stop for me. About the fourth time I stayed over, I couldn't help but notice that visitors were pouring into the house at a fairly rapid pace. Sure, their visits didn't last too long, but man, it seemed like the open invite to meet the hardcore legend was kind of a breach of trust. I mean, inviting a few people was cool, but on this one day, I thought the guy was overdoing it. Beside, these guys were sleazy, even by my standards.

I had to force myself to settle down, get a grip on things, stop being so judgmental. Things were different now. WWE was a ratings phenomenon. I was the WWE champion. These were my fans, the people who made me, and I had to be respectful and appreciative of them, no matter how gross they were. Still, I couldn't help but feel slightly used by the sheer number of visitors, perhaps two dozen throughout the morning.

A few days later, I received a call from my friend. "Look, I'm sorry about all those people coming by the house," he said.

"Look, I understand. I'm the champ now. It's only natural for people to want to meet me."

"Mick, they weren't there to meet you," he said.

"They weren't?" I said, trying to maintain my sense of dignity despite the hurt involved in finding out the sleazy guys weren't fans of mine. "What were they there for then?"

"Um, my girlfriend is a crack dealer."

No, I haven't been back to that house in Indianapolis. I haven't stopped by many people's houses after that particular eye-opening episode. Not unless I know the people really, really well, for a really, really long time.

From time to time, throughout the book, I may have hinted at my disapproval of President Bush, his administration, his policies, and his use of wrestling interviews to shape foreign policy. In 2004 I did go on record, as part of WWE in their "*SmackDown* Your Vote" campaign, as an outspoken critic of the president. I realized my views might alienate some of my fans, but I just don't think I could have lived with myself, if a state like Ohio had been lost by ten votes, knowing that my voice could have made a difference. I dreaded feeling like Oscar Schindler at the end of *Schindler's List,* convinced he could have done more to help.

I even talked Vince into setting up a political debate at the University of Miami, one night before the first real presidential debate at the same institution. Actually, I had suggested a series of debates at a variety of campuses, but Vince, being Vince, decided to do it right, complete with *ABC World News Now* live coverage of the event.

So I debated John Layfield—or JBL, as our fans know him—before the cameras and several hundred enthusiastic students. John is an unabashed Bush supporter, and a powerful public speaker, and came across very well in his comments. Fortunately, my years of near-obsessive political research served me well, as I was able to fend off many of John's conservative contentions, and score with a potpourri of progressive counterpunches and some sensible centrist slams. I even came close to knocking out the former NFL player turned wrestler, turned financial analyst, turned radio talk show host, with a historic LBJ quote, "The richest nation in the world can afford to win the war on poverty." Even a crowd that had been told not to applaud our statements couldn't help but shower the hardcore legend with cheers after that one. Which, come to think of it, may have been my only showering experience of that entire week.

As in life, just about anything in politics can be more easily dissected by using an example from WWE. Hence, my decision to tell the world (or at least *World News Now*) of George W. Bush's "Suck it" presidency. Years ago, during the heyday of WWE's attitude era, it seemed to me that thought-provoking promos had gone the way of the eight-track, record albums, or quality Al Snow matches, replaced instead by the slick catchphrase. Sure, Promoland may have closed its doors for good on May 29, 2006, but the whole place seemed to be on the brink of creative bankruptcy back in '97 and '98. I mean, why try to get people to think when you could get them to yell "Suck it!" instead?

Sports entertainment, it seemed, had passed me by. But I couldn't help but think that a day might come when our fans would need more than "Suck it!" from their sports entertainers; that eventually they would require more from our guys than just a simple sodomatic slogan. Fortunately, that day did indeed arrive, issuing a second chance for guys like me who had been swept to the curb during the catchphrase craze.

President Bush, having learned a thing or two from WWE, knew all about

Sharing a laugh
with JBL at our
political debate.

the power of the catchphrase. Hey, why make valid points that might require the patience and attention of our country when you can continually score with the same old stale catchphrases such as, "Freedom is on the march. We're fighting them over there so we don't have to fight them over here. As they stand up, we'll stand down," and "Bring 'em on"?

These catchphrases, I told the Miami audience, were indicative of a "Suck it presidency." In time, our country would require more of its elected leaders than just a series of catchphrases, but by that time, I feared, it would be too late. He'd already be reelected.

JBL, during his rebuttal, issued the line of the night: "You just said, 'Suck it,' during a presidential debate."

I hadn't hung out with John for a long time, maybe years, before that night. But I will always fondly remember hanging out with him after the debate, both of us feeling like proud Americans who had stood up for our own personal beliefs in respect to the future of our country. And I will always have the utmost respect for Vince for allowing me a forum in which to speak my mind.

I was thirty-four years old when I retired from full-time wrestling. Which is fairly young to have time to stand back, get a good look at the world, and realize it doesn't all revolve around me. Before that, I was simply too busy to pay much attention to the fate of those less fortunate around the world. I mean, who had time for genocide in Rwanda when there was a big show coming up at the ECW arena? How could I be expected to worry about the uninsured in America when my right ear was being thrown into a garbage can in Germany?

So, at an age when most people are dedicating most of their time and energy to work, I was able to travel around the country, do appearances, meet people, ask questions, and truly see how rough much of America has it. Sure, we live in a great country, but it is also a place where millions of working people simply cannot afford to raise a family with the sweat of their brows. The United States used to be a place where hard work was the key to success. Now, it's the key to a door leading down the path to nowhere.

Which is probably the reason Senator John Edwards's campaign involving the story of the "two Americas" resonated so strongly with me. As a fairly well known entertainer, I straddle these two Americas almost every single day. And I realize that the only reason I am able to live in the one America is because so many people in the other America think enough of me to spend their hard-earned money on the books, action figures, wrestling events, and Pay-Per-Views that make it possible. To walk away from them and their problems would simply seem like an act of betrayal. At least, I thought so in 2004. I'm not sure I'll get as involved in 2008.

I have read articles ranging from speculative to scientific on the physical, genetic, or psychological differences between conservatives and liberals, which basically deal with whether political sensibilities are a learned or instilled behavior, or a combination of both. For me, it all comes down to my traumatic raccoon experience. A couple years ago, I was heading out onto the highway, about half an hour into a four-hundred-mile trip. I've always loved the peace and solitude of the open road, especially when accompanied by some good tunes or a few promos to cut in my head during the course of a late-night sojourn. As a matter of fact, it's probably the thing I miss most about life on the road.

I was really looking forward to this particular drive when a raccoon suddenly darted out into the middle of the highway. I swerved to avoid the little masked bandit, but in doing so, hit a second raccoon whose presence had, until that last split second, been unknown to me. It was a direct hit, a sickening thud that left no doubt as to its victim's fate—roadkill for sure. I turned to my right to see the first raccoon scamper off into the safety of the roadside brush. And in that one moment, my entire trip was ruined. No number of quality tunes could assuage the sadness I felt. Not so much for the dead raccoon, for his demise had been quick, relatively painless, and honorable—after all, it had been the hardcore legend who got him. No, my sorrow was reserved for the surviving raccoon, who would be left to wander aimlessly, ransacking suburban garbage cans without the special friend my Chevy Impala had made such an impression on.

Look, there's no way to rationalize this type of reaction. You're either going to care about the sadness of a surviving raccoon or you're not. You're either going to hit that thing, pop in a CD, and continue your drive unaffected, or you're going to do four hundred miles behind the wheel with a heavy heart.

So if that makes me a bleeding heart, I guess I'll wear that badge with pride. In an odd way, it's probably helped me. Because subconsciously I think our WWE fans know I care about that raccoon. And I think it makes them like me.

That political debate must have gone very well. For later that night, I heard a knock on my Miami hotel room door. I checked the clock. One-thirty in the morning. At first I thought of drunk college students and put a pillow over my head, hoping that if I ignored the noise, it would somehow go away. No such luck. Instead, the knocking grew louder, more persistent, until I leapt up from my bed, fully intent on giving the inconsiderate door knockers a little taste of the 1995 Cactus Jack. Man, did I have a promo in store for them.

But when I flung the door open, I was greeted by the ominous sight of two Secret Service agents flanking the tall, lean frame of Democratic presidential candidate Senator John Kerry. "May I come in?" he asked politely, yet with a sense of utmost urgency, as if the country's very future was at stake.

"Of course," I said, ushering in the senator and his security team. "How can I help you?"

The senator scanned the room, looking for security bugs, or a possible hooker whose services I'd solicited. Finding nothing, he said, "This is a matter of utmost urgency—the country's very future may be at stake."

Yes! I'd been right! But how could I be of any help to Senator John Kerry?

"I need your advice," the senator said.

"Well, for starters, when you go to Wendy's for a photo op, don't order the soup. It's insulting to the public. I don't care if you have to put a well-manicured finger down your throat when you get back on that bus. You order a double with cheese, fries, and a Frostee, and you smile when you're eating it. Got it?"

"No, no, no," the senator said, backpedaling as if he was a young Michael Jackson, trying to avoid father Joe's stinging right-left combination. "I'm talking about . . . advice on my debate tomorrow."

"Really?" I said flabbergasted. "Why me? Haven't you guys been rehearsing that thing for days now?"

"Yes, that's true," the senator admitted. "I believe I know the issues, but after seeing you in action at your debate, it occurred to me that you might be able to help in the presentation department."

Little Mick and the eyes
that God gave him.

"You saw me? You were there?"

"Well, I wasn't there. ABC News. You know, it's tough to sleep with such a big debate tomorrow."

"Okay, I understand," I said. "And I'm flattered that you would come to me. But I'm afraid you're not going to like what I have to say."

"Well, remember when I said that I voted *for* the war spending bill before I voted against it? It turns out a lot of people don't like what *I* have to say. Be honest with me, Mike."

Sure, he'd just called me by the wrong name, but I let it slide. After all, this debate was probably the first time he'd seen me, unlike the president, who had modeled his entire foreign policy around one of my wrestling promos.

"Well, Senator, you're much more intelligent than the president . . ."

"But then again, aren't we all?" the senator said with a hearty laugh. I reached up to give him a high five, but Kerry left me hanging on it. I'm not sure he even knew what the hell I was doing.

When the laughter subsided, I said, "You're boring, Senator. You know your stuff, but you're boring. If you go out there with that same dull demeanor, the president is going to look like the winner, even it he doesn't know Dick." A reference to the vice president, which I will admit was slightly confusing.

"Well, what can I do?" the senator asked, clearly dejected. "I am as God made me."

"That's true," I said. "But then again, we show up at WWE as God made us, and then Vince changes us around, he give us gimmicks."

"Gimmicks?" the senator asked.

"Yes, gimmicks. Look, I'd been Cactus Jack for eleven years when I showed up in Vince's office. He thought I looked sleazy, like I wasn't a star, so he put a mask on me, and as Mankind, I went on to be a WWE legend, one of the biggest stars the business has ever seen."

"Do you think a mask would help me?" he asked, confused.

"Of course it would. Look what it did for Tim Woods as Mr. Wrestling II, or Bill Eadie as the Masked Superstar, or Al Snow as Avatar?"

"You mean I'll have to change my name?"

"Well, sure, but just for the debates. Besides, everyone will know it's you. We'll make you a mask that augments your really big chin. We'll make it purple, call you the Purple Heart, really play up your wartime heroics."

"I don't know," Kerry said. "I don't want to draw too much attention to my three—count them, three—one, two, three—purple hearts. It might seem gratuitous."

"Yeah, you're right," I said.

Suddenly Kerry snapped his fingers. "I've got it," he said. "America needs a straight talker, a guy who calls them like he sees them. Right?"

"Yes."

"Then why beat around the Bush? No pun intended." Kerry let out a little chuckle. "I'll be debating in a mask, right?"

"Right."

"So, I'll call myself just that!

"Tomorrow night, I will do verbal battle with President Bush, but not as the old, boring, monotone, soup-at-Wendy's-ordering John Kerry. No, tomorrow night, right here, at the University of Miami, will mark the debut of—"

"Of who?" I asked. Kerry had me hooked. Who would he be? Who would he be?

"I'll be THE MASKED DEBATER." Kerry paused. "Do you think it will work? Do you think I'll be popular?"

"Senator, I think the Masked Debater will be beating people off with both hands."

Dear Hardcore Diary,

I should have written this entry two nights ago, following my visit to Walter Reid Army Medical Center. But I ended up spending several hours at my friend Marissa Strock's apartment, eating dinner and just hanging out with her and her mom, Sandy. Marissa, twenty-one, an Army PFC (private first class) had both her legs amputated following an improvised explosive device (IED) attack in Iraq.

The imminent dinner had been the subject of a slight debate between me and Colette, who was still mildly upset about the Christy Canyon interview. She was, however, not upset in the least at the prospect of me having dinner with an attractive young lady and her attractive mom at their apartment.

"So what you're telling me, Colette, is it's okay to have dinner with one woman at her apartment, but it's not okay to do an interview with another one at a radio station. Right?"

"But that's different, Mick," she said.

"Why, because one of the women had her legs blown off?"

"Yes."

"Well, isn't that kind of a double standard?"

Colette admitted that it was, indeed, kind of a double standard, but the truth is, most wives wouldn't let their husbands do either thing—the interview or dinner. My wife gives me an awful lot of latitude to do things she knows are important to me, including my fairly frequent Washington, D.C., road trips.

It's kind of hard to explain exactly why a guy like me who has so many reservations about the war in Iraq feels so compelled to visit the troops who are doing the fighting. Perhaps a psychologist might be able to shed some light on the subject, but I'm guessing a good professional could shed light on a lot of the subjects I've covered in the course of this book. I do know the reason I took my first trip to Walter Reed in November 2003: sheer guilt.

For a full year, I'd seen images of the war on television, but had remained oddly detached from it, as if it was some movie or fancy video game. The war really hit home with the injury of a Long Islander, Lieutenant Fernandez, a recent West Point graduate, who had lost one leg and part of another foot. I didn't know the lieutenant, but some of my friends knew him from his lacrosse-playing days at Rocky Point High School, about fifteen minutes from where I grew up.

A short while later, I read a *Washington Post* article about the injured troops at Walter Reed. Sheryl Crow had been there, singing a song in each wounded service member's room. Hulk Hogan had been there as well. Maybe I wasn't quite Hulk Hogan, but nonetheless most of the injured troops I read about were young—nineteen, twenty years old—and would therefore have been impressionable high school kids back in my WWE heyday. I felt the guilt start to mount. Were there injured troops who might actually like to see me? Could I actually make a difference?

I called Sue Aitchison, who handles a great deal of WWE's community relations work. Even when I'd been estranged from WWE, I'd kept in touch with Sue, and would occasionally represent the company at different fund-raising events. Did we have a connection with the USO, who arranged these hospital visits?

I was put in touch with Ellen Brody of USO's Washington Metro office, and was in Washington, D.C., two days later. Ellen made everything so easy for me, and she and USO's superwoman Elaine Rogers have become valued friends during the course of my two-and-a-half-year association with their group.

"Slim Jims and wrestlers," Ellen said on the phone prior to my first visit. "I don't understand either of them, but that's what our troops like. So that's what we try to give them."

"How long do these visits usually last?" I asked.

"Oh, they vary," Ellen said. "But on average I'd say two hours. Of course, Wynona was here last week, and she stayed for seven hours."

"Is that the longest visit?"

"I think so," Ellen said.

"Then I'm going to stay for seven, too."

With Chris Nowinski and General Peter Pace, chairman of the joint chiefs of staff.

I did stay for seven hours on that first visit—a visit I really felt would be my only one when I embarked on it a night earlier. I thought the trip would be depressing. Instead, I found it inspiring. Soldiers and marines who'd left arms or legs in Iraq or Afghanistan talked of returning to be with their unit. At first I assumed they were kidding, but found out I was wrong—they simply had a dedication to their country that was inconceivable to an outsider like me.

As I finished my visit, I thought of all the hours spent, all the rooms visited, all the photos taken, and realized I hadn't even talked all that much.

Instead, I'd done a whole lot of listening; to stories of their injuries, their families, their fallen brothers and sisters in arms. They'd felt comfortable with me around. I guess I'd been a part of their lives for so long that I seemed like someone they knew.

I prepared to leave, but was told I needed to visit one more room, which had not been on our list. The USO is great about letting troops know who is coming by to visit, so they can get an accurate idea of who actually wants to meet certain guests. It really eliminates the guesswork so that I wasn't just walking blindly into rooms. Everyone I met had actually expressed an interest in meeting me.

The soldier I was to visit last had been in a bad accident, having lost a leg extremely high on his hip, almost at his midsection. His name was Josh Olsen, a young staff sergeant from Washington State, whose devastating injury had caused his body weight to drop almost in half, from a rock-solid 190 to slightly over a hundred pounds.

I talked quietly with the young man for a few minutes, and noticed his mother was crying. I didn't know at the time that she wasn't the only one. I found out later that his nurses had been crying and holding each other during the course of my short visit. It seemed that I was the first person Sergeant Olsen had shown any interest in talking to during his month-long stay in the hospital.

His eventual stay lasted much longer—many months as an inpatient, followed by well over a year as an outpatient. Yet when I returned a month later, he seemed like a new man, buzzing around the hallways in his wheelchair, e-mailing his buddies back in Iraq, working incredibly hard at rebuilding his body and his life.

Over the months I saw Josh regularly, and each time, he was making great progress. His prosthetic was proving to be a very difficult situation, as even the surgeons and specialists at Walter Reed had never seen an injury quite like his, an amputation quite that high. So he made it a point to rebuild the rest of his body, tearing up the weight room, gaining back his lost size and strength with a determination I can't really comprehend.

Ellen Brody gave me regular progress reports, prompting me to leave a late-night, drunken, teary-eyed message on his machine, telling him how much I admire him and how proud I was to call him a friend. Well, it wasn't all that late, and I'd only had two beers, but I'm a lightweight, and two drinks is all it takes to send me into sentimental mode.

I had dinner with Sergeant Olsen's parents about a year ago, at a casino out in Idaho, near the Washington State line, where I was part of an independent wrestling show put on by one of my old Texas wrestling opponents, "Maniac" Matt Borne.

His mom asked if I was still visiting the hospital regularly. I told her yes, I still tried to get down to visit the troops every month. I kept that pace up for about a year and a half, but have slacked off since, visiting only five times in the last year.

"Why do you keep coming back?" she asked.

I thought it over for a second. I knew the answer, but didn't know if I could actually get it out in front of them. "Well, I think I keep coming back because of your son. Because he made me feel like I made a difference."

My Dinner with Wolfie

As I sat down at the groundbreaking ceremony for the new amputee wing at Walter Reed Army Medical Center, I felt my blood run a little cold. Something was among us, some reptilian form, some snake or miserable air-breathing gill fish. I don't know if there even is such a thing, but what better way to describe the man in front of me, Deputy Secretary of Defense Paul Wolfowitz. Mr. Wolfowitz is now head of the World Bank, but at his most influential, he was something of an architect of the Iraqi war. No, he didn't draw up invasion plans, but it was his persistence, along with that of a few key others in the neoconservative movement, that helped President Bush make the decision to invade Iraq.

The meeting was inevitable. What was I going to say? If I said, "Nice to meet you," I was a liar. But there had to be a way to say hello and be respect-ful, while still maintaining my integrity.

I needed to be diplomatic. Wait, I had it! My greeting. When he turned to me, I would simply say, "Hello, Mr. Wolfowitz, how are you? I know the troops appreciate your support." Good, right? Polite, but true. For reasons I don't quite comprehend, the troops not only appreciate his support, they actually like the guy.

I try to give credit where its due. Even if I don't like the guy. Even if it's Wolfowitz. But I'll admit, the guy has been relentless in his support for the wounded troops. He is a frequent visitor to Bethesda and Walter Reed, and often hosts the Friday-night dinners for the wounded troops and their fami-lies at Fran O'Brien's, a venerable steak house in downtown Washington.

During the course of my visits, I have often tried to gently dig up some dirt on Wolfowitz, whenever I discover he has made a previous visit to a ser-vice member I am speaking to. It would probably be inappropriate to ask lead-ing questions like, "Isn't Wolfowitz a dick?" Instead, I ask more open-ended questions, like, "Oh, you met Deputy Secretary Wolfowitz, what's he like?"

And damn, I hate to say this, but they all like him. They say things like, "He's a great guy." Or, "They don't get any better than him." I guess the clos-est I got to negative was one soldier who said, "Oh, yeah, he was nice, he should be—he's the reason I'm here." Which, come to think of it, *is* kind of negative.

Same thing with Bush. The troops love the guy. And he does seem to care. I've seen family photos of the president on visits, hugging the parents, sitting on patients' beds, pinning Purple Hearts on chests. They all glow about Mrs. Bush, too. Especially about Mrs. Bush. Hey, who am I to argue? They've met the guy and his wife; I haven't.

I managed to escape the groundbreaking ceremony without incident or Wolfowitz greeting but wondered if I'd be so lucky at Fran O'Brien's later that evening. I imagined the scene at Fran's—a long table in a back room, fairly intimate, maybe fifteen people, twenty tops. But as I made the rounds through the hospital, especially in physical therapy and occupational therapy, it seemed that everyone I spoke to was going to the dinner.

Fran O'Brien's was packed. As I should have guessed, there were far too many injured troops to sit around one long wood table. There were troops everywhere, a hundred or so, in various stages of the healing process. Some sported new prosthetics, learning to walk on fiberglass legs instead of muscle and bone. Some were in wheelchairs, awaiting procedures that would help them to walk.

I had talked to a buddy of mine, Chris Walker, who I'd known since middle school, and I apologized for hitting D.C. so often without stopping by to see him in Baltimore. Like a lot of people, Chris felt detached from the war and wished he could somehow feel better connected to something other than CNN or Fox News. So he had jumped at the chance to go with me to Fran's, to meet some of the men and women who had given so much, and, last but not least, to pilfer free food.

Chris and I were both surprised to find Doonesbury creator Garry Trudeau at our table. Trudeau's political satire can be razor-sharp at times, but the troops love the guy because he listens to them, values their feedback, and tells their side of the story in his Pulitzer Prize–winning work.

I got up to use the restroom and was introduced to Mark Bowden, a fine political journalist and author of *Black Hawk Down*, which was turned into a successful movie of the same name. "I can't stand that guy," I told Bowden, upon seeing Wolfowitz about ten feet away.

Bowden laughed. "I'm here with him," he said. "I'm writing an article on him."

"Oh, sorry," I said. "Maybe you shouldn't include that in the article."

I did read the article a few months later in the *Atlantic Monthly*. As Bowden had told me, it wasn't meant to be either pro- or anti-Wolfowitz; just a way for people to better understand a very polarizing figure. I really do understand him a little better now. I still don't like him. But I don't hate him either. He just happens to view the world in a way that I don't. Not to mention the fact that he was way off the mark with his prewar assertions.

After my short bathroom break, I was introduced to Fran's proprietor, who told me he wanted to introduce me to a good friend of his. I turned to see Wolfowitz. Holy crap! What should I do? Luckily, I was on autopilot. I'd played out this scene in my mind and knew just what I'd do. "Hello, Mr. Wolfowitz, how are you? I know the troops appreciate your support."

The deputy secretary of defense opened his mouth and let loose a blast of bad breath that would have killed a lesser man. He mentioned meeting one of our guys (Batista) at the Pentagon and then tried to make some kind of joke about the Divas, but humor, I surmised, was not the guy's strong suit. Neither is foreign policy, for that matter.

I got back to the table and was immediately questioned by Trudeau, who had seen the Wolfowitz incident in all its halitosic glory. I ran him through the dialogue, taking great care to note that no actual lying had taken place during the course of our short conversation. Someone from Fran's came over to ask Trudeau if he too would like a meeting with Wolfie.

"You know, I think that I'll pass," said Trudeau. "And if he's read my work, I think he'll pass, too."

I wandered off for a while, visiting tables, dispensing Cactus Jack T-shirts and *Wrescal Lane* copies to the troops. Suddenly, I felt a wave of excitement crash across the room. I turned to see Gary Trudeau and Paul Wolfowitz shaking hands, as if at some kind of peace summit, both of their bodies bathed in the bright lights of cameras. Then it was over. Just like that. Photographers retreated, and both combatants went back to their respective corners: Trudeau at my table, Wolfie raising hell at the bar, margarita in hand, licking salt off a barmaid's bare boobs. Yeah, I made that part up.

I hit up Trudeau for some details. What had been said? What had gone down?

"Well," Gary started. "I took your advice. I tried to be polite without lying."

On the way back to Baltimore, my friend Chris started laughing.

"What's so funny?" I said.

"It just seemed so surreal, so bizarre," he said.

"What did?"

"The conversation."

"Which one?" I asked.

"The one with you and Gary Trudeau," Chris said. "I can't believe Gary Trudeau told a friend I've known for twenty-five years that he took his advice on how to talk with the deputy secretary of defense."

A week later I received a call from Ellen Brody of the USO. "You've been invited to have dinner at the Pentagon," she said.

"Wow, that's exciting."

"Yeah, but there's something you should know," Ellen said.

"What's that?"

"It's hosted by Paul Wolfowitz."

"Oh," I moaned, "I can't stand that guy."

"I know," she said. "But it's a very big deal. All of the joint chiefs will be there. And . . ."

"And what?"

"And Mr. Wolfowitz asked for you by name."

Update—On February 5, 2007, I had my third dinner with Wolfie. I'd like to report that Dr. Wolfowitz's breath was minty fresh, and that our conversation was enjoyable and extensive. Honest. I am even looking forward to my fourth dinner with Wolfie.

Dear Hardcore Diary,

It's a huge day for our show. A make-or-break show. As I headed into Monday night's *Raw*, I admitted to myself that I'd basically given up on the angle. Admitted that I was a defeated man. I accepted that this ECW show was going to be a disaster, both creatively and financially, and that I'd have to chalk it up as a giant and very expensive learning experience.

At one point, Kurt Angle, Edge, and I sat down to talk over our promo. Kurt was supposed to say a line that read, "If I were a true Mick Foley rip-off, I'd be selling out to whoever flashed the biggest wad of cash in front of my face."

Kurt looked at me and jokingly asked, "Is that true, Mick?"

I laughed. "No, actually, I'm taking quite a financial hit on this one."

Kurt and Edge both exploded in laughter. Man, on this day, laughter really was the best medicine, and I needed its anesthetizing quality. Whether it was one wrestler comparing the creative team to a bunch of art lovers, each one intent on putting their own little touch on the Mona Lisa—a pair of glasses, a bigger smile—or Terry Funk telling a ridiculous story about a doctor sticking hard-boiled eggs and a doughnut up his ass in order to lure a tapeworm out of its anal lair, I laughed an awful lot on Monday.

I had accepted my fate as a headliner on the worst show in recent history. Still, I attempted to make a last-minute appeal to Vince, more to ease my conscience than to actually get anything done, because I sincerely doubted that it would succeed.

But I hit Vince with as much truth as I could, going on

record with saying the angle sucked, having been watered down to the point of being unrecognizable. I pushed for Terry Funk. I pushed for Tommy Dreamer. I pushed for a video package that could feature both guys at their best and could convey in a few short sound bites just how important this match was to both of them.

I reminded Vince that my pitch in Stamford specifically called for the use of the ECW video library, which would definitely showcase the passion of my past feuds with Dreamer and Funk. I astutely pointed out that none of that had actually been done, and even went so far as to say, "Vince, this has been screwed up so badly that it made me think of WCW, where people speculated that it was being done badly on purpose, to derail angles and Pay-Per-Views, just to maintain the status quo."

Okay, maybe I went too far with that last one, as Vince seemed to take offense at the insinuation.

"Mick, why don't you write all that down, so we can try to get some of it done for Wednesday." Then he stood up and, leaning in toward me, said, "I may not be a good person, but I am always a good businessman."

"I disagree, Vince," I said, shaking his hand. "I think you are a good person." Vince seemed stunned as my nose grew five inches in an instant, turning to wood and sprouting small branches that a trio of tufted titmice twittered on triumphantly.

Actually, I do think Vince is a good person. I've known him for a long time, and I know he is, deep down, a caring, warm human being. I once asked him for a day off in 1999, due to a death in the family. Vince's eyes teared up immediately, so quickly that he couldn't possibly have faked it. Sure, some of the things he does make me shake my head in disbelief, or even disgust, but the fruit of his labor, WWE, has entertained so many millions around the world, and has put smiles on countless faces that don't often have a reason to do so.

A few minutes later, I was approached by Paul E., my saving grace. "Vince said you have some ideas," he said. "Talk to me, I'm writing the show for Wednesday."

Earlier in the day, I had spoken to Paul about the "whore" accusation. Actually, I didn't do it in a confrontational manner, or even use the w word. But I did say, "I know you think I do a lot of things in this business just for the money. That's true. But this wasn't about the money. This was all about the vision."

"I know," he said.

Having Paul at the helm gives me hope. He knows the audience. He knows emotion. He will do whatever is possible to make Wednesday's show as good as it possibly could be. We need those two hours on Wednesday as a last-chance endorsement for *One Night Stand*. We have two hours to do the hardest sell job in sports entertainment history. Like a traveling salesman of old, we'll be going door-to-door, via the miracle of cable and satellite, telling millions of people all about our product and why they can't afford to live without it.

We had a very good *Raw*. From a wrestling perspective, I'm not sure what happened, but from an ECW perspective, it was just what we needed. I finally felt the buzz. The ECW buzz that had been so prominent before last year's show had finally returned, along with a host of ECW alumni.

The show itself seemed to gain new meaning. I no longer felt that I was carrying the weight of the world on my shoulders, that my one match would either make or break the show. Of course, if the buy rate is good, I will try to claim that I did indeed make the show, but that's another fight for another day.

John Cena did a hell of a job, even better than usual, with his contract-signing segment. Cena has become incredibly good at shifting emotional gears, interchanging humor and serious dialogue effortlessly, hopefully impressing on his legion of fans just why this match is so important.

I'm really looking forward to my potential *SummerSlam* match with John, provided my knee holds out, or we don't have a last-minute creative shake-up. Maybe someone will decide that Mona Lisa needs a coonskin cap or a tattoo.

My knee actually feels a little better. Doc Rios said it was possible that my Baker's cyst had ruptured, allowing me some relief from pain, and better movement, too. Earlier in the week, I'd had trouble just walking. I'd even taken a pain pill one afternoon, which I took as a sign of personal weakness and failure. It is one thing to take medication to get through a six-hour red-eye in coach; another to pop a pill just to get through the day. It was a failure I do not intend to repeat.

⋅ ⋅ ⋅

Somewhere around 10:30 P.M., after Beth Phoenix broke her jaw, but before a great Vince–Shane–Triple H segment, I was summoned to the writers' room for a talk with Paul.

"I've got a promo for you on Wednesday," he said. "I'm not sure we're going to get the package you wanted, but I'm going to make sure that you get a chance to talk. We're going to show the 'Cane Dewey' promo, and then we'll go to you, in a room, horror lighting, no fans booing, no cheap pops. Just you and your promo."

Then Paul gave me my promo. Sure, I take great pride in coming up with my own stuff, but when something is real good, I'm more than happy to steal it. And this was real good. So good that I can't wait to steal it. So good that I'll put my own little touch on it and practically dare people not to buy this show. So good that I may just do the unthinkable—push the doors to Promoland open just enough so I can squeeze in and go on one last heart-pumping ride.

12:18 P.M.—time to go to Dayton

Dear Hardcore Diary,

Okay, here's the fact sheet from the June 7 WWE vs. ECW show from Dayton. There was no video package. No Funk promo. No Dreamer promo. Tommy Dreamer officially heads into *One Night Stand* as a main eventer of sorts, despite the fact that the vast majority of our fans don't even know what his voice sounds like. Actually, Terry did get to cut a promo (and a very good one), but it was for the Internet only; not exactly the casual fans Terry needs to convince his worthiness to. The "Cane Dewey" promo did show, but only for about thirty seconds—not long enough to make fans feel they knew my mindset back in '95. I did get to do that promo. I did get the horror lighting. But it wasn't just me in a room—it was me in the middle of the ring.

Unfortunately, the gap between what I wanted to do with that promo and what I actually did do with it was a wide one. It was like the verbal equivalent of Evel Knievel's infamous Snake River Canyon jump. Man, did I ever want to make history with this promo, but in much the same way that Evel's courage (or rocket ship) failed him back in '74, my confidence, testicular fortitude, or talent took a hike almost immediately, causing me to fall back on a few worn-out clichés and a whole lot of yelling. As I was doing it, I was aware it wasn't sucking, but I was also well aware that it was far, far from what I wanted it to be. I was looking for a 1971 Reggie Jackson All-Star game type of blast. Instead, in my moment of truth in Dayton, I unveiled a whole lot of warning track power. At least, I thought so at the time.

Despite the cryptic nature of the previously mentioned facts, I thought we had a tremendous show. There was a definite ECW buzz, although the buy rate will ultimately tell if the show was too little, too late, or just enough, just in the nick of time.

I was given some verbiage for my promo but decided not to look at it, opting instead for the potent cocktail of my memory of Paul's previous night's promo, my emotional ride to Dayton, and the heartfelt hope and belief that the right words would hit me when the spotlight was on. And on this one night, the spotlight would literally be on. As per Paul E.'s request, I would be sitting in a chair in center ring, house lights off, only a single spotlight illuminating me.

I wasn't required to rehearse my promo—just the lighting. Damn, it looked good. Not "good" as in "handsome" good. But "good" as in "different" good. Eerie good. Moody good.

Seeing my face in such lighting, in such an extreme close-up, gave me two immediate thoughts. One, I would need to tweeze my nose hairs before I went out there. Which I eventually did. The second one was a little trickier. To do it, I would need two separate approvals: one from Terry Funk, and one from Vince.

I spotted Terry at ringside right after my lighting test. "Hey, Terry," I said, walking up into whispering range. "Did you see how good that lighting looked?"

"Yes, I did," Terry said.

"Might be a good time for a hardway."

Terry raised an eyebrow and looked quickly around. "It might be," he said. "But you know it's dangerous."

"Yeah, I know. But it might really make this angle."

"Okay, let's do it," he whispered, "but its going to hurt like a mother blanker." Actually, he had an alternate word for "blanker."

Now I needed to sell Vince on the idea. There are some things that are best done in secret. I judged that this particular hardway idea was not one of these things. Sure, I'd tried to do a top-secret hardway with Randy Orton— but this was different. Vince loved me back then. I could afford to call an audible that would piss him off. That was April 2004. In June of 2006, I believed that Vince McMahon had taken about as much of Mick Foley's grief as he was willing to. A move that he interpreted as "devious" could well lead to either the removal of my promo or the removal of the close-up that would make the hardway seem memorable.

Besides, that 2004 hardway idea hadn't worked out so well.

"Hey, Vince," I said, trying to figure out a way to cozy up to my favorite billionaire without seeming smarmy or too deferential.

"Hello, Mick," my favorite billionaire said.

Keeping in mind that Vince was up to his Mick Foley limit, I decided to forgo a deep psychological preamble about why the time was right for such a unique step. So I just dove right in. "I think tonight's a good time for a hardway."

"Why do you say that?" Vince said. Great, he wasn't instantly disgusted. He was going to allow me the opportunity to sell it to him.

"Well, the lighting's just incredible. No one's seen a hardway in years, and Terry's about the only guy left in the business who still knows how to do them. I think it will really make a difference in the angle."

"If it's too bloody, we won't be able to use our close-up."

"I don't think it will be, Vince—an eyebrow doesn't usually bleed too much."

"Okay, if you're okay with it, let's do it."

Technically speaking, I'd done a hardway in January of 2004. But that was self-inflicted. I really can't remember the last legitimate, intentional hardway in WWE.

I gave Terry the thumbs-up and, one at a time, told all three handheld cameramen, Marty, Rico, and Stu, to get real tight shots of Terry's postmatch punches. The production of WWE shows is so top-notch that we often take the work of so many people for granted. Still, when something is really needed, I try to consult with the guys on the ground, and when something is done really well, I do my best to let them know how much it's appreciated.

The crowd was hot, enthusiastic in their support of ECW. They seemed to enjoy being live witnesses to this historical head-to-head adventure, and thrive on getting behind the underdog promotion. A company-versus-company battle royal was well received, and then it was my turn. Normally, a role as Edge's second, kind of a Kenickie to his Zuko, wouldn't be much cause for personal anxiety. Few jobs in life are as easy and fun as getting paid to watch WWE from the best seat (or standing area) in the house. But this was somehow different. I was nervous. Nervous because I knew I had to deliver on this promo. Or, maybe more accurately, because I knew I had to deliver on it right after getting my eyebrow split open by Terry Funk.

Edge is a pro. He understands that our biggest problem is the credibility issue our opponents have with Vince (and with some of our fans), so he used the match to try to "make" Tommy Dreamer. It was a hardcore match; no rules, very physical, and, with the exception of Edge missing a table on a backdrop and landing in a precarious manner on his surgically repaired neck, it was a success.

There I go again, mixing up my past and present tenses whenever I describe a match or interview. I hope you'll just try to live with it.

Lita interferes, causing Terry to get involved, which causes me to wrap a piece of barbed wire around Terry's neck. Terry and I roll outside, and I watch as Edge spears Tommy for the win. Good match. Now it's my turn . . . to get punched in the eye. Hardway time.

I see two handheld cameramen in position, and I know the "hard camera" in the stands is on us, too. There's no way to miss this. Terry rears back with that big left hand, and "bam," fist meets flesh. Yes, we've done it! Except I'm not sure we have. I don't feel the telltale trail of hot blood charting its course down my cheek. Terry rears back again. Damn, this means we didn't get it the first time. Oh, man, this is going to hurt. I had prepared myself for one shot. "Bam!" Fist meets flesh, part II. Still no trail. No warmth. Terry rears back again. There's no blood on his knuckles. This is not going well. Take three . . . and rolling. The third punch is different. It lands below my left eye. So does punch four. Number five may or may not have broken my nose. The crowd is actually chanting my name. They feel bad for me. Hell, they should. *I* feel bad for me. This idea sucked.

Finally, left hand number six, or nine, or sixteen, sends me down to the ground, where my legs promptly get tangled up with a barbed-wire bat—an everyday discarded item in these types of matches.

Wait a second. I feel something. Something warm. I touch my fingers to my head, pull them back, look at them. Yes! Genuine hardway blood. It may look the same as other blood, but it's not. There's something special about hardway blood. It's earned blood. There's just a little of it, but it doesn't really matter. It's enough. My hardway joy is short-lived, however, as the Funker slaps me hard, cutting off my moment like a nosy mother walking in on a teenage pickle-tickling session.

Finally, mercifully, Edge intercedes, and I head up the ramp, trying to clear the cobwebs in time to cut the promo of a lifetime. I've got a three-minute commercial break, and then I'm on. Magic time. Time to reap the harvest of all those late-night seed-planting rides. I've got all the ideas I need in my head. It's just a matter of allowing them to come out.

I head out to the ring with a chair. Per my request, I am not accompanied by music. It feels more real this way. Besides, my music is just so damn peppy. I sit in the chair, and I get my cue—I'm on the air, live.

But the moment I open my mouth, I know I'm off my game. I wanted a slow build, a gradual escalation of emotion and volume. Instead I'm yelling. I'm also trying to make a comparison between ECW and an old girlfriend, but this crowd doesn't seem to be in a metaphor-buying mood. Besides, it's a crappy metaphor. Not only that, I've lost my storyteller's touch. Maybe this isn't the right crowd for stories. After all, it's Ohio, a battleground state. A red state, a Bush state. A sound bite state. No wonder I'm dying out there. I'm trying to pitch Updike to a "Suck it!" readership.

I really had imagined that ball clanging off the lighting tower in centerfield of Detroit's old Tiger Stadium. I still remember where I was: in a tent at Lake George, New York, listening to that game on the radio—that home run as fresh in my mind now as it was at the moment of impact, thirty-five years ago.

It's strange how my two most vivid baseball memories, Jackson's All-Star heroics and Chris Chambliss's game-winning home run in the '76 American League Championship series, were both radio experiences. Maybe the spoken word simply has the power to fire the imagination that a visual moment does not.

But what about the famed 1960 Kennedy/Nixon debate, the first to be aired live on television? JFK kicked Tricky Dick's ass all the way back to California in that one. Or did he? Depends on who you ask. To those who saw the debate, the handsome, confident senator from Massachusetts had an easy time with the pasty-faced, sweating Nixon. But those who only heard the debate thought Nixon had won.

That debate is often looked at as a pivotal moment in television history, because it helped prove the power of the visual image. Perhaps a video of my Dayton interview can be put into some type of time capsule as well, as further proof of that power. Because last night, after catching a 6:00 A.M. flight home and taking my younger children to the zoo, I settled down into my cracked white leather recliner and fired up the TiVo, fully prepared to wallow in the mire of depression that my lackluster promo promised to bring.

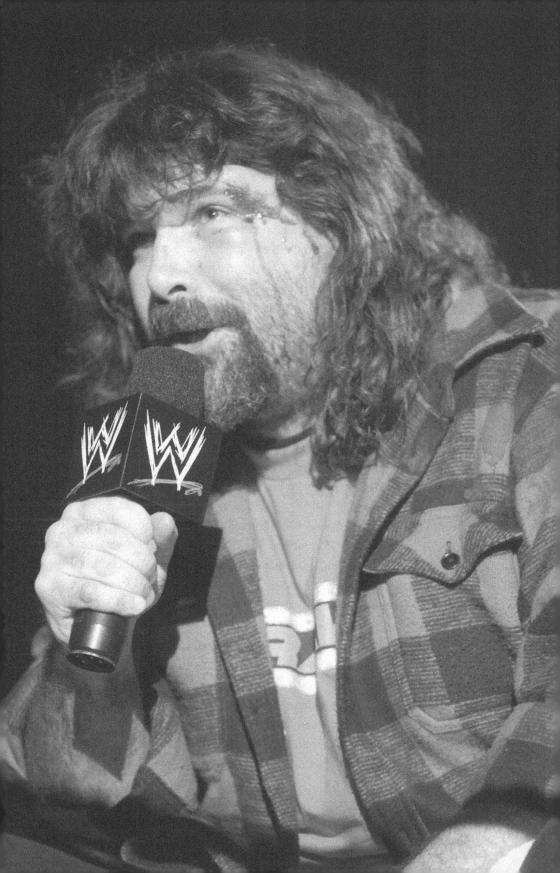

Here's the promo. Read it for yourself.

MICK FOLEY: Where the hell do any of you get off telling me I sold out? Where do you get off, where do you find the nerve, to call me a whore? You think I hate ECW? I loved that place. I loved that place. But ECW simply didn't love me back. She was like the girl I can't let go of, but the one who makes me sick upon seeing her. She wanted too much blood, too much of my heart, too much of my life! So I left. And I found fame and fortune in WWE. And Paul Heyman was right. There's only one real difference between me and Tommy Dreamer; I'm a whore, and he's not. You see, about seven years ago, I pulled a sock out of my pants and made Vince McMahon laugh, and the doors of opportunity opened wide for Mick Foley . . . but not for Tommy Dreamer. All he's got is his heart, his pride, and the initials ECW. And I want to tell Edge that I went back and I watched our *WrestleMania* match, "the greatest Hardcore match of all time," I said. Well, the truth is, maybe it wasn't quite as good as I thought. Maybe, Edge, you and I are going to have to be tougher than ever, hungrier than ever, sicker than ever to walk into that steaming cesspool that is the Hammerstein Ballroom. Twenty-five hundred sickening, twisted fans screaming for our blood. Because Tommy Dreamer can do everything I can, and maybe with more passion. He's going to beat us up all over New York City! He's going to bludgeon us. Terry Funk, the greatest wrestler I ever saw. If you look at Terry Funk and see an old man, you're not seeing the real Terry Funk. His slaps hurt worse than most men's punches. His punches dole out concussions. And when he picks up a weapon, he can use it like no man ever has. He is in excruciating pain waking up every single day, looking for one more chance to have one great last match. I blew the son of a bitch up in Japan, and he came back and hugged me. I set him on fire in Philadelphia, and he put his arm around me. He doesn't put his arm around me anymore. I don't want your arm around me, Terry Funk. Tommy Dreamer, the only differ-

The Dayton hardway promo.

ence between me and you is, I had the guts to go to WWE! Because when I go to the Hammerstein Ballroom, Edge and I are prepared to take the beatings of our lives. And I will do that to exorcise the sick, twisted whore that is ECW. I want her out of my life. You've seen me thrown off cells. You've seen me slammed on tacks. You've seen me go through a burning table at *WrestleMania*. It is nothing compared to the horrors I will unleash on Dreamer and Funk! Because, ECW, I'm going to take the hearts of your heroes, and I'm going to shove them down your throats for making me fall in love with you to begin with! You stepped on my heart! You stepped on my soul! You took everything I believed in, and you threw it away! And now, when I walk into that ring at the Hammerstein Ballroom, as a WWE legend, you, Terry Funk, and you, Tommy Dreamer, will learn about loss. Have a nice day.

There you go. Not so great, right? Grammatically incorrect, indecisive, vague, not especially thought-provoking.

But the image saved it. It didn't just save it. It made it work. Thank goodness for Terry Funk and his plethora of punches. There wasn't much blood, but it was enough; in its own subtle way, it was far more memorable and powerful than the gushers guys hit so regularly on Pay-Per-View.

My eye was swollen too, courtesy of punches three, four, and five. They had sure hurt at the time, but watching on TiVo, seeing how the eye literally swelled and changed color during the course of the promo, made the pain I'd endured seem like a small price to pay.

I watched that promo five or six times, each time marveling at the lighting, the blood, the swollen eye, the haunting message. It was the first time since '98 I'd watched any of my stuff more than once. That was Hell in a Cell. Hopefully this promo will raise one-thousandth the number of goose bumps as that infamous match did. Hopefully it will serve as a bridge between the true believers and the intrigued but hesitant.

Come on over, everybody. Come on over and watch *One Night Stand*. It may not turn out to be as lonely a viewing experience as I had previously thought.

Dear Hardcore Diary,

Everything I am doing to prepare for this match is wrong. I knew exactly what the correct path of preparation was. Following last night's personal appearance at a video store in Brooklyn, I should have headed into New York City, checked into a hotel for two nights, and committed myself to preparing mentally and getting enough rest for such a big match.

As I have mentioned earlier, writing a book about my adventures was probably not a bright idea. Stopping by the Linda Ronstadt show at the Westbury Music Fair (it has a new corporate name, but I refuse to acknowledge it) and writing until 3:30 A.M., sleeping in a child's bunk bed and being woken up by a three-year-old at 6:00 A.M., will probably be looked at as a mistake when my tongue is dragging on the floor tomorrow night.

My knees were begging for a rest today, but instead of listening to them, I took Hughie and little Mick to a nature fair for a couple of hours, walking around, looking at animals, buying a variety of foods of negligible nutritional value. Snow cones, cotton candy, popcorn—by the time we made it to McDonald's, Chicken McNuggets seemed like health food. Then it was on to Noelle's softball game, where I was nice enough to help the kids polish off their McFlurries. My weight was at 304 yesterday—down eleven pounds, but obviously not quite what I'd hoped for going into *One Night Stand*. I can't help but feel that I'd have been far more successful with my weight issue if I hadn't had the rug pulled out on me so many times over the last six weeks. The knee injury didn't help either, as it caused me to alter workouts and seek solace in ice cream and candy. Maybe I should have sought solace in Christy Canyon instead. Sure I would have been wracked with guilt, causing me to confess my transgression, leading to the loss of wife, children, and half of everything I own. But at least Christy would have constituted a noncaloric consumption. Unless, of course, there was some type of whipping cream or chocolate sauce involved.

Even this hardcore diary entry is suffering for my decision. Instead of completing my last offering in solitude and silence, there is a constant cacophony of confusion calling out to me, permeating even the inner sanctum of the Foley Christmas room. The dog is barking. The Belmont Stakes is on. Dewey was thoughtful enough to let a fart make its way into my world before he left the room.

We've got a leak in our pipes as well, the source of which, at this juncture, has yet to be detected by the plumber. Mickey wanted a flashlight so he could join the plumber. "I want to look like a plumber," he said. "I want to look like a plumber."

"Mickey, come here," I said. Once the little guy was close enough, I pulled his sweatpants halfway down his butt. "There you go," I said. "Go upstairs and tell Mommy that you look like a plumber now." Which is exactly what he did, eliciting a big laugh from Mommy, and giving me temporary sanctuary from my concerns.

Little Mick's personality is something of a sanctuary for me. I get the biggest kick out of the little guy, even if his recent (as in last five minutes) inaction during the Los Lonely Boys song "Heaven" has made me rethink my whole plans for tomorrow. Mickey, you see, is supposed to sing "Heaven" in the church choir tomorrow. As you already know from reading my May 14 diary entry, his performance in the choir has been a little less than clutch. Indeed, the chances of him choking under pressure again are almost guaranteed. Yeah, it will be fifteen kids and me up there again, except this time I've got a huge black eye, just in case the missing teeth and hair down to my shoulders didn't make me conspicuous enough.

He's laying on the floor now, listening to "Heaven" for the sixth time without the slightest hint of singing along, and has just asked me about Jesus' exact positioning on the cross at the time of his crucifixion. "Were his arms like this [palms down] or like this [palms up] when he died?"

"I'm pretty sure they were up," I told him.

"How come my teeth are so sharp?" he said.

I really don't know if I'll stick with plan A: church choir, Noelle's softball

The day before **One Night Stand** with little Hughie.

game; or go with plan B: get a good night's sleep in a hotel and prepare for the match without a single thought of my kids. Except I know that's not an option, for if I miss out on church and softball, I'll do nothing *but* think about my kids during my prematch preparation. Why am I forced to walk the earth with this conscience? Maybe, if there's such a thing as reincarnation, I can come back down to earth and just trample all over people without giving a damn about anyone but myself. That would be awesome. That's it—in my next life, I'm coming back as a conservative.

Hopefully, the poor quality of this final prematch entry will not be indicative of the match itself. I really would have liked to have sent all of you into *One Night Stand* with a provocative, heartfelt written account of my ambitions and fears surrounding this vital match in my career. But as this entire six-week experience has shown me, very little of what I counted on has turned out to be true.

I'll check back in with you in a couple of days, following my match, and a trip to Six Flags Great Adventures, where my battles to fit into roller-coasters never intended for asses the likes of mine will make my struggles with Vince, the creative team, and the hardcore duo of Funk and Dreamer look woefully wimpy by comparison.

Dear Hardcore Diary,

I would have loved to have written this final entry in the luxury of some fine hotel room immediately following the climactic *One Night Stand* conclusion. Unfortunately the reality of WWE sometimes gets in the way of fairy-tale endings, and with *Raw* airing from Penn State University the next night, I was looking at a very anticlimactic five-hour postmatch drive.

I had made an allowance for a nice hotel in the Foley budget for this particular night, but as 3:00 A.M. rolled around, the Budget Rest motel on Interstate 80 started looking really good. Sure, the mattress was a little lumpy and had probably been witness to sexual encounters by hundreds of travelers over the years, but nonetheless, this place was still way ahead of some of the dives I'd stayed in over the years. Besides, I was fairly sure there would be no parade of crackheads streaming in to say hello.

I set a pillow up underneath my knees, to alleviate the stress that these types of motel beds tend to cause my back. I lay down, making sure to rest my upper back on the towel I'd placed on the bed. I had five large ugly gashes on that back, like a paw swipe from some angry bear, and I feared having a bedsheet of questionable cleanliness sticking to my wounds come morning.

No, this was not the way I'd pictured my postmatch routine. Usually, after a big match, I order room service and a Pay-Per-View movie, then lie in bed thinking about how great my performance was. Come to think of it, I think I skipped that part of the routine after my September 2005 Carlito match, as there was not a whole lot of greatness to digest.

But this routine was vastly different, not just because of my one-star accommodations, but because of the unique hardships my variety of hardcore injuries caused. Uh-oh, I was in trouble. I turned on the light and examined my hands. Underneath a swath of gauze, reminiscent of Boris Karloff in *The Mummy*, I had a litany of lacerations on both hands. I wished I could have put the problem off, but it was an increasingly urgent one, a problem that simply would not go away. A problem that was presenting itself at the most inappropriate time. Slowly, I made my way into the bathroom and looked into the mirror at the kaleidoscope of blues, purples, and yellows that Terry Funk had painted on my face with the painful, hardway brushstrokes of his left hand. I saw that face turn into a mask of confusion. How exactly, I wondered, was I going to wipe my ass?

Though I had long since abandoned the foolish notion that I was going to achieve some kind of wrestling immortality with this whole ECW thing, I still felt as if the ultimate chapter (this diary entry) could be either happy or sad, depending on the quality of our match. In the words of the poem "Invictus," "I am the captain of my fate, and the master of my soul." Despite the fact that my idea had been greatly altered, minimized, and, in terms of confidence in both Tommy Dreamer and Terry Funk, had suffered from an embarrassing case of premature evacuation, I still held out some hope that we could all have a hell of a match, and a great deal less hope that I could wrestle some type of admission of misjudgment out of Vince.

I made it to church to see little Mick really give "Heaven" his all . . . in rehearsal. Man, he was really working the fret board of his blue blow-up guitar, as if he was Angus Young hitting the "Stiff Upper Lip" solo. Then, come show time—nothing. He didn't even make it to the front of the church, choosing instead to say, "I don't really want to be here," over and over, while sitting on Dad's lap.

I made it to Noelle's game too, to watch her squad lose a heartbreaker, 11–10 to the team coached by a guy who helps run the league. Actually, the game seemed like a tie, until the coach unveiled a secret error in the scorecard that allowed his team the victory.

This coach has the distinction of being the only guy in my youth league experience that I've questioned, raised my voice to, or yelled at. It's just that some of these "win at all costs" parents strip all the fun out of the game. I remember limping onto the playing fields a couple of years ago, right after my *Backlash* injury, and watching in shock as this guy's team stole base after base, including double steals, during the course of the game. I asked our coach if stealing was even allowed. "Yeah," he said, "but so far the coaches have had a gentleman's agreement that there would be no stealing." This coach, however, didn't want anything to do with this agreement. For his girls, it was off to the races.

I did a little research on the subject of stealing bases in ten-year-old girls' softball games. I interviewed many people associated with the league, including the head of umpiring, and no one, it seemed, could recall a *single* instance where a girl had been thrown out stealing. Not a single one.

Why such a lopsided percentage of say 100 percent to 0 percent in the steals/caught stealing ratio? At Noelle's next practice, I lined up the girls at home plate and asked each of them to attempt a couple of throws to second. Noelle came closest—a high arching lob that landed a good ten feet from the bag. The other girls did not fare quite so well. Some couldn't reach the pitcher's mound.

I called the head of the Little League (not the head of softball) and asked why a rule in which failure was virtually guaranteed would be allowed. "Well, we want to encourage the girls to practice skills that they'll need as they head into middle school."

I thought about that logic for a second, then said, "When they get to middle school, they will be mature enough to reach second base. Right now, you're asking ten-year-olds to defend the indefensible. My experience shows me that when someone has no success whatsoever at a certain skill, they will simply stop trying."

"That may be true," the man said. "But at least the rule is fair to both teams."

"Actually, it's not," I said. "It favors the better team."

"How do you figure that?"

"Because the better team makes less mistakes, gives up fewer hits, and allows fewer base runners. A bad team may get an extra run or two a game out of a stealing rule, but a good team can just trot around the bases at will. This is what leads to the blowouts, the 16–2 games that make adults sick and make little girls cry. This is what leads to kids never wanting to play sports again."

I hung up, having made my point, but I wasn't satisfied. The image of that damn coach arguing every little call while his team treated the base paths like a track meet just wouldn't go away. Now I know how Mets fans felt when Mike Piazza was behind the plate. I only wished I had the power to change things. Wait a second, I did have the power. The power of the pen.

A day later, I called the Little League office. I know that most of the coaches and volunteers involved in youth sports have only the best interests of the kids at heart—including the head of our league—but it bothered me to see one guy (the coach) affecting the lives of children and their parents with his self-imposed rule changes (he had made up the stealing rule at the younger age group) and petty, selfish attitude. So I invoked the power of the pen.

"Hi, Mr. Jones [not his real name], this is Mick Foley, the parent who talked to you yesterday. Good, thanks, how are you? Listen, I'm not sure if you're aware of it, but I've written a couple of *New York Times* bestselling books, and therefore, when I expressed an interest in doing a story on fanaticism in youth sports, *Newsday* [a Long Island paper] was very interested. So I'd like to get some comments from you and Coach Steiger [not his real name] for my article."

I never did write that article. I'm not sure I ever really had the intention. And Steiger's team beat ours handily in the championship game. But seeing that loudmouthed coach sitting meekly on the bench, opening his mouth only to offer the mildest of encouragements, gave me a feeling of great pride and power.

"What's wrong with Steiger?" I heard our team's parents ask repetitively. "He's just sitting there." I shrugged my shoulders for a few innings, as if I too was baffled by the case of Steiger's inaction, before finding myself unable to contain the story of my great power any longer.

"It was the pen that got him," I said. "The power of the pen." The confused faces of our team's parents gave me the necessary excuse to unveil my literary past, and unearth such notable references as "towering number-one bestseller," "a million copies sold," and "wasn't ghostwritten like the president's was." So from the jaws of softball defeat I was able to snatch moral and literary victory.

Now that I got that softball tangent out of the way, let me see if I can snatch wrestling victory out of Vince's hungry jaws of defeat. Wow, what a weak segue, even by my limited literary standards.

Trying to make six people happy in a match like this can often be a difficult proposition. Participants often have their own agenda, their own interests to look out for down the road, and can therefore often be difficult to appease in such a wild setting. After all, everyone wants to get their stuff in. "Stuff" is not usually the word used in such a sentence, as most wrestlers opt for a more excretory euphemism to describe their repertoire of moves in one-word fashion.

We're lucky. Everyone's on the same page. Everyone feels screwed. Everyone feels betrayed by Vince and the creative team, and everyone wants to prove them wrong. There is only one way to do that—tear the house down! We're all together on this one.

I had a few ideas for a basic structure of the match. Luckily, everyone agreed. One by one, the participants chipped in with ideas, some accepted, some discarded, but each one given in the best interest of the match. It may have been the easiest Pay-Per-View negotiating session I'd been a part of. We had a few great gimmicks (foreign objects, or "international objects," as they were called in WCW in the name of political correctness), a few dramatic transitions, a few huge surprises, and one great finish, courtesy of Paul E. A few weeks earlier, I had expressed concern that involving Lita and Beulah in the finish might strike many (including me) as a cheap way out. What sense would it make to leave a bad taste in people's mouths? With the news of a new plan, I am no longer concerned.

This is about the point where I will start using past and present writing tenses interchangeably. I apologize ahead of time for the grammatical incorrectness. But, in order to take you guys on a harrowing journey through the match, I have to feel like I'm living through it all over again. So screw the grammar, the past and present tenses, and the punctuation as well. And as far as Dreamer, Funk, and Beulah go, I've got three simple words: "Bring 'em on!" Oh, man, I hope the president didn't read that.

It's twenty minutes before the match, and I'm in an oddly mellow state. I can't help but contrast this mellowness to my pre-'Mania mindset, where I had worked myself into a frenzy. Back on April 2, I had found a private corner of the building and rocked back and forth for minutes, listening to "Winter" by Tori Amos, a beautiful, haunting song that for some reason continues to give rise to goose bumps and thoughts of hardcore destruction, thirteen years after first being touched by it in Maxx Pain's car on a long forgotten WCW road trip.

Kane later told me that he walked by and opted not to say hello, seeing the altered state I was in the process of entering.

But all the mental preparation in the world couldn't hide the doubts, concerns, and even fears I faced heading into 'Mania. I remember heading up to the gorilla position, mere minutes—two or three—before match time. I saw Edge and Lita and, without even thinking about my words, asked them if they would say a prayer with me before we went out there. A prayer for safety, not for performance, although I was so scared that I was willing to take whatever the big guy was willing to give me.

Words are like that sometimes—they just kind of sneak out. Although the last time I remember being that surprised by my own words was back in 1987, on one of my weekly 800-mile round trips from college to Dominic DeNuccis's wrestling school, when I asked a hitchhiker if she would touch me in a not so innocent way while her boyfriend slept in the backseat. Wow, where did that come from? I swear, I was a really shy kid back then.

The poor woman didn't really know what to say. Keep in mind that I'd been very polite about the idea, and that it was presented as a question/suggestion so that there was no need for fear, or bold action, like slashing me with a hidden blade, or jumping out of a moving car. In an odd way, she seemed genuinely flattered by the remark. Finally, she said, "I'd like to, but it would be kind of disrespectful to my boyfriend."

"How long have you two been together?" I asked.

"We met earlier today."

About an hour later, the long-term boyfriend woke up and, yawning, asked a question from his prone position on the cracked burgundy interior of the Ford Fairmount's backseat. The woman turned in her seat to face him and, in the process of doing so, grabbed a hearty handful of the future hardcore legend's most private parts.

A few minutes later, I dropped them off. She said good-bye with a wink and a sly little smile that I interpreted as a victory of sorts. Sure, as far as victories go, it was devious, and morally bankrupt, but at that point in my life, I was willing to take victories wherever I could find them.

• • •

An unforeseen factor almost makes a most unfortunate mark on our match. Dreamer reported a sense of queasiness and gastric pains an hour or so before the match. Unbeknownst to me, my partner Edge was almost indisposed for his entrance music, having sought emergency relief in the Hammerstein Ballroom restroom. A day later, following *Raw* at Penn State University, I fall victim to some sort of intestinal virus—severe enough to keep me bedridden for three full days.

Vince McMahon's prediction had almost come true before the match could even begin, as it was damn close to being "the shits" in a far more literal sense than Vince probably could have imagined.

Speaking of imagination, my entrance yields far less response than I would have previously thought possible. As I stand in the ring, I try to rationalize the funereal atmosphere. Where the hell is the reaction? I would have thought I'd have a ton of heat, but this crowd is lukewarm at best, bordering on downright brisk in its response. Well, I rationalize, they don't want to cheer me because I am playing the part of the ECW turncoat. The crowd has been so wild, and has been such an integral part of the show, that a turn against ECW protocol could be seen as a detriment to the show. These people, by virtue of their love for ECW and their willingness to go to great lengths to procure these tickets, are already rebels. To rebel against their rebellious nature could really be confusing. So there are very few cheers. But there aren't a whole lot of boos either. Maybe they respect me too much to boo. Maybe some of them realize the lengths I've gone through to create our match scenario. Or maybe, just maybe, they don't really care a whole lot, one way or another. Yeah, I think, that's it.

Edge and Lita have considerably more heat for their arrival. Edge has got the hardcore title held proudly aloft and seems to be enjoying the unique atmosphere of this particular party. I really enjoy watching how much pride he takes in accepting the boos that come his way, and firmly feel that I am in the presence of the top bad guy in the business.

"Listen, you don't want to mess with these idiots," he says to me. "Because this is their night. This is like their Christmas. Only their Santa Claus is Jewish, fat, bald, and gives out an endless supply of bullshit instead of presents."

What a great line. I know I sometimes seem down on the writers, but whoever came up with this line (I think it was Gewirtz) deserves a round of applause. Edge and I had wondered about the appropriateness of the

Preparing for
hardcore battle
with my tag
partners, Lita
and Edge.

"Jewish" comment, but Gewirtz, who is himself Jewish, seemed to think it wouldn't be a problem.

"All you idiots are going to go home," Edge says, pointing to the fans, "and you're going to go text your imaginary girlfriends about how good this show was. Then you're going to hop on the Internet, and you're going to pleasure yourself looking at pictures of my *actual* girlfriend."

Lita shows off a dose of gravity-defying cleavage, and she and Edge engage in the most graphic French kissing I've seen since Christy Canyon and Ginger Lynn swapped saliva for my viewing pleasure on Playboy radio.

Lita grabs the mike, and refers to Tommy Dreamer as "the innovator of silence," a remark that unfortunately hits way too close to home, but which nonetheless gives me and Edge reason to celebrate with a daring white-guy jumping high five. Lita does a remarkable job of maintaining her composure during her speech, considering that "She's a crack whore" chants threaten to drown out her voice. By the time she finishes, the "crack whore" chant seems almost quaint, having been replaced by not so subtle suggestions for her to kindly stop speaking.

Now it's Funk and Dreamer's turn to enter, which they do to the accompaniment of loud cheers, nondescript techno rock music, and Tommy's real-life wife Beulah. The Funker looks great—fired up and ready to go, ready to prove Vince McMahon wrong. At least, I hope so. Tommy looks . . . stoic, which I'm not sure is a compliment. But hell, at least he doesn't look soft and doughy, like yours truly. Fortunately, I've got quite a following. But, for those just tuning in, I honestly don't look (or feel) like the most dangerous guy in the world. More like somebody's slightly offbeat biker uncle, who had a few too many drinks and decided to enter a local tough-guy contest.

The crowd is coming alive, though, chanting, "ECW, ECW." Beulah, noting Lita's rumored fondness for threesomes (fictional, by the way), suggests making the match a three-on-three, mixed-gender Tag Team match. A couple of girl slaps later, and the match is on. The fans have bought the concept, and the bell rings. All the planning, phone calls, arguing, and frustration become a thing of the past. The match is all ours. Our chance to make a difference—to create a lasting work of art on our own twenty-by-twenty piece of canvas.

Edge and Dreamer start the match. Nobody (and I mean nobody) is expecting this match to be a technical classic, so the main purpose of the opening minute—a headlock, headscissors, etc., etc.—is just an excuse to get to the fun stuff.

The Edgester tags me in, and I make it very clear that I want Terry Funk in the ring; eager to dispense a little payback for my swollen, discolored eye, which I do my best to point to every couple of seconds. In actuality the entrance of Funk, awash in a chorus of "Terry" chants, is merely a means to an end. I am willing to take nine more slaps to the face in return for the privilege of uttering two of the greatest lines of my career.

"This wasn't a good idea," I say to Edge as I step through the ropes, my night in danger of reaching a very premature conclusion. "I don't really want to be here."

Okay, maybe the lines don't seem to be so great, at least on the surface. But perhaps the beauty in these words lies not in their delivery but in the knowledge that they were stolen from my five-year-old son, who only hours earlier had said those exact same words to me while sitting on my lap, watching the rest of his church choir mates sing "Heaven" to the congregation. "I don't really want to be here. I don't really want to be here."

Despite my heartfelt admission, Funk is in no mood for compassion, and the match proceeds to break down into mayhem, with me and Funk spilling to the outside, and Tommy and Edge following suit. The girls view the ugliness from afar, knowing they will have a pivotal role in the latter stages of the match.

I'm all over Funk, until he tosses a random chair my way, and it finds its mark—the top of my skull. To this day, this move remains the sole property of Terry Funk, probably because any right-thinking person wouldn't particularly care for the trail of lawsuits such a move could likely leave in its wake.

Terry is all over me, throwing his big left hand repeatedly. In my opinion, it's still the best-looking punch in the business and still hurts like hell as well, although considerably less than the hardway punches of six nights earlier.

Meanwhile, Dreamer has stopped Edge, and unveils a motley collection of foreign objects; the beginning of what I will refer to as "the progression of the gimmicks." Start slow, and build. A road sign. A garbage can. Boom, boom! Not bad, but we all know it's just a simple starting point.

Funk and I "take a walk," fighting up the aisle, while Edge brings a ladder into the ring. The progression of the gimmicks has entered its second stage. So has the chanting, which appears to be veering into R-rated territory, courtesy of the "F—— you, Edge" chant that has been birthed by the creative minds of the ECW faithful. Where do these chants come from? And how exactly do they grow?

Edge props the ladder in the corner and readies himself for the spear that will drive Dreamer back-first into the steel. But Tommy sidesteps it and hip-tosses Edge, and spine meets metal, to the delight of the partisan crowd.

Terry rolls into the ring and shoulders the ladder, spinning with it in a "whirlybird" maneuver, knocking down me, Edge, and even Dreamer with Three Stooges precision. Actually, it doesn't look all that good, and we are in momentary danger of losing the interest of the crowd until Terry sets the twelve-foot apparatus up and begins to ascend.

Edge foils the plan, however, stopping Dreamer before tipping the ladder, sending the sixty-one-year-old Funk into an *F Troop*–like free fall to the canvas below. I lay a couple of boots into Funk, knocking him from the ring. Now it's time to play. The progression of the gimmicks is about to speed up. Way up. Business is about to pick up, courtesy of the barbed-wire board.

I'd used boards like this on dozens of occasions in Japan. But this board, courtesy of "Magic Man" Richie Posner, puts the other versions to shame. It's thicker, longer, heavier, and laced with considerably more barbed wire (real stuff) than it's Japanese counterpart. Together, Edge and I lift the board over-head and drop it suplex-style on the prone body of Dreamer, who, truth be told, doesn't seem to enjoy it. Indeed, his screams of agony seem especially realistic, and Edge seems intrigued by the stubborn barb that just won't leave its new home in Tommy's head.

The Edgester and I ready ourselves for a second deadly drop, but Funk is ready, and manages to grab hold of the legs of both me and Edge, sending us sprawling backward to the canvas, the board close behind, a devastating reminder of how real our imaginary world can sometimes be. Edge manages to avoid much of the impact, but the board catches me good, immediately slicing through the palm of my hand, creating a continuous stream of blood; dark, deep red, almost burgundy.

The board is then set up in the corner, and I am peppered with jabs from both Funk and Dreamer, who then proceed to throw me backward into the board. My head and shoulders crash into the lower part of the board, eliciting wails of hardcore satisfaction from the Hammerstein crowd—and a genuine scream of anguish from me, as I realize my hair is entangled in the unforgiving wire. My right forearm has been shredded as well, and blood flows freely from that second body part. My hand, however, remains my biggest problem, and I can see a chunk of meat peeking out through the blood. Even amid the wild verbal onslaught of ECW fans, I have the foresight to predict a future problem.

"THIS IS AWESOME!" the fans chant, as flattering a cheer as I've ever heard. It is a chant that has actually become fairly common at smaller wrestling shows around the world, but as a first-time recipient of the chant, I'm pretty touched by it.

Meanwhile, Edge has stopped Dreamer again, and although he's cut off by Terry, gives me the time I need to free myself from the grasp of the barbs, allowing me to use the board as a weapon on Terry when he returns from educating Edge on the subject of his boots.

Terry returns, and wham, I launch the board at him. Funk goes down hard, the board atop him, and reemerges moments later in a bad way, his face a crimson mask—the point of origin seemingly his eyebrow.

Lita hands me a small coil of barbed wire, and I proceed to work over the general area of Funk's left eye; dropping a couple of quality barbed-wire-wrapped forearms before blatantly grinding the wire into the affected area.

"You sick guy," the crowd chants. Actually, they had a more colorful substitute for "guy" that rhymes with "truck." It's not quite as flattering as "This is awesome," but it's close. Funk proceeds to do a very convincing job of making everyone—even me—believe his life may be coming to an end. After the show, Kirwin Siflies, one of WWE's incredible directors, who has seen literally hundreds of men ply their crafts in WWE rings, remarked that he was very impressed by Terry. "He does things that no one else does. He says your name when he's hurt. He asks for help."

Indeed, Terry *does* do things differently. He always has. His style has always been effective, and it always will be. Despite the naysayers and predictors of doom, Terry Funk is proving me right. He's doing a hell of a job in turning this match into a memorable mess—a four-star fiasco. And we're not through yet. The gimmicks still have a way to go to reach their ultimate progression.

Terry Funk is carted off, and Edge and I proceed to decimate Dreamer with the barbed-wire bat. Lita even joins the fun, executing a legdrop on the bat that conveniently covers Tommy's genital area. The crowd chants, "We

Squaring off with the Funker.

want Sandman," but little do they know that Sandman is being saved for a later segment, in which he will interrupt a poem by Eugene, complete with the beautiful imagery, "ECW isn't phony—I want to hug Balls Mahoney."

Now it's Socko time. I don't know why I didn't milk the arrival of my little cotton sidekick. Maybe because the match was running longer than Vince had hoped for. So almost immediately after reaching into my pants and pulling out the limp white object (the sock, the sock), I pulled off a surprise of sorts by applying the dreaded Socko claw to the beautiful Beulah, even managing to pull her into the ring, proving that I am capable of impressive feats of strength when my opponent weighs 105 pounds.

The move raises the ire of Dreamer, who temporarily breaks free of Edge—long enough to windmill me a couple of times with ineffective blows before being cut off once again by Edge.

Now it's Socko time for Tommy, and "the innovator of silence" tastes the sock, and then feels the wrath of Edge's Spear. It is the same lethal combination that dropped Dreamer in Anaheim, and the match is all but over. Except, Edge doesn't want it to be over. Not yet. Not until he's had his way with Beulah.

The "Rated R Superstar" picks up the fallen Beulah and toys with her, taunting her, placing her in position for the sexually suggestive pumphandle slam. Jeez, where the hell is Terry? We're kind of expecting him, but so far he's a no-show, prompting Edge and me to kill some time with yet another white-guy high five. Where is he? Where the hell is he?

Finally, we hear a rumbling, and turn to see Terry making his way through the crowd, a barbed-wire-wrapped two-by-four held aloft. His eye wound is wrapped in dramatic "Spirit of '76" fashion. Please don't tell me you've never heard of a "Spirit of '76" comeback. Remember the fife and drum? Oh, come on.

We all know it would seem completely ridiculous not to acknowledge the slothlike speed of the Funker's return, so

This is going to hurt.

Edge, Lita, and I turn to face it, fully intent on beating it back, with the help of our superior numbers and trusty barbed-wire bat. But Dreamer will have none of it, and, in a moment that will go down in the Party Poopers Hall of Fame, administers a double low blow to the hardcore title coholders. This leaves Tommy face-to-face with Lita, who promptly bails, leaving Edge and me to face a barbed-wire bombardment.

I am the first recipient. Wham! A shot to the stomach. Wham! A second to the back. Edge is next up, and he takes a similar two-shot to the stomach and back. But Funk isn't through. Though it seems to take forever, Terry is able to light the board on fire, and in an instant it is a mighty blaze, eliciting a roar of approval from the crowd.

The first blow is to my gut. The fire is hotter than I had imagined, and the flame seems to linger a moment near my midsection before swirling into hardcore heaven.

I'm not so fortunate with the second blow. It's to the back, and it's a good one; sending me down to my knees, where I come to the vague realization that my back is on fire. I should have stopped, dropped, and rolled, like all schoolkids are taught. Had I done so, the red and black flannel would have probably been extinguished. Instead, I crawl outside the ropes, waiting for blow number three, which will spell an end to my evening.

Here it comes. Wham, to the chest, and I'm propelled backward, off the apron, into the waiting barbs of the board below, which has been propped up against the guardrail only moments earlier by Tommy Dreamer. "Oh, my God," screams ECW announcer Joey Styles, adding drama to the moment with his classic phrase. The impact puts out the fire, but I am soaked down with a chemical fire extinguisher anyway, as in the case of fire—which should never be used in any type of wrestling match—it's always better to be safe than sorry. This may seem hypocritical, but it's true. I've used fire two times during the course of my eleven-year association with WWE, and on both occasions, the stunt was approved by the fire marshal, who made sure every precaution was taken to ensure an exciting but safe maneuver.

The fire extinguisher makes breathing difficult, and the landing hurt like hell, creating the clawlike gouges on my back, but despite my predicament, I am gratified by the rabid "ECW" chants that permeate the building. My night is over. I am now free to lie back and enjoy the rest of the match, from the relative comfort of my barbed-wire bed.

Oooh, damn! I guess I was wrong! Funk just landed on me. He was knocked off the apron by Edge and landed right on me. What the hell? It seems as logical a way as any to see the ending; stuck in a bale of barbed wire with my friend and mentor, Terry Funk.

Dreamer stops Edge with a DDT and proceeds to apply a submission hold with the creative use of barbed wire thrown in for good measure. Edge later admitted that he was being choked out for real, and found Lita's breakup of the move to be a genuine relief.

Lita turned to Beulah, and the catfight was on. Beulah on top, Lita on top, Beulah on top, Lita on top—until Dreamer grabs hold of Lita's long mane of red hair and plants her on the canvas with a Death Valley driver. It is a stunning lack of chivalry, but one that the ECW faithful is in full support of. I guess one must actually have a girlfriend to hold a door open for her.

Tommy and Beulah strike a pose of unity, enabling Edge to sneak up from behind with an Edgeomatic, yet another example of the creative use of barbed wire in this very creative bloodbath. Beulah goes toward her man, checking up on him—an act of love that proves to be a very costly mistake, and the cause of the end of the match. For when she turns to Tommy, Edge readies himself for the Spear. Beulah recognizes her error, but not in time, for Edge is upon her, sailing through the air, crashing into her midsection with a Spear for the ages.

"Oh, my God," Styles yells. "Edge damn near broke Beulah in half." Which really doesn't seem like much of an exaggeration, given the tremendous impact of the move. I give Beulah all the credit in the world for this. She's not a wrestler. Her instinct must have surely been to turn from the impact. But she hung in there and took the blow, and allowed a tremendous exclamation point to be added to the very odd, but very effective story of suffering we'd just written in the Hammerstein Ballroom.

But wait, the story wasn't quite over yet. Edge was about to add an exclamation point of his own, with the seediest, most provocative pinfall cover in sports entertainment history. Okay, maybe Verne Gagne and the Crusher had done something like . . . Never mind. It was the type of cover that even Jake Gyllenhaal and Heath Ledger might object to, saying, "Hey man, isn't that just a little bit too much?"

Now it's time to relax, once I get the hell out of the wire, which I finally do with Edge's help. I know this type of match isn't for everyone, but I also know it's among the best of its kind that I've been in—and I've been in a lot of them. Time seemed to fly by—the match went almost twenty minutes—

and my conditioning was never a factor. I may not be so lucky in the Flair match, but on this one night, I feel lucky indeed. Lucky to have had a match that lived up to its billing. Lucky that I wasn't more seriously hurt, given the risks that were taken. Lucky to have been in a match of such magnitude with the true hardcore legend, Terry Funk. And most of all, lucky that I'd have a chance to see Vince McMahon the next day, where I would demand an admission of misjudgment on his part. He had been wrong.

Afterword

Dear Hardcore Diary,

"Yes, Mick, you had a very good match," Vince said.

"So, you're admitting you're wrong?" I asked.

"Yes, Mick, I was wrong."

Just like that it was over—the shortest, most direct admission of error in the history of sports entertainment. One night earlier, I'd drifted off to sleep, comforted by the anticipated images of a vanquished Vince McMahon, his mouth filled with figurative poop, choking out an agonizing confession of major mat misjudgment and fundamental wrestling wrongdoing.

What a letdown! So brief. So direct. No hemming and hawing. No anguish. No shit in the mouth. Just a simple, "Yes, Mick, I was wrong." What a small price to pay for all the frustration his error in judgment had caused me.

Speaking of errors in judgment, I guess I've got a confession to make as well. Remember my prediction that *One Night Stand* was going to be a financial disaster? Remember how I predicted that it might end up as the least watched Pay-Per-View in WWE history? Well, it turns out that I was, uh, wrong. Oddly enough, *One Night Stand* turned out to be a surprising financial success, far exceeding WWE's initial projections, and decimating my forecast of impending doom. At this point, it looks to have a chance of eclipsing last year's total of 335,000 buys, which in and of itself was considered a major success.

So, how to explain this success? Well, some of it stems from an increase in international purchases, which in general have been a major boon to WWE Pay-Per-View profits.

WWE has done an amazing job of opening and exploiting new revenue streams, utilizing international marketing and promotion, as well as remaining on the cutting edge of new technology to maintain its status as a very successful entity.

But international buys were not the sole source behind the success. I'm actually at a loss to explain it, with any degree of certainty. It probably goes back to the Dayton show, the late buzz, the Cena interview, the hardway promo. Maybe it was just enough to encourage an awful lot of people on the fence to take a chance. Or maybe, just maybe, the whole Foley/Edge/Funk/Paul E./Dreamer story was more effective than I thought. Though I doubt that possibility will ever enter Vince's mind. By my own estimate, Vince McMahon has given me credit for the success of exactly *one* Pay-Per-View—the February 2000 Hell in a Cell with Triple H. And when it comes to dishing out the credit for the success of *One Night Stand*, I believe Vince is going to "stay the course" with that anti-Foley philosophy.

Perhaps *One Night Stand*'s greatest, if least obvious, legacy is that it helped maintain Edge's status as a certifiable main event performer. Much as I had hoped, Edge's affiliation with me, from our *'Mania* buildup through the ECW show, was accepted by fans as a lateral move, not a step backward, and he emerged professionally (if not physically) unscathed from the June 11 carnage, ready to rejoin the WWE Championship picture.

So, by the time Vince called me into his office at the June 12 *Raw* at Penn State University, I had already accepted the possibility that Edge, not me, might be wrestling John Cena at *SummerSlam*.

So I wasn't surprised, or even upset, when Vince said, "Mick, we think you and Ric have too much potential to just blow off your program at *Vengeance*."

I saw where he was going, and decided to fill in the blanks, saying, "So you'd like me to work with Ric at *SummerSlam*?"

"Do you have a problem with that?"

"No," I said. "As long as you and I can still do our angle after *SummerSlam*."

"Which one was that?" he asked.

"The one with Melina. The 'Kiss My Ass Club' one."

"Oh, yes," Vince said, "we'll still do that."

Yeah, as you'll see, we still did it, but the fact that Vince had to be reminded about the idea should have given me an indication that it wasn't going to be treated with the degree of importance that I had hoped for.

Here perhaps is the biggest shocker of all—I really liked working with Ric Flair. I may have been disappointed with my actual in-ring wrestling performances, but the buildup and the promos were among the most enjoyable things I've taken part in.

In an odd way, Rob Van Dam's misfortune was my good fortune. For following my *Vengeance* match with Ric, which was really just a glorified, bloody teaser for *SummerSlam,* I was set to take part in a six-man tag match on July 3, teaming up with Edge and Van Dam (or RVD) to take on the team of Cena, Sabu, and Flair. Personally, I would have preferred to hold off any physicality with Flair for several weeks. I had left Ric laying in a puddle of his own blood at *Vengeance,* and wanted to exploit that image for a little while longer. I really didn't see how this six-man tag would advance our story, but didn't think it would be politically wise to argue for scrapping it. After all, there were sure to be important creative battles worth fighting for in the future. I was willing to sit this one out.

I don't know all of the technicalities of the fateful Van Dam/Sabu road trip that had been inconveniently interrupted by an officer of the law a few days earlier. But an hour before match time, a decision was made to ditch the six-man in favor of an Edge/Van Dam single match, in which the Edgester won the title that RVD had won from Cena at *One Night Stand.*

I decided to stick around, asking writer Ed Kosky if I could perhaps try out an interview after the show. Hey, if they didn't use it, no big deal. But if they did, it would save me a trip to the teeming metropolis of Sioux City, Iowa, for the next week's *Raw.*

So, in a sense, I pried the doors to Promoland open for an after-hours visit, summoned forth some real-life anger, circa 1994, and strapped myself in for a hell of a ride.

Of course, the promo had its detractors. Quite a few, from what I'm told. But fortunately, Vince was not one of them, and he green-lighted not only the Philadelphia pretape for Sioux City, but two additional weeks of pretaped promos as well. Those promos had their detractors as well. I was making Flair look bad, they thought. I will admit that I rode Ric hard in these promos, but I thought he would see them as a challenge, and respond accordingly. If I thought for one second that Ric Flair wasn't capable of handling my best stuff, and knocking it out of the park, then I wouldn't have gone at him quite so hard. I wasn't sure he *would* knock it out of the park when we finally met face-to-face (which was scheduled for the July 31 *Raw* in New Jersey), but I did know he had the potential to do so.

Besides, as I explained to Vince and Brian Gewirtz, WWE Superstars weren't exactly lining up to propose scenarios in which they would suffer the most devastating loss in recent memory, to be followed by the most humiliating act of degradation and betrayal imaginable. I knew where I wanted to end up, and Vince trusted my unconventional method of getting there.

Flair trusted me, too—at least, I think he did. And I like to think that trust paid off for everyone—me, Ric, Vince, the fans—when we finally did face-to-face verbal battle in New Jersey. It really felt like we were making magic out there, feeding off each other, working from a loose basic outline but with a genuine sense of real emotion, the likes of which WWE fans rarely see. I hoped it could be a historic promo of sorts, the one that would finally put to rest the idea that Ric Flair only gives "eighties 'rasslin' promos." Surely his effort in New Jersey would serve as a harbinger for a post-*SummerSlam* Flair push.

Despite all the emotion of the promo, it was actually a hokey comedy line, delivered prior to Flair's ring entrance, that will live on (if only in my mind) as one of my finest sports entertainment moments.

"Ric Flair and I were really not that different," I told Melina, who had served, at my request, as my personal ring announcer.

"After all, Ric Flair and I both have famous friends. You see, Melina, Ric Flair is a personal friend of the president of the United States."

Which is kind of true. Ric does know the current president, although he was better acquainted with the first President Bush.

"And I am personal friends with hardcore porn icon Christy Canyon." Christy, I must say, received a much more friendly and enthusiastic response than the president.

"Now, one of our friends," I told Melina and the crowd, "got to the top by screwing an awful lot of people . . . and the other one appeared in adult films."

Yes! Now admit it, that's a good line. Even if you do like President Bush, you have to admit that's a good line. Hey, I just had lunch today with

Attorney General Alberto Gonzales, and even he admitted it was a good line. Okay, maybe he didn't say anything remotely like that, but I really did have lunch with him at chairman of the Joint Chiefs of Staff General Peter Pace's house. Same house, different tables, limited (five or six words) conversation between us.

One of my relatives didn't care for the joke. It actually caused quite an ugly scene at my cousin Kelly's wedding the day before *SummerSlam*. The relative had never actually heard the line, but nonetheless, the very fact that I'd made a political joke was an affront to his heartfelt belief that celebrities should never use their status to advance political beliefs. Fair enough. He's entitled to his opinion. But his feeling that he "shouldn't have to listen to Vanessa Redgrave's politics at the Academy Awards" as his primary argument was a little weak. Why? Because he'd never actually heard her speech. And because the speech took place in 1977.

My mother thought the line was quite funny. She did, however, have one question for my wife, which Colette later relayed to me.

"How does Mick know a porn star?"

"What did you tell her?" I laughed, guessing that this was not exactly a typical mother-in-law–type conversation point.

"Well, I said that you were on her radio show and that you really liked her because she'd helped children overseas." Which is true, although her philanthropic tendencies never really crossed my mind when I first started liking her about twenty years ago.

Christy herself got quite a kick out of it. Although she didn't see the show (I don't know if she's ever seen *Raw*), her phone apparently rang repeatedly over the next few hours, prompting the joyous voice mail I received the next day.

"Hey, Mick, this is your hardcore porn icon friend calling. You are so awesome." Followed by several minutes of interesting life observations by someone who views life through a slightly different lens. I think I've only talked to Christy twice since our lone meeting in that Los Angeles radio studio, but I have been on the receiving end of many of her meandering (but never boring) stream-of-consciousness messages, leading me to believe that Christy Canyon may be to voice mail what Garrison Keillor is to public radio. Of course, Christy does occasionally throw in choice verbiage not regularly heard on the *Prairie Home Companion*.

•　•　•

Wow, where the hell was I? Oh, yeah, Ric Flair. During the course of my pre-taped interviews, I had dared Ric to bring his "A" game to New Jersey. He did. He also brought his "A" game to Boston for *SummerSlam*. Unfortunately, I left my "A" game somewhere else, maybe at home, maybe in New Jersey, maybe at my cousin's wedding, opting instead to bring my "C+/B-" game to town.

It wasn't a bad match by any means, in fact it was pretty good. Maybe if I'd been an outside observer, I would have thought it was very good; it was certainly an intense, bloody spectacle, with many barbaric moments sprinkled liberally into the mix. (Although I doubt Ric would want any derivative of the word *liberal* used in connection with his name.) Take, for example, the classic Ric Flair open-hand chop to the chest, seen literally thousands of times by millions of fans over the last thirty or so years. Our match, however, saw the first "hand wrapped in barbed wire" variation of that chop—an idea that seemed great at the time of delivery, but somewhat less so while receiving twenty-five stitches in my chest after the match.

But I wasn't an outside observer. I knew how good it should have been. And I know who was to blame for it coming up short. Ric! No, just kidding, Ric was great. I'm the guy to blame. Basically, I had a game plan for a match that would have been somewhat akin to a sweeping Hollywood epic. Maybe a complete thirty-minute drama, twenty-five minutes from bell to bell, plus entrances and aftermath. Except I couldn't get thirty minutes to work with. I got twenty. So I began thinking of ways to lop off scenes, kind of eliminating the dialogue that would have made the action more memorable. I gave up on the idea of a sweeping thirty-minute epic, and settled instead on trying to give fans an incredible twenty-minute action movie. Except I became so consumed with giving WWE the twenty minutes they wanted that I forgot to deliver the three extra minutes I really needed.

Damn, I wish I had those three minutes over. What a difference they would have made. The difference between an intense, bloody spectacle and a hardcore classic for the ages.

In the end, I guess I changed my opinion of Ric Flair. Or, to be more accurate, I changed my opinion about his opinion of me. I think he respects me. He might even like me. But I think both of us are glad that we were able to put our past problems behind us and put together an inspired body of work.

But that's not to say that I've completely forgotten about what he said about me in his book. Because I think it's changed me; caused me to become less concerned about my career and whatever legacy it might leave in the wrestling business. I no longer expect my peers to say nice things about me. Quite the opposite. If they do happen to say, or write, something nice—great. If not, well, I guess that's life. I guess now is as good a time as any to throw in a random Ricky Nelson quote, so here goes: "You can't please everyone, so you've got to please yourself."

I have come to accept that not everyone is going to be a fan of my particular style, be it in the ring or on the mike. Fortunately, Vince McMahon liked my style. Sure, it took me eleven years to get to WWE. Sure, Vince may have thought I looked sleazy, like I wasn't WWE material. And sure, it may have taken years of prodding from J.R., as well as a few words of support from guys like Undertaker and Kevin Nash, for me to even get my foot in the door. But ultimately it was Vince who made the decision to hire me, to push me, and eventually to treat me like I was one of his top guys—even if he was stingy when it came to Pay-Per-View credit attribution. Ultimately, it was Vince McMahon, "the decider," overruling all of the potential "persuaders." It was Vince who became like a second father to me, who told me to treat his house like it was my house, who . . . Okay, maybe I'm overdoing it a little.

As of the writing of this afterword, Vince has been made aware of the worst of the criticisms expressed in this book, and found them to be alternately amusing and insightful. The fact that he allows criticisms about him in a book that he publishes speaks very highly of either his belief in freedom of speech or his apparent joy at courting controversy wherever possible.

The fact that I feel free to express this criticism toward the man who pays me speaks well of either how confident I am in our unique relationship, or how many times I've been hit in the head with steel chairs.

All right, all right, that's enough kissing Vince's ass in the *literary* sense. Let's move on to kissing it in the *literal* sense. As those of you who skipped to the color insert may have noticed, I did indeed join Vince's special club. Yes, Vince kept his word, and I got to do my big angle with Melina—the one I proposed in Anaheim, where I agreed to kiss Vince's ass to save her job. But by the time the big moment rolled around, the day after *SummerSlam,* I had grudgingly accepted that the idea was not going to come off as the big deal that I had imagined.

We weren't given much time—six minutes for everything—and I was well aware that the angle's main purpose to Vince was to serve as a backdrop to his continuing adventures with DX. But even with the short time allotted and even with all sense of subtlety stripped from the sequence, I still held out hope that strong personal performances could make the idea a success. The performances were indeed strong. Melina more then lived up to my faith in her, with genuine tears streaming from her eyes as she begged me to reconsider my commitment to Vince's crevice. And Vince and I slipped effortlessly back into our old chemistry together, probably because deep down, we share a small, but very real, dislike for each other. Maybe even a little bigger than small. At least on my part.

Sure, the whole thing wasn't played up as big as it could have been. But Melina was so genuinely grateful and happy afterward that it made the mere consideration of disappointment on my part seem foolish. I even got choked up when I said good-bye to Johnny Nitro, thanking him for being a hell of a guy who never made me feel like I was hovering around his girlfriend, or treating her in any way but with the utmost respect.

As I headed out onto the road, for home and the seven-month vacation that my public firing would bring, I received a call from Barry Blaustein, who marveled at how I had been able to turn an act of degradation (kissing another man's ass) into an act of defiance. Which is exactly what I had hoped to do, although in truth, following Blaustein's call, not one other person has echoed his cinematic sentiment.

If only it had all ended there, I would have labeled the entire experience, from *One Night Stand* to *SummerSlam*, as a success. If only. Unfortunately, it didn't end there. I sat in front of my television every Monday for the next several weeks, a helpless observer, watching in vain as everything I had worked for vanished. There was no new Flair push—no mike time at all—just a few meaningless matches with the Spirit Squad. The spotlight I had hoped would be shone on Melina, the one I was sure Vince would take full advantage of, turned out to be a momentary flicker. Within three weeks, it was as if our angle had never existed.

I took it all as a personal defeat, and as a personal slap in the face from Vince and the creative team. The conspiracy theorist in me surfaced, and I began to internally question everything about my last several weeks with WWE, from the lack of any meaningful promotion of my *Raw* segments with Ric to what I viewed as Vince's preoccupation with everything DX. For a few weeks, I just flat-out lost my mojo, and couldn't seem to get it back. On more than one occasion, I woke up in a cold sweat thinking about the Flair match, wishing I could have those damn three minutes back. I questioned whether I even belonged in the ring any more. I looked back at the DVDs of my most recent matches, the 2006 comeback matches, and couldn't help but think that something was missing. The fire in my eyes was gone.

I even came to compare my return to WWE—the contract I'd signed in September 2005—to a fictional decision to get back together with an old flame. At first I was constantly reminded of why I'd fallen for her to begin with, but as the months went by I became more and more aware of just why we'd parted, and for several weeks after *SummerSlam*, I found myself wondering what the hell I'd ever seen in her. I felt like Jack Nicholson in *The Shining*—the beautiful woman in room 217 had become a nasty, pus-filled, decaying, putrid cadaver right before my horrified eyes.

A kind and considerate text message from Melina served as a temporary oasis from my desert of disenchantment. The segment with Melina, understandably, was not among my wife's personal favorite Mick Foley moments. But Colette agreed that it was a nice message.

A few days later, I called Flair, just to tell him how much I'd enjoyed the match (I didn't tell him it was causing me nightmares), and that I was sorry it hadn't led to anything resembling a decent push.

"Hey," Flair asked, "did you get my text?"

"No, but I just wanted to tell you—"

"Hold on," Ric interjected, "before you say anything, let me send it again."

So, I waited a moment, my cheap cell phone vibrated, and there it was— Melina's text message! Holy crap, it wasn't even her text, it was Flair's all along. Colette thought that the text from Flair was the nicest thing. I guess I did too, I even saved it. Why? Because he's Ric Flair. The same reason his book bothered me so much. Because he's Ric Flair. The same reason why I outright refused to even think about winning at *SummerSlam*. Because he's Ric Flair.

In fairness to Melina, she was kind enough to forgive me for having sin-gle-handedly built her hopes up, leading her to believe (as I expressed earlier in the book) that our angle was going to be the biggest break of her career. Indeed, I think the guilt I felt over seeing her storyline amount to little more than nothing, combined with the embarrassment I felt over having dedicated so much *Hardcore Diary* energy to it, may have been the primary culprits behind the tragic loss of the Foley mojo.

Fortunately, that mojo has largely returned (in a steady trickle, not a flood), so that I am now better able to see the larger picture in a slightly more positive light. Hopefully, you the reader have escaped from the downer zone I just sent you journeying into, without too much psychological trauma.

After all, the outcome wasn't all bad, was it? I had some good matches. I did some good interviews. I even got a chance to romp around Promoland, long after I'd assumed it was closed for good.

I'm proud of myself, too. I came back for six months of ideas, angles, interviews, and matches, and I don't think I ever looked or felt like I was coasting or resting on my laurels. I gave the fans a different version of Mick Foley, and I think, for the most part, they enjoyed the effort. I know I did— at least, some of it. Despite the frustration, I really did enjoy much of the process. The in-ring promo with Funk, teaming up with Edge, proving Vince wrong, making magic with Ric Flair. Hey, let's not forget about Melina's hand touching my "guys." Sure, that hand was balled up in a fist and was traveling at high speed when that contact with the "guys" was made, but, hey, it's my book and I'm going to count it. Yes, I am aware that I made a similar stupid joke in *Foley Is Good*.

No, I never really got to "wrestling immortality." Those two balls I could have sworn I'd hit out of the park (the April 25 pitch in Stamford, and the May 8 pitch in Anaheim) barely reached the warning track. But at least I took my best swings. When it comes to this whole experience, maybe I need to quote President Clinton from his now infamous September 24, 2006, interview: "I tried . . . and I failed. But at least I tried."

Besides, time may be the final judge as to whether this whole thing was ultimately a failure. Maybe we can reexamine the Vince McMahon and Melina possibilities when I return. Who knows, with the benefit of a little creative fertilization we may yet see growth from those seeds planted on August 21 in Bridgeport, Connecticut. The promos have already started to sprout in my mind—they should be ready to harvest when I return to WWE. Unless, of course, Vince isn't interested in any more of my crop (another winning pun from the best-selling author), and opts instead to bury the fruits of my mental labor.

Pretty lame agricultural analogy, huh? I probably should have just stuck with the Promoland theme.

So now for the big question. If I had known then what I know now, would I still have pitched my idea in Stamford, the idea that served as the basis for *The Hardcore Diaries?*

Let me see, I just quoted Bill Clinton earlier, so perhaps I should quote another famous statesman here. How about the Texas Rattlesnake, Stone Cold Steve Austin, who might very well say, "Oh HELL NO!"

No, I wouldn't have shown up in Stamford.

But I think my mistake made for a good book.

Acknowledgments

Thank you first and foremost to Vince McMahon, for suggesting the idea of another autobiography, and for allowing me to share my story in its entirety.

Special thanks to my editor, Margaret Clark, for her feedback corrections, grammatical expertise, belief in this project, and for all the many other tasks required in transforming over six hundred pages of handwritten notebook paper into actual book form. The transcriptions of the live speeches were provided by Sue DeRosa, Michael Dalvano, Anwar Fennell, Ben Williams, and Matt Yackeren from WWE. Thanks also go out to Richard Oriolo for his design, and to Dean Miller at WWE and Erica Feldon at Pocket Books for their support.

Thank you to my family for toleration of my extended writing session in the Foley Christmas room.

I'd like to thank Michael Zimmerman for his friendship and inspiration.

Lastly, thanks to all the wrestlers, service members and special kids who have touched my life. To quote an old rocker, "You've made me a better man."